D1736624

THE PROJECT OF INDEPENDENCE: ARCHITECTURES OF DECOLONIZATION IN SOUTH ASIA, 1947–1985

Martino Stierli
Anoma Pieris
Sean Anderson

The Museum of Modern Art, New York

PORTFOLIO

IN FOCUS

TRANSFORMATIVE PROJECTS

Allianz, MoMA's partner for design and innovation, is proud to sponsor *The Project of Independence: Architectures of Decolonization in South Asia, 1947–1985* at The Museum of Modern Art. This exhibition will shed light on modern architecture culture in South Asia from the end of British rule in 1947/48—when the emerging nations we today call India, Pakistan, Bangladesh, and Sri Lanka increasingly used architecture to articulate their visions for a new society—to the formation of a more collective regional identity in the 1980s. By focusing on the diverse work created by local rather than international architects, designers, and planners, *The Project of Independence* considers the region's architectural production as an active force in the drive for self-determination.

At Allianz, we are pleased to support an exhibition that celebrates the work of key architects from the subcontinent such as Balkrishna V. Doshi (India), the only South Asian winner of the Pritzker Architecture Prize; Minnette de Silva, the first woman architect of Sri Lanka; and Yasmeen Lari, the first woman architect of Pakistan, to name a few.

About Allianz
The Allianz Group is one of the world's leading insurers and asset managers, with more than 100 million retail and corporate customers in more than 70 countries. Allianz customers benefit from a broad range of personal and corporate insurance services, ranging from property, life, and health insurance to assistance services to credit insurance and global business insurance. Allianz is one of the world's largest investors, managing around 766 billion euros on behalf of its insurance customers. Additionally, our asset managers PIMCO and Allianz Global Investors manage 1.7 trillion euros of third-party assets. Thanks to our systematic integration of ecological and social criteria in our business processes and investment decisions, we hold the leading position for insurers in the Dow Jones Sustainability Index.

FOREWORD

The Project of Independence: Architectures of Decolonization in South Asia, 1947–1985
explores architectural production in the second half of the twentieth century in a region
that served as a blueprint for political independence from colonial rule across the globe.
Transnational in approach, this exhibition brings together for the first time a wealth of
archival materials, architectural models, found footage, and vintage as well as contemporary photography to document a unique moment when modern architecture embodied
societal and political aspirations, reflected a new sense of national identity, and was
embraced as a tool for social progress. Much more than just an investigation of a specific
regional narrative, *The Project of Independence* seeks to enhance our understanding of
the shared histories among newly independent countries, as well as the conditions that
are shaping present realities in the Global South.

The exhibition reflects the commitment of The Museum of Modern Art's Department
of Architecture and Design to expanding its outlook beyond the European and North
American canon that until recently informed the majority of its exhibitions. In 2015 the
Museum presented *Latin America in Construction: Architecture 1955–1980*, a landmark
survey of modern architecture in Latin America. Subsequently, attention shifted more
explicitly to questions of decolonization and self-assertion with *Toward a Concrete Utopia:
Architecture in Yugoslavia, 1948–1980* (2018); a focus that is further explored and enhanced
by the present exhibition, which covers a similar time frame as part of a sustained archae-
ology of the recent past. Even before this current undertaking, MoMA dedicated large
exhibitions to South Asia, including the celebrated *Textiles and Ornamental Arts in India*
(1955), which introduced the richness of the region's craft and textile traditions to an
American audience less than a decade after the country's political independence. The 1963
exhibition *Le Corbusier: Buildings in Europe and India* explored the Swiss-French architect's groundbreaking design for Chandigarh, the new state capital of Indian Punjab,
in the context of his global practice. With its thematic focus, *The Project of Independence*
takes a different approach, one that celebrates the work of the first generation of post
-Independence South Asian architects and engineers, whose work so powerfully gave form
to an overarching societal vision. The unequivocal embrace of progressive values and
of newly founded institutions by this generation of architects and intellectuals has lost
none of its relevance in our contemporary moment, when many achievements of the
mid-twentieth-century social contract are under attack.

Many years in the making, *The Project of Independence* was in a critical phase of
planning and research when the COVID-19 pandemic transformed the world as we knew
it and for many months brought essential aspects of museum work to a standstill. We owe
enormous gratitude to the many private and institutional lenders in South Asia and beyond,
as well as many individuals both inside and outside the Museum who helped ensure that
the curatorial vision could be realized with few concessions. In this sense, *The Project of
Independence* is a powerful testament to the spirit of collaboration and collegiality.

The Project of Independence was organized by Martino Stierli, The Philip Johnson
Chief Curator of Architecture and Design; Anoma Pieris, a professor at the Melbourne
School of Design, The University of Melbourne; and Sean Anderson, Associate Professor,
Department of Architecture, Cornell University; with Evangelos Kotsioris, Assistant
Curator. Research for *The Project of Independence* was facilitated by an advisory board of
scholars and architects whose insights and expertise were indispensable to the success of
this ambitious project.

We are indebted to MoMA's partner for design and innovation, Allianz, and to
Xin Zhang and Shiyi Pan, whose crucial support made this exhibition possible. We're also
deeply grateful to The International Council of The Museum of Modern Art and to the
Graham Foundation for Advanced Studies in the Fine Arts for their generous contributions.

Glenn D. Lowry
The David Rockefeller Director
The Museum of Modern Art

INTRODUCTION

Martino Stierli and Anoma Pieris

South Asia holds a unique place among the many regions of the world where modern architecture served both as an instrument and an active agent of social progress in the second half of the twentieth century. Architects, planners, and engineers in the newly formed nation-states of what had been British India and the Crown Colony of Ceylon after the end of colonial rule in 1947/48 made a significant contribution to the project of independence. Through their work, they articulated a powerful vision of a self-determined postcolonial society. This aspiration was expressed in new cities and spaces of political representation, and in the construction of formally and typologically innovative buildings. By responding to the social and material conditions on the ground, they asserted a cosmopolitan worldview that was uniquely situated in the subcontinent. In so doing, Pioneering South Asian architects set in train processes that disrupted the colonial hierarchy of center and periphery by challenging modernism's universalist claims in ways that would reverberate across Asia, Africa, the Caribbean, and beyond.

The four countries that are the focus of this book and the exhibition it accompanies—India, Pakistan, Bangladesh, and Sri Lanka—all had a centuries-long history of (British) colonization;[1] they are therefore often represented as a shared cultural space, whose identity is defined as much by an interconnected history in the precolonial and colonial periods as by the ways in which, after Independence, they reimagined themselves as progressive, egalitarian, predominantly secular nation-states. This holds true notwithstanding the trauma, in India and (East and West) Pakistan, of Partition—which left hundreds of thousands dead and led to one of the largest refugee crises in human history—and nationalist armed conflicts including that which led to the independence of East Pakistan as Bangladesh in 1971. If the transition to independence in Sri Lanka (then Ceylon) was in many respects more organic and gradual, minoritarian challenges to hegemonic state-building would escalate into a bloody civil war that began in 1983 and would last three decades.

Having achieved political Independence, these respective South Asian territories forged distinctive pathways to self-determination against the backdrop of ongoing Cold War political tensions and rivalries. Despite various and in some cases shifting alignments with the Soviet Union and the United States, whose strategic interests were reflected in funding priorities, the notion of a shared space is also evident in political bids for greater self-determination through India, Ceylon, and Bangladesh's membership of the Non-Aligned Movement during the 1960s and 1970s (Pakistan ultimately joined in 1979) and the formation of the South Asian Association for Regional Cooperation (SAARC) in 1985. That year marks the end point of our project, as it also coincides with the increasing dominance of regionalist tendencies in South Asian architecture. The tenets of regionalism in many ways paralleled the emergence of postmodernist discourse in the West, which constituted a separate but related indication of an increasing disenchantment with the unfulfilled utopian visions of modernism.[2]

Our focus, then, is on a period of architectural production shaped more by secular "statist" goals than these later "culturalist" agendas. *The Project of Independence: Architectures of Decolonization in South Asia, 1947–1985* seeks to acknowledge the agency of architects in devising a built trajectory of self-determination for their respective countries while also accounting for the larger political and economic parameters that made their work possible. To this end, it is addressed in the pages that follow alongside various facets of the project of independence, among them politics and urbanism, industry and housing, and the role played by new institutions in shaping greater self-reliance and self-determination, generally giving less emphasis to more private commercial commissions. The relative dominance afforded to India in this narrative is a consequence of its sheer size and population compared to those of the three others. It is also a result of the greater availability of architectural archives.

1   Other countries that are commonly considered to be part of the region, such as Afghanistan, Bhutan, Maldives, and Nepal, have different political histories and diverging cultural trajectories, and are for this reason not included in this survey of post-Independence architectural production.
2   Among the factors symptomatic of and contributing to the rise of regionalist idioms from the late 1970s onward was the establishment of the Aga Khan Award for Architecture in 1977 and its journal, *Mimar*, which began publication in 1981.

Much of the original material, in terms of sketches, architectural drawings, and plans, is presented here for the first time to a wider audience. And while several prominent South Asian architects have in recent years received monographic exhibitions, this project is the first attempt to consider their impressive and significant output within the ideological frameworks of its creation and the political context of the region as a whole.[3]

In her recent study *Worldmaking after Empire*, Adom Getachew presents a powerful argument for understanding the political project of decolonization in the mid-twentieth century through a reconceptualization of "anticolonial nationalism as *worldmaking*."[4] Translated to the context of South Asian architecture from Getachew's primary focus on the Black Atlantic world and the sphere of international politics, this position implies a practice of design and construction that speaks not only to the immediate needs of the newly founded nation-states and their respective desires for self-representation, but also to the aspiration to be part of a larger international conversation about modernity. The construction of a new built environment was an important dimension of postcolonial cultural production that gained aesthetic agency and symbolic meaning by aligning with political goals. Hence, in post-Independence South Asia, modern architecture can be considered a constitutive part of the process of postcolonial political and cultural decolonization within a broader project of worldmaking that sought to create what Getachew calls an "egalitarian international order."[5] Nationalism and cosmopolitanism, from this perspective, are not to be understood as mutually exclusive, but rather as interdependent forces that defined the politics of decolonization in the Global South.

Our project thus intends to speak to the productive intellectual double-bind between nationalism and internationalism. What the literary scholar Alpana Sharma has identified for some of the most prominent first-generation, post-Independence writers from the region, such as Mulk Raj Anand, Attia Hosain, and Raja Rao, is relevant for their architectural colleagues as well, namely that "modernism is the natural idiom of these writers in so far as it provided them with a sharp-edged tool with which to chip away at the edifice of colonialism."[6] Thus, while recent research across disciplines has powerfully asserted the degree to which modernity and colonialism were and are intertwined and unthinkable without each other, it is worth emphasizing that modernity—and modernism as its cultural articulation—was also embraced as a powerful tool in the process of decolonization, not least through the ways in which it embodied and expressed the collective social aspirations of the region's newly independent nations. It was only consequential in this context that many architects turned away from British models of architectural pedagogy and versions of the modern—such as Art Deco, which had been popularized in urban centers such as Bombay under colonial rule, or the incorporation of aspects of traditional monumental architecture in the colonial-modern "Indo-Saracenic" style—and instead looked to align themselves with a Continental conception of modernism, often filtered through the so-called International Style in the United States, but adapted to the very different economic, cultural, climatic, and technological situation of South Asia.

Modern architecture, in this light, can be understood as serving as an instrument of cultural emancipation not only from the weight of political and cultural colonization but also from a rigid conception of modernism as uniquely developed by the West and considered from a Western perspective. South Asian post-Independence architecture stands in a specific relation to the concept of cosmopolitanism—"ways of thinking, feeling, and acting beyond one's particular society"[7]—which has held center stage in postcolonial theory since its introduction by thinkers such as Homi K. Bhabha, Gayatri Chakravorty Spivak, and Arjun Appadurai.[8] Related theories of "cosmopolitics" explored the situated and embodied character and

3   Two exhibitions surveying Indian architecture were produced in the context of the government-sponsored Festivals of India in the 1880s, both accompanied by catalogues: Raj Rewal, Jean-Louis Véret, and Ram Sharma, eds., *Architecture in India* (Paris: Electa Moniteur, 1985); and Carmen Kagal, ed., *Vistāra: The Architecture of India* (Bombay: Tata Press, 1986).

4   Adom Getachew, *Worldmaking after Empire: The Rise and Fall of Self-Determination* (Princeton, NJ: Princeton University Press, 2019), 2.

5   Getachew, *Worldmaking after Empire*, 2.

6   Alpana Sharma, "Decolonizing the Modernist Mind," *South Asian Review* 33, no. 1 (July 2012): 18.

7   This definition is from the text on the back cover of Carol A. Breckenridge, Sheldon Pollock, Homi K. Bhabha, and Dipesh Chakrabarty, eds., *Cosmopolitanism* (Durham, NC: Duke University Press, 2002).

8   See Homi K. Bhabha, "Unsatisfied: Notes on Vernacular Cosmopolitanism," in *Text and Nation: Cross-Disciplinary Essays on Cultural and National Identities*, ed. Peter C. Pfeiffer and Laura García-Moreno (Columbia, SC: Camden House, 1996), 191–207; Arjun Appadurai, *Modernity at Large: Cultural Dimensions of Globalization* (Minneapolis: Minnesota University Press, 1996); and Gayatri Chakravorty Spivak, "Foreword: Cosmopolitanisms and the Cosmopolitical," *Cultural Dynamics* 24, nos. 2–3 (July 2012): 107–14.

complexity of cosmopolitanism.[9] Building on the work of a generation of postcolonial scholars who have opened up new decentered points of view by considering the multiplicity and entanglements of modernist architectures and urbanisms, Duanfang Lu conceptualizes the "distinctive meanings, practices, trajectories, transformations, and consequences" of what she calls "Third World modernism."[10] Lu writes: "Recognition of other modernities has to be posited at the level of epistemology in order to imagine an open globality based not on asymmetry and dominance but on connectivity and dialogue on an equal basis."[11]

In this spirit, we do not dwell at length on Le Corbusier and Louis I. Kahn, the two seminal Western figures who have been celebrated many times previously for their bold contributions to architectural modernism in South Asia. Nor do we offer an expansive discussion of the many other foreign architects who were realizing projects in the region after Independence, among them figures such as Richard Neutra, Edward Durell Stone, and Gio Ponti. Instead, the focus is on significant projects of the first generation of post-Independence architects who either were born in the region or settled there permanently. Many members of this generation trained in the West, and upon their return to the region adapted and interrogated their education in addressing the social, economic, cultural, and material conditions on-site, furthering the notion of a hybrid approach that speaks to both global and local frames of reference. While some of these efforts have in the past been judged harshly as having aligned too closely with Western precedents, these architects' highly reflexive design processes were shaped by competing notions of identity: one anchored in a sense of transnational modernity and the other rooted in the specificity of place. It is in this tension between the universal and the specific that the historical and aesthetic significance of the impressive body of work of the first generation of post-Independence architects in South Asia is situated. The plurality of voices and approaches evident in their architectural production is reflected by the range of the essays by leading scholars in the field gathered in this book, through which we hope to illuminate the significance of South Asia's modern architecture in the histories of global modernism.

9   See Pheng Cheah and Bruce Robbins, eds., *Cosmopolitics: Thinking and Feeling Beyond the Nation* (Minneapolis: University of Minnesota Press, 1998), 3.
10   Duanfang Lu, introduction to *Third World Modernism: Architecture, Development and Identity*, ed. Lu (London: Routledge, 2011), 3.
11   Ibid., 24.

THE POLITICS OF CONCRETE: INDUSTRY, CRAFT, AND LABOR IN THE MODERN ARCHITECTURE OF SOUTH ASIA

Martino Stierli

Fig. 1   Woman carrying cement at the Capitol Complex, Chandigarh, India, in front of the Secretariat (1951–58) designed by
Le Corbusier (Charles-Édouard Jeanneret, 1887–1965). 1956. Photograph: Ernst Scheidegger

The photographs showing some of the countless laborers involved in the construction of Chandigarh between 1951 and 1967 exert a particular fascination (fig. 1). In Le Corbusier's "official" documentation of his designs for the new capital city of the Indian Punjab in his *Oeuvre complète*, the Swiss-French architect heavily privileged drawings, sketches, and (his usual) retouched photographs, yet even he included a small number of photographs of workers in action on his Capitol Complex buildings.[1] Similar imagery of concrete construction and labor can be found in a book by the Swiss photographer Ernst Scheidegger, who repeatedly traveled to Chandigarh in the early 1950s to document the construction process.[2] The workforce was made up primarily of unskilled local workers, many of whom were women, as can also be seen in film footage included in Yash Chaudhary's short documentary *Chandigarh* (1969), and Alain Tanner's poetic *Une ville à Chandigarh* (1966), narrated by John Berger.

Part of the fascination of these images for Western viewers might be grounded in a taste for the "exotic" and thus be an Orientalist reflex, part of the process of othering that, as Edward Said famously argued, has long informed and tainted the Western perception of Asia, North Africa, and the Middle East.[3] But the deployment of labor-intensive processes on one of the most ambitious construction projects in modern history also brings into play the critical question of how the universalist project of modern architecture was modified by the situation on the ground in South Asia. While concrete held promise as a relatively novel industrial material during the period of decolonization, architects had to negotiate the reality of preindustrial labor skilled in the production of brick structures and the lack of

machinery for the production and transportation of concrete, which was in many cases mixed on the ground and placed into small baskets carried on the heads of laborers.[4]

As we shall see, among the many technologies and signifiers of the modern in circulation in the colonial and postcolonial world, for a whole generation of architects, concrete served as a symbolic representation of modernity tout court. Although concrete had been used in India even under the British raj, primarily for infrastructural construction by British military engineers and in the lavish Art Deco buildings designed for the urban elites in Bombay and elsewhere,[5] the ostentatious display of exposed concrete at Chandigarh was closely associated with the belief in social transformation advocated by the progressive elite of the newly independent nation. This belief is epitomized in the famous observation of India's first post-Independence prime minister, Jawaharlal Nehru, in 1959: that Chandigarh "hits you on the head . . . it makes you think."[6] In this narrative, modernity has been absorbed through materiality.

The specific meanings of concrete construction within the framework of the political project of decolonization in South Asia after independence from British rule were highly ambivalent. While some architects and intellectuals regarded the use of concrete as an emancipatory tool that would allow architecture to become an active agent in the progressive project of social transformation, others considered it inappropriate for the specific sociocultural and economic context of the subcontinent, and therefore a neocolonial application of Western standards.

I am indebted to Anoma Pieris, Evangelos Kotsioris, and Vikramaditya Prakash, whose comments have greatly helped me advance and sharpen my argument.

1   Le Corbusier et son atelier rue de Sèvres 35, *Oeuvre complète*, vol. 6, *1952–1957*, ed. W. Boesiger (Zurich: Editions Girsberger, 1957), 81, 86–87. For more on the role of labor in images by Le Corbusier's second official photographer, architect Jeet Malhotra, see Atreyee Gupta, "Dwelling in Abstraction: Post-Partition Segues into Post-War Art," *Third Text* 31, nos. 2–3 (March–May 2017): 9–17. For a strong critique of Le Corbusier's own perception of Chandigarh, see Vikramaditya Prakash, *Chandigarh's Le Corbusier: The Struggle for Modernity in Postcolonial India* (Seattle: University of Washington Press, 2002), 82–87.
2   These photographs were only published in 2010, perhaps indicative of a more recent interest in question of labor and process as opposed to artistic parti and product. Stanislaus von Moos, ed., *Chandigarh 1956: Le Corbusier, Pierre Jeanneret, Jane B. Drew, E. Maxwell Fry; Photographs by Ernst Scheidegger* (Zurich: Scheidegger & Spiess, 2010).
3   Edward W. Said, *Orientalism* (New York: Pantheon, 1978).
4   As much is indicated by Scheidegger's photos; see in particular von Moos, *Chandigarh 1956*, 72. See also Stuart Tappin, "The Early Use of Reinforced Concrete in India," *Construction History* 18 (2002): 84. Tappin's article describes how reinforced concrete was used in British India, from the late nineteenth century onward, mainly for infrastructural projects by military engineers.
5   For a discussion of the use of modern building technology and materials during British colonial rule, see Peter Scriver and Amit Srivastava, "Rationalization: The Call to Order, 1855–1900" and "Complicity and Contradiction in the Colonial Twilight, 1901–1947," chaps. 1 and 2 in *India*, Modern Architectures in History (London: Reaktion, 2015).
6   Jawaharlal Nehru, "Inaugural Address by Shri Jawaharlal Nehru, Prime Minister," in *Seminar on Architecture*, ed. Achyut Kanvinde (New Delhi: Lalit Kala Akademi, 1959), 3.

This dispute relates to one of the big debates about India's future, the "rift in visions . . . between industrializers and Gandhians."[7] While Nehru saw the future of independent India in the industrial urban metropolis, Gandhi advocated for the preindustrial village as a model for a self-reliant future.[8] The ideal of *swaraj*, or self-rule, that Gandhi and his followers pursued entailed a rejection of imported models of industrial modernity, and a return to craft and agricultural traditions on a small, local scale. By contrast, Nehru and his comrades-in-arms maintained that true independence and self-sufficiency could be achieved only by ending economic imperialism through investment in nationalized heavy industry.

ORIGINALITY AND OTHER MODERNIST MYTHS

To appreciate the role of concrete construction and modern building technologies in post-Independence South Asia requires critically revisiting the conventional Eurocentric narratives of architectural modernity as essentially an expansion from the European/Western center to the global periphery—the so-called developing world. The vibrant conversation on concrete construction in other parts of the Global South, in particular postwar Brazil, strengthens the case for replacing these origin myths with an approach based on the specificity of each given cultural context. Dipesh Chakrabarty in his *Provincializing Europe* makes the pertinent observation that wherever they are to be found, "the universal concepts of political modernity encounter pre-existing concepts, categories, institutions, and practices through which they get translated and configured differently."[9] Rather than privileging a linear view of modernism's history, in other words, we need to pay attention to how ideas and technologies get translated, transformed, and differentiated across space and time. But Chakrabarty also calls into question the very agency behind the universalist

project of global modernity: "The project of provincializing Europe has to include . . . the understanding that this equating of a certain version of Europe with 'modernity' is not the work of Europeans alone; third-world nationalisms, as modernizing ideologies par excellence, have been equal partners in the process."[10]

What is at stake is the myth that architectural modernism (or for that matter modernity more generally, with all its technological, historical, social, and cultural repercussions) was an essentially Western project that was later exported and applied on a global scale. According to this colonialist logic, global modernisms are by definition epiphenomena; a series of uncomfortable attempts to align modernism's universalist claims with often fundamentally different local socioeconomic and cultural conditions. The resulting "epistemic colonization" is still widespread in Western historiographies of modernism,[11] despite numerous efforts to challenge such narratives. In architectural historiography in particular, what is needed is not so much a mere expansion of the canon, but a more radical process of unlearning. Rather than retelling obsolete myths or constructing ever-repeating lineages of alleged "influence,"[12] we must investigate the *performativity* of architectural modernisms in specific historical situations.[13]

From this perspective, the notion that Chandigarh (and subsequent modernist projects in South Asia) represents a simple transfer of Western knowledge to a new setting seems glaringly reductive. Postwar modernism, it could be argued, was a constituent element of a non-Western trajectory of (political) emancipation from Western (in this case British) dictate, and for this reason at least as much a rejection of that dominance as its alleged expansion. Chandigarh was not merely the result of an export

7   Sunil Khilnani, *The Idea of India* (1997; repr., New Delhi: Penguin Books India, 2004), 73.

8   See Prakash, *Chandigarh's Le Corbusier*, 9–10.

9   See Dipesh Chakrabarty, "Preface to the 2007 Edition," in *Provincializing Europe: Postcolonial Thought and Historical Difference*, (Princeton, NJ: Princeton University Press, 2008), xii. I am indebted to Vikramaditya Prakash for reminding me of the acuity of Chakrabarty's argument for my own historiographical attempt.

10   Chakrabarty, *Provincializing Europe*, 43.

11   I am borrowing the term "epistemic colonization" from Prakash, *Chandigarh's Le Corbusier*, 25.

12   For a critique of the concept of influence, see Michael Baxandall, *Patterns of Intention: On the Historical Explanation of Pictures* (New Haven, CT: Yale University Press, 1985), 58–59. For a discussion of Baxandall's critique in an explicitly decolonial framework, see Partha Mitter, *The Triumph of Modernism: India's Artists and the Avant-Garde, 1922–1947* (London: Reaktion, 2007), 8–9.

13   My argument here is in line with Vikramaditya Prakash's observation: "The important questions of historiography, I would argue, often do not lie in determining origins, but in assembling situational explanations, coherences whose validity can be judged within the context of their production, rather than against principles that are claimed to be foundational and universal. This is critical historiography—an assemblage of situational explanations, a textual strategy of reading." Prakash, *Chandigarh's Le Corbusier*, 26. This approach is further supported by Adrian Forty's observation regarding concrete construction: "Concrete is an example of a technology where innovation matters a lot less than use. . . . What matters is not where, when or how these inventions happened, but the use that has been made of them." Forty, *Concrete and Culture: A Material History* (London: Reaktion, 2012), 40.

of architectural knowledge from Paris to the Punjab, but rather a project fundamentally shaped and enabled by the specific historical and socioeconomic conditions on-site. Indeed, the formal and aesthetic qualities of Chandigarh owe as much to the work of the local laborers and the traces they left as they do to the parti of the architect. The construction of an entire city from scratch would anyway hardly have been possible in the time frame under consideration in the West, and could only happen through the bold embrace of architectural modernism as an instrument and agent in the political project of decolonization.[14]

GOLCONDE GUESTHOUSE

But for a survey of the material history of exposed concrete in the subcontinent to begin with Chandigarh is questionable in any case. In chronological terms, the first building in the region that made extensive use of reinforced concrete not only structurally but also as a means of aesthetic expression was the Golconde guesthouse, built between 1937 and 1942 as a dormitory for the Sri Aurobindo Ashram in the then French colony of Pondicherry. Designed by Tokyo-based Czech American architect Antonin Raymond (1888–1976) in collaboration with Japanese American architect and furniture designer George Nakashima (1905–1990) and Czech architect François (František) Sammer (1907–1973), as well as Chandulal Shah (d. 1945),[15] the building was an astonishing architectural feat (see pp. 170–73; Portfolio, no. 14). But it was also the result of a major logistical enterprise, with the construction equipment arriving from Japan and the steel shipped from France. Since Pondicherry did not have a wharf, the freighter had to anchor in the Bay of Bengal as the steel was brought to shore on boats made from palm trunks—a perfect illustration of how an industrialized construction economy was translated to the local context, harnessing traditional techniques based on hand-made production.[16]

Besides its pioneering and experimental use of reinforced concrete, Golconde was also an ingenious essay in bioclimatic design, as is apparent in features such as the individually adjustable concrete louvers on its facade for the natural circulation of air. The building could have become a model for adapting modernism to the subcontinent's tropical climate; and indeed the Sri Lankan architect Minnette de Silva (1918–1998), in a letter she wrote to the architectural historian Sigfried Giedion in 1950, called Golconde "one of the few significant modern buildings in India," indicating her intention to feature it in the Bombay-based magazine *Marg* (see Singh, pp. 135–41).[17] For the most part however, the impact of Golconde on the development of modernist architecture in the region remained relatively modest.[18]

BÉTON BRUT

Recent scholarship has underscored that exposed concrete—often under the moniker Brutalism—became a global phenomenon in these years, a new architectural lingua franca.[19] The "invention" of the traces of labor and production as a rhetorical

14 The only two comparable projects of the time were Brasília and New Belgrade, both of which equally formed part of their respective countries' politics of decolonization, albeit with very different meanings. See in particular Styliane Philippou, *Oscar Niemeyer: Curves of Irreverence* (New Haven, CT: Yale University Press, 2008); and Jelica Jovanović and Vladimir Kulić, "City Building in Yugoslavia," in *Toward a Concrete Utopia: Architecture in Yugoslavia, 1948–1980*, ed. Stierli and Kulić (New York: The Museum of Modern Art, 2018), 58–63.

15 See Pankaj Vir Gupta, Christine Mueller, and Cyrus Samii, *Golconde: The Introduction of Modernism in India* (New Delhi: Urban Crayon, 2010).

16 See George Nakashima, *The Soul of a Tree: A Woodworker's Reflections* (Tokyo: Kodansha, 1981), 64.

17 Minnette de Silva to Sigfried Giedion, January 3, 1950, gta Archives, ETH Zürich, Switzerland. Golconde was indeed featured in *Marg*, but not until 1963 and only in a very brief descriptive text along with a selection of photographs. See "Golconda [*sic*] Guest House," *Marg* 17, no. 1 (December 1963): 44–45.

18 The only other mention of Golconde in a South Asian professional publication of the period seems to have been in the editorial in the December 1954 issue of the *Indian Concrete Journal*, where it was described as "Indian construction . . . set in a locality subjected to the worst vagaries of the weather." "Editorial: Architectural Concrete," *Indian Concrete Journal* 28, no. 12 (December 1954): 473. Two Western publications from the 1950s also referenced the building, focusing on the movable louvers made of asbestos concrete. See Francis Meynell, "Architecture Today," *Concrete Quarterly*, no. 27 (October–December 1955); 27–37; and "A Photographer's Dream," *International Asbestos-Cement Review* 4, no. 4 (October 1959): 52. By the 1980s, however, it had become widely acclaimed, featuring in the catalogues to two of the Festivals of India exhibitions (see Singh, p. 140), with Charles Correa describing it in 1986 as "without doubt the finest example of modern functional architecture built in India in the pre-independence period." Correa, "Golconde, Aurobindo Ashram, Pondicherry," in *Vistāra: The Architecture of India*, ed. Carmen Kagal (Bombay: Tata Press, 1986), 111.

19 See in particular the recent, highly useful *SOS Brutalism: A Global Survey*, ed. Oliver Elser, Philip Kurz, and Peter Cachola Schmal (Zurich: Park Books, 2017), as well as Forty, "The Geopolitics of Concrete" and "Politics," chaps. 4 and 5 in *Concrete and Culture*. For an Eastern European case study, see Stierli and Kulić, *Toward a Concrete Utopia*. For the region that is the focus of the present volume, see Peter Scriver and Amit Srivastava, "South and Southeast Asia," in Elser, Kurz, and Cachola Schmal, *SOS Brutalism*, 299–303.

Fig. 2   Unité d'Habitation, Marseille, France. 1945–52. Le Corbusier (Charles-Édouard Jeanneret, 1887–1965). Exterior view of northwest corner. Between 1949 and 1952. Photograph: Lucien Hervé

Fig. 3   Sunil Janah (1918–2012). Untitled, from the series Industrial Documents. View of the Konar Dam under construction, Jharkhand, India. c. 1948–55. Gelatin silver print, 9 1/16 × 11 in. (23 × 28 cm). Swaraj Art Archive

Fig. 4   Faculty of Architecture and Urbanism, University of São Paulo, São Paulo, Brazil. 1961–69. João Vilanova Artigas (1915–1985) and Carlos Cascaldi (1918–2011). Interior view. c. 1970. Photograph: José Moscardi

Fig. 5   Hall of Nations, Pragati Maidan, New Delhi, India. 1970–72. Demolished 2017. Architect: Raj Rewal (b. 1934). Engineer: Mahendra Raj (b. 1924). Detail view. 1974. Photograph: Madan Mahatta

device in exposed concrete is usually associated with Le Corbusier's Unité d'Habitation in Marseille from 1945–52, where the *pilotis* and the undercroft exemplify what would become known as *béton brut* or Brutalism (fig. 2), a term that underwent a number of semantic shifts but eventually came to essentially signify the aesthetic of rough, exposed concrete. As Réjean Legault has argued, the reason for this "invention" was accidental: the insufficient availability of skilled labor made it impossible to achieve the desired (smooth) quality of the finishes, prompting the architect to decide to leave these traces of workmanship in their unrefined state after the wooden formwork was removed.[20] This ostentatious display of imperfection and the lack of finesse not only corresponded with the obsessions of contemporaneous artists such as Jean Dubuffet and his *art brut* but also constituted a rebuke to the prewar myth of concrete as the "precise, 'machine-age' material."[21] In this (European) context, *béton brut* came to signify something more than industrial progress: it could now be seen as architectural modernism's self-reflexive neo-humanist turn—a turn that to European architects, critics, and historians was informed by the experience of the devastations of war. Adrian Forty, for instance, argues that in Europe Brutalism came to signify a notion of postwar melancholy, reflecting the shattering of the belief in technology as a benevolent force.[22]

In South Asia, by contrast, the traces of construction formwork left on the surfaces of concrete buildings conveyed a different set of meanings. If the use of exposed concrete had been accidental in the case of the Unité d'Habitation, in Chandigarh it was a direct and deliberate representation of the locally available means of production. While the material had previously been used in colonial India by the Public Works Department for the construction of roads, railway infrastructure, and military installations, after Independence concrete came to embody modernity first and foremost in ambitious industrial and infrastructural projects such as the famous dams (fig. 3) that Nehru hailed as the "temples of the modern India."[23]

But it was in Chandigarh that local labor processes and raw aesthetics for the first time found an expression in architectural form, with concrete representing both an embrace of the industrial age and a socialist ethos. As Peter Scriver and Amit Srivastava have argued, the coarseness of the skins of the Chandigarh buildings and their imperfection came to signify a "bloody-minded commitment to moving forward"; and in fact, the lack of finesse in the finishes even offered "an opportunity to comment poetically on the struggles of the developing world."[24] Chandigarh's raw exposed concrete thus stands less for a neocolonial gesture enacted by a foreign architect and more for the process of decolonization that the nation was embarking on. This would align also with Nehru's aspiration for Chandigarh. For him, the Punjab capital was to be "a new town symbolic of the freedom of India, unfettered by the traditions of the past . . . an expression of the nation's faith in the future."[25] Nehru emphasized that modern architecture in India could contribute to an international conversation while at the same time reflecting the specific socioeconomic conditions of the subcontinent: "A modern European building, as you may call it, is a building coming out of industrialism. You may call it a building of the industrial age. If the industrial age comes to India, it will bring something like that but it will have to fit in with our function, climate, etc. So it is not European or Indian but something fitting in with the general structure of society, technological advance, climate, function, etc."[26] In unequivocally embracing industrialization as the way forward for his nascent country, Nehru saw modern architecture as providing the futuristic iconography for that embrace. Inasmuch as industrialization was only just beginning on a large scale (and would remain an incomplete project), the visual presence of the traces of manual labor on the concrete surface of Chandigarh's buildings epitomize Nehru's view of modernity adapting itself to the realities of the present. This demand for site-specificity also seems to indicate that Nehru's progressivist vision had perhaps more in common with Gandhi's culturalist model than is often acknowledged. Moreover, the quoted passage

---

20   See Réjean Legault, "The Semantics of Exposed Concrete," in *Liquid Stone: New Architecture in Concrete*, ed. Jean-Louis Cohen and G. Martin Moeller, Jr. (Basel: Birkhäuser, 2006), 47. The author here revisits Le Corbusier's own account of his invention in Le Corbusier, *Oeuvre complète*, vol. 5, *1946–1952*, ed. W. Boesiger (Zürich: Editions Girsberger, 1953), 191.
21   Reyner Banham, *The New Brutalism: Ethic or Aesthetic?* (New York: Reinhold, 1966), 16.
22   See Forty, *Concrete and Culture*, 128.
23   Jawaharlal Nehru, "Temples of the New Age," in *Jawaharlal Nehru's Speeches*, vol. 3, *March 1953–August 1957* (New Delhi: Ministry of Information and Broadcasting, 1960), 3.
24   See Scriver and Srivastava, "South and Southeast Asia," 300–301.
25   Nehru in an article in the *Hindustan Times*, July 8, 1950, as quoted in Ravi Kalia, *Chandigarh: The Making of an Indian City* (1987; repr., New Delhi: Oxford University Press, 1998), 21.
26   Nehru, "Inaugural Address," in Kanvinde, *Seminar on Architecture*, 9.

demonstrates that for him, modern architecture was not just a rigid set of technological and aesthetic rules that would be translated from one primary cultural context to the peripheral other. Instead, it offered a highly flexible matrix of parameters that would be adapted fluidly to given specific conditions, and allowed for innovation and a feedback loop between perceived center and periphery along the way.

GLOBAL MODERNISMS

The project of independence from British rule in South Asia in the late 1940s set an example that would reverberate across the globe in the decades to come. The ways in which architecture was employed as an agent in social and political transformation in the subcontinent made it one of the "key laboratories in the world of mid-twentieth century architectural design where Brutalism was being forged in original terms."[27] In newly independent nations and across the Global South, exposed concrete would come to represent the (initially) idealistic and progressive politics of the period.[28]

Postwar Brazil was another laboratory for concrete construction, and can be instructively compared to India, despite its remarkably different history. Like their South Asian counterparts, Brazilian architects developed a highly articulated language of exposed concrete based on a radically different set of parameters from those that pertained in Europe. Brazil had not experienced the destructions of the war, nor could it look back to a previous level of technological development whose unilaterally optimistic meaning could now, in hindsight, only be mournfully remembered and memorialized. Rather, raw exposed concrete in Brazilian postwar architecture simply was the most advanced construction technology available within the framework of limited economic means.

One of the champions of concrete in Brazil was the Paulista architect João Batista Vilanova Artigas (1915–1985), perhaps best known for his extraordinary building for the Faculty of Architecture and

Urbanism at the University of São Paulo (1961–69; fig. 4). In a short essay from 1988, Artigas pointedly rebuked the notion that his architecture had anything to do with Brutalism as it had been theorized by Reyner Banham and others in the West.[29] Instead, Artigas argued, "The ideological content of European brutalism is something other. It brings with it a cargo of irrationalism."[30] In Adrian Forty's paraphrase, Artigas made the case that "architectonic form, despite its appearance of technical determinism, was in fact arrived at through arbitrary or accidental aesthetic choices."[31] Even though this claim is debatable, it served his polemic, according to which the use of exposed concrete was, in Brazil and the Global South more broadly, somehow a direct and authentic representation of the local socioeconomic conditions.

Artigas's design for the Faculty of Architecture and Urbanism represented not only the country's underlying conditions of production but also a rejection of Western narratives about the meaning of concrete.[32] It is worth remembering Italian-born Brazilian architect Lina Bo Bardi's scathing commentary on the use and promotion of earth and raw brick construction in developing countries by nonprofit organizations: "*mud* for the third world, and concrete and steel for those above the equator." This distinction, in her view, primarily served to exclude the Global South from the club of the privileged nations in the usual fashion.[33] In the South Asian context, the situation was certainly not as clear-cut, with Gandhi explicitly favoring the use of earth and raw brick as an appropriate material palette to reflect the subcontinent's unique socioeconomic conditions. His thinking fundamentally differed from Nehru's techno-scientific approach and the concomitant preference for explicitly modern building materials such as concrete.

From this perspective, concrete construction in Chandigarh and South Asia more generally could be seen as offering a synthesis between idealism and a radical realism: idealism by means of the belief in architecture's capacity to transform society toward a progressive image of itself; and realism by means

27 Scriver and Srivastava, "South and Southeast Asia," 302.
28 Ibid., 299–303.
29 See Reyner Banham, "The New Brutalism," *Architectural Review* 118, no. 708 (December 1955): 335, 358–61; Banham, *The New Brutalism*; and "New Brutalism," special issue, *October*, no. 136 (Spring 2011).
30 João Batista Vilanova Artigas, "Em 'Branco e Preto,'" *AU: Arquitetura e Urbanismo*, no. 17 (April–May 1988): 78. Quoted from the English translation in Forty, *Concrete and Culture*, 128.
31 Forty, *Concrete and Culture*, 128.
32 See ibid., 129.
33 Instituto Lina Bo e P.M. Bardi, ed., *Lina Bo Bardi* (Milan: Charta, 1994), 242.

of the embrace of the fundamental economic and social conditions that such endeavors encountered on-site.[34] Even though this kind of "reality-check" seems, as suggested above, already to have been present in Nehru's progressivist thinking about Chandigarh and modern architecture on the subcontinent more broadly, the double-bind between idealism and realism could also be understood as a synthesis between, on the one hand, Western-centric progressivism and, on the other, Gandhi's culturalist position, which emphasized the local and the handmade as India's path forward.

THE HALL OF NATIONS COMPLEX

Besides Chandigarh, another key example of the meaning of concrete within the larger context of India's project of independence was the Hall of Nations Complex on New Delhi's Pragati Maidan fairgrounds, designed by architect Raj Rewal (b. 1934) in collaboration with structural engineer Mahendra Raj (b. 1924) (fig. 5; see Portfolio, no. 29). Erected as a multifunctional exhibition space for the Asia '72 international trade fair, organized in commemoration of the twenty-fifth anniversary of India's independence from British rule, the Hall of Nations was to showcase the commerce of various participating countries, while the adjacent, smaller Halls of Industries served as a symbolic representation of India's industrialization (see pp. 218–21). The Hall of Nations was—in the terms of Nehru's famous metaphor—one of the temples of the new, modern India in which "the sacred, the secular, the commercial, and the industrial found an accord."[35]

The building has received a variety of interpretations. Giordano Tironi foregrounds the architecture's ability to filter light and the resulting sense of animation in the interior,[36] while the awe it evoked is apparent in Rewal's comparison of the Hall of Nations with London's Crystal Palace (1850–51).[37]

Architectural historians Peter Scriver and Amit Srivastava characterize the complex as an iconic example of the "tendency toward structural expressionism,"[38] which, they argue, became a hallmark of the progressive vision of post-Independence India. On another level, the Hall of Nations Complex is paradigmatic of how concrete construction epitomized the ethos of self-reliance in a country proudly having come of age.[39]

The formal resolution of the Hall of Nations, like that of many of India's concrete buildings during these decades, was the result of a veritable pas de deux between engineer and architect. Indeed, the "tendency toward structural expressionism" is to a considerable degree a result of the towering contribution of Mahendra Raj, the eminent Indian structural engineer of his generation and one of the outstanding figures of his field in the latter half of the twentieth century. Raj had launched his career on the construction sites of Chandigarh, where in 1952 he and Gulzar Singh were tasked with the structural design of Le Corbusier's High Court building.[40] Based on this experience, Raj was promoted to executive engineer and assigned to design the Secretariat, where he contributed significantly to the final layout of the intricate web of brise-soleils on the main facade (fig. 6).[41]

In subsequent years and decades, Raj would collaborate with many of the country's leading architects, including Balkrishna V. Doshi (b. 1927), Charles Correa (1930–2015), and Achyut Kanvinde (1916–2002). These collaborations resulted in some of the most iconic structures of post-Independence modern architecture in India, among them the Sardar Vallabhbhai Patel Municipal Stadium (with Correa; 1959–66; see pp. 190–93; Portfolio, no. 4) and Tagore Memorial Hall (with Doshi; 1963–67; fig. 7), both located in Ahmedabad; the Shri Ram Centre for Art and Culture (with

34   I am using the term "realism" here in line with the Italian *neorealismo* movement; see Maristella Casciato, "Neorealism in Italian Architecture," in *Anxious Modernisms: Experimentation in Postwar Architecture Culture*, ed. Sarah Williams Goldhagen and Réjean Legault (Cambridge, MA: MIT Press, 2000), 25–54; see also Manfredo Tafuri, *History of Italian Architecture, 1944–1985*, trans. Jessica Levine (Cambridge, MA: MIT Press, 1989), 9–20.

35   Giordano Tironi, *Humanisme et architecture: Raj Rewal, construire pour la ville indienne* (Lausanne, Switzerland: L'Âge d'Homme, 2013), 132.

36   Ibid., 131–35.

37   Raj Rewal quoted in Richi Verma, "Call To Save Pragati Maidan Hall," *Times of India*, April 14, 2015.

38   Scriver and Srivastava, *India*, 243.

39   These ideas are related to Adom Getachew's recent discussion of "self-determination" in post–World War II postcolonial politics: see p. 7 of the introduction to this volume, and Getachew, *Worldmaking after Empire: The Rise and Fall of Self Determination* (Princeton, NJ: Princeton University Press, 2019).

40   See Mahendra Raj, "My Initiation into Structural Engineering," in *The Structure: Works of Mahendra Raj*, ed. Vandini Mehta, Rohit Raj Mehndiratta, and Ariel Huber (Zurich: Park Books, 2016), 26–27.

41   Ibid., 28.

Fig. 6   Secretariat, Capitol Complex, Chandigarh, India. 1951–58. Le Corbusier (Charles-Édouard Jeanneret, 1887–1965). Exterior view during the final stages of construction. Mahendra Raj Archives

Fig. 7   Tagore Memorial Theatre (Tagore Memorial Hall), Ahmedabad, India. 1963–67. Architect: Balkrishna V. Doshi (b. 1927)/Vāstu Shilpā. Engineer: Mahendra Raj (b. 1924). South facade with ten trapezoidal folded plates. 1965. Vāstu Shilpā Foundation Archives

Fig. 8   Shri Ram Centre for Art and Culture, New Delhi, India. 1968–72. Architect: Shiv Nath Prasad (1922–2002). Engineer: Mahendra Raj (b. 1924). Exterior view during construction. 1968. Photograph: Madan Mahatta

Shiv Nath Prasad) in New Delhi from 1968–72 (fig. 8; see Portfolio, no. 2);[42] the National Cooperative Development Corporation Office Building (with Kuldip Singh) from 1978–80 (see pp. 234–37; Portfolio, no. 36), also in the capital;[43] and the Hall of Nations Complex, under consideration here.

The striking space-frame structure of the Hall of Nations (fig. 9) was based on the modular repetition of a concrete tetrahedron shape to form a truncated pyramid. In other words, the form of the building as a whole was a consequence of the multiplication of the constituent geometry of its structural system, which thus served as its defining aesthetic characteristic. The logic of the modular construction was immediately legible and apparent to the visitor. The space frame provided a sense of a facade that was not an applied surface but had its own spatial dimension, a sense of "depth" or volume to it, which was, however, highly translucent and permeable, thus creating an overwhelming effect of filtered light in the interior space.[44] Indeed, the Hall of Nations could be seen as a built manifestation of Chakrabarty's illuminating metaphor of "translucence," a term with which he describes "the partly opaque relationship . . . between non-Western histories and European thought,"[45] in this case one that plays out through the translation of architectural modernism.

In the economic context of early 1970s India, architects had virtually no access to commercially available space-frame systems that could have been imported from overseas.[46] The choice of concrete (as opposed to steel), although based on cost considerations, was a leap of faith taken after overcoming the engineer's initial hesitations, as a space frame in reinforced concrete in these dimensions had thus far not been built anywhere: the Hall's footprint measured 240 by 240 feet, and it was a hundred feet high. Industrial prefabrication would have been the logical choice for the modular elements,[47] given how prefabricated concrete lends itself to a Fordist and Taylorist streamlining of the production process in what Michael Osman has called the "managerial aesthetics of concrete."[48] Indeed, it is precisely concrete's seeming affinity to systematization and scientific management that made the material so appealing to many modernist architects in their quest to fundamentally reform the construction process and to align the ancient art of architecture with the logic of the assembly line. However, all but one of the contractors for the Hall of Nations Complex preferred in-situ casting and construction. One reason for this, besides the ready availability of a cheap labor force, would have been transportation costs: the lack of modern systems of circulation and a pertaining logistical apparatus rendered prefabrication uneconomical in most cases.[49] The decision against prefabrication may have delayed the building's completion, although plentiful inexpensive labor made work hours a secondary concern. Nevertheless, the choice drew criticisms, mainly from Western observers, among them R. Buckminster Fuller,[50] a fervent advocate of prefab construction. But his preference reveals a Western-centric worldview that failed to account for how the prevailing lack of funds and the economics of scarcity forced an adaptation of the design to given conditions and became essential drivers in technological and formal innovation.[51] With the Hall of Nations Complex, Rewal and Raj acknowledged the "facts" of Indian construction, summarized in another context by Adrian Forty as "concrete, abundant unskilled labour, lack of productive capital."[52]

The Hall of Nations Complex thus chimed with the ideas Artigas developed with reference to Brazil discussed above: the building was by no means a

42   For a discussion of this seminal project, see Rajat Ray, "Shri Ram Centre for Performing Arts," in Elser, Kurz, and Cachola Schmal, *SOS Brutalism*, 318–21.
43   See Peter Scriver and Amit Srivastava, "National Cooperative Development Corporation," in Elser, Kurz, and Cachola Schmal, *SOS Brutalism*, 328–31.
44   See "Permanent Exhibition Complex, New Delhi," in *Raj Rewal: Innovative Architecture and Tradition*, by Raj Rewal et al. (Noida, India: Om Books International, 2013), 66.
45   Chakrabarty, *Provincializing Europe*, 17–18.
46   A detailed account of the decisions behind the Hall of Nations' design is given by the engineer himself in Mahendra Raj, "Hall of Nations & Halls of Industries," in Mehta, Mehndiratta, and Huber, *The Structure*, 142–51; regarding space-frame systems, 143.
47   Ibid.
48   See Michael Osman, "The Managerial Aesthetics of Concrete," *Perspecta* 45 (2012): 67–75. For a detailed discussion of the implications of concrete construction on skilled and unskilled labor, see Forty, "Concrete and Labour," chap. 8 in *Concrete and Culture*.
49   Anoma Pieris, personal communication with the author, April 23, 2020.
50   See Tironi, *Humanisme et architecture*, 133.
51   The argument of economy has to be qualified, of course: while the on-site construction eliminated the need for steel plates and erection bolts, the costs for the (wooden) formwork were higher. Raj, "Hall of Nations," 150.
52   Forty, *Concrete and Culture*, 128. Forty uses this enumeration in relation to the architecture of Artigas, but it is equally applicable to the Indian context.

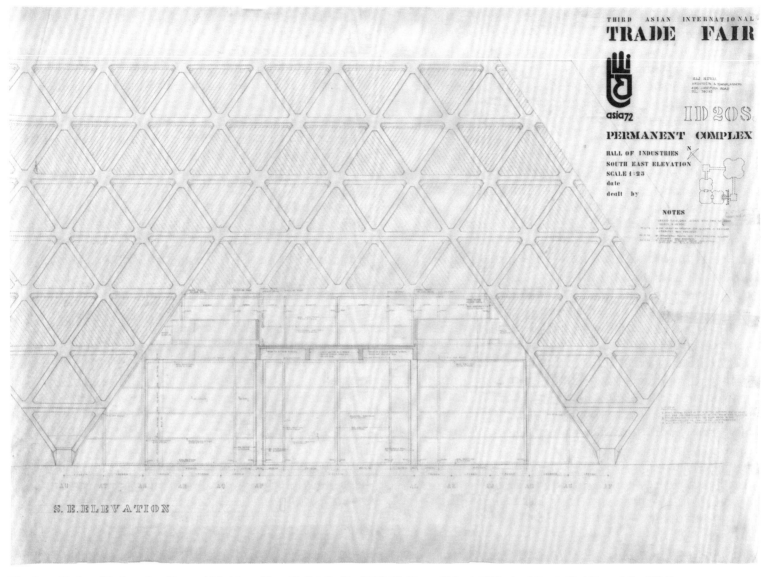

Fig. 9   Halls of Industries, Pragati Maidan, New Delhi, India. 1970–72. Demolished 2017. Architect: Raj Rewal (b. 1934).
             Engineer: Mahendra Raj (b. 1924). Drawing of northeast elevation. 1970. Pencil on tracing paper, 40 × 55 in. (101.6 × 139.7 cm).
             The Museum of Modern Art, New York

Fig. 10   Premabhai Hall, Ahmedabad, India. 1956–74. Architect: Balkrishna V. Doshi (b. 1927)/Vāstu Shilpā. Engineer: Mahendra Raj
             (b. 1924). Interior view of the entrance hall. 1976. Vāstu Shilpā Foundation Archives

mere expansion of Western industrial technology and architectural sensibility to a perceived "periphery" but, to the contrary, an example of architectural modernism whose very existence was fundamentally a consequence of India's specific socioeconomic conditions, not least its limited access to capital and advanced industrial technology. As in Brazil, architect and engineer made constructive use of these preconditions, here in order to arrive at a genuinely South Asian version of modern architecture that proudly asserted what India could do on its own terms.

Thus the Hall of Nations—like many other contemporaneous South Asian buildings—entails a rejection of what Chakrabarty calls the "historicist" model of global historiography. As he puts it, "Historicism is what made modernity or capitalism look not simply global but rather as something that became global *over time*, by originating in one place (Europe) and then spreading outside it."[53] This concept of temporality relegated South Asia (and the Global South more broadly) to what Chakrabarty famously calls the "imaginary waiting room of history";[54] a conception than was (ab)used to justify colonization, as it allowed for non-Western cultures to be portrayed as backward and in need of colonial intervention. What the history of the construction of the Hall of Nations Complex illuminates, conversely, is the entanglement of a purportedly universalist conception of modern space and the material culture of manual labor. The fact that it was precisely the reciprocity between these two seemingly asynchronous factors that produced a highly innovative and unique modernist structure shows the necessity of rejecting the historicist model and acknowledging modernity as a condition of synchronous heterotemporalities.

STRUCTURAL EXPRESSIONISM CONTINUED (PLUS A NOTE ON GENDER)

Mahendra Raj's aptitude for structural expressionism is further exemplified in his collaborations with leading architects on designs for two stadiums, in Ahmedabad and Srinagar (in the Kashmir valley),

respectively. The Sardar Vallabhbhai Patel Municipal Stadium in Ahmedabad, designed by Correa with Raj for the Ahmedabad Municipal Corporation, is a proud expression of the progressive city government's objective of democratizing access to spaces of social gathering that had in colonial times been reserved for the elites.[55] Correa and Raj's design for the stadium may have been the first anywhere to use a modular folded-plate frame structure with a cantilevered roof.[56] The resulting highly recognizable formal and spatial quality of the building is best perceived in the interstitial spaces on the exterior, created through the rhythm of the inclined "legs" of the folded plates and the underside of the seating terraces.

Raj would return to a more conventional use of the folded-plate technique a few years later for the facade of the aformentioned Tagore Memorial Hall. A decade after that, the drama of experiencing the underside of a vast concrete volume that seemingly hovers effortlessly above the spectator was pushed to the extreme in the entrance lobby of the stunning Premabhai Hall (1956–74; fig. 10; see Portfolio, no. 3), in the old city center of Amhedabad. This was another collaboration with Doshi and further proof of the bold architectural and civic aspirations of the city's enlightened elites.[57]

The Indoor Sports Stadium, constructed much later (1979–82) in Srinagar, the summer capital of the union territory of Jammu and Kashmir, was a collaboration with the Delhi-based office of Kanvinde (fig. 11). Outwardly reminiscent of the triangular grid of the concrete space frame of the Hall of Nations from a decade earlier, the Srinagar stadium is based on an entirely different structural concept consisting of triangulated plates that taper outward from a cross-shaped base in order to house the seating system.[58] Together with the Hall of States (architect Raj Rewal; 1982) at New Delhi's Pragati Maidan, and the New Delhi Municipal Corporation Headquarters (Palika Kendra) (architect Kuldip Singh; 1973–83; see Portfolio, no. 28), the Srinagar stadium brought to a conclusion Raj's exploration of the aesthetic possibilities of the structural

53   Chakrabarty, *Provincializing Europe*, 7.
54   Ibid., 8.
55   See K. M. Kantawala, "Growth of the City of Ahmedabad," *Social Welfare* 10 (1964): 43.
56   Mehta, Mehndiratta, and Huber, *The Structure*, 64.
57   The aesthetic sensation of massive concrete planes hovering above empty spaces is equally a characteristic of the Brazilian Paulista school of architecture, from Lina Bo Bardi's Museu de Arte de São Paulo (completed 1968) to Paulo Mendes da Rocha's Museu Brasileiro da Escultura e Ecologia (completed 1995). For a short discussion of Premabhai Hall, see Vikram Bhatt, "Premabhai Hall," in Elser, Kurz, and Cachola Schmal, *SOS Brutalism*, 304–7.
58   Mehta, Mehndiratta, and Huber, *The Structure*, 256–57; see also Tanuja Kanvinde and Sanjay Kanvinde, eds., *Achyut Kanvinde: Ākār* (New Delhi: Niyogi, 2017), 231.

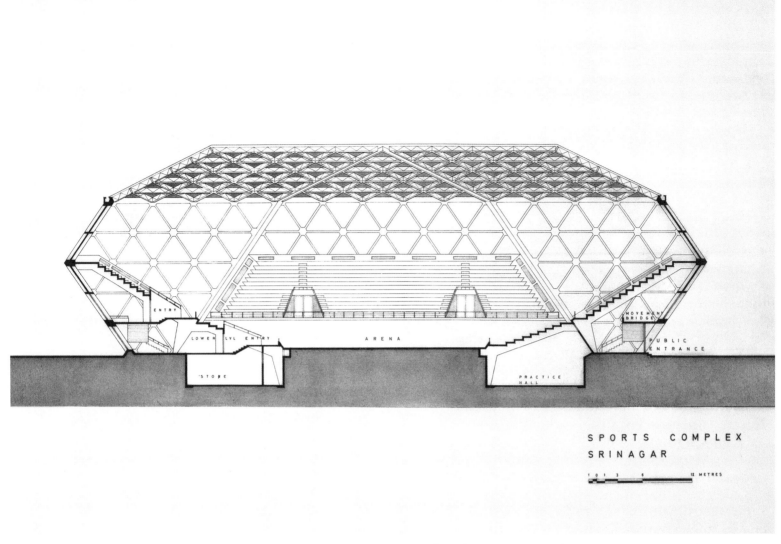

SPORTS COMPLEX
SRINAGAR

Fig. 11   Indoor Sports Stadium, Srinagar, India. 1979–82. Architect: Achyut Kanvinde (1916–2002). Engineer: Mahendra Raj (b. 1924).
Section. 1982. Mahendra Raj Archives

Fig. 12   Yasmeen Lari House, Karachi, Pakistan. 1973. Yasmeen Lari (b. 1941). Exterior view from garden. 1987.
Photograph: Kazi Khaleed Ashraf
Fig. 13   Yasmeen Lari House, Karachi, Pakistan. 1973. Yasmeen Lari (b. 1941). Interior view. 2012. Heritage Foundation of Pakistan

expressionism of concrete. The bold manifestation of daring feats of engineering was, however, by no means limited to the work of Raj, nor to India. The house that Yasmeen Lari (b. 1941), Pakistan's first woman architect, designed for herself in Karachi, completed in 1973, features cantilevered balconies that dramatically extend toward the lower garden level (fig. 12). The house speaks not only to Lari's experimentation with concrete and her determination to push the material to its limits, but also to optimism and the belief in a future wide open for new possibilities, architecturally and politically. The muscular expression of structure may also be seen as an act of self-assertion by a pioneering woman architect.[59] For Lari, concrete was a powerful emancipatory tool with which to destabilize preconceived gender politics in a conservative society and a notoriously male-dominated profession. As she explains, "I wished to challenge the notion of feminine or delicate architecture that would so logically be prescribed to me as a female."[60] The building's split-level, open interior plan was as novel to Pakistani architecture as the expressionism of the exterior (fig. 13). The living room features a coffered exposed-concrete ceiling based on a grid of squares, whose geometry could be taken as an avowal of both modernism's universalism and its translatability.[61]

TECTONICS

The aforementioned Achyut Kanvinde counts as one of the most prolific and innovative figures among the first generation of Indian architects after Independence. His use of concrete shows how the material could be made to demonstrate the elementary constructive principles of architecture by means of their ostentatious display and aesthetic expression—which is to say, by means of tectonics. Inasmuch as concrete architecture metonymically stood for the construction of a new society according to the principles of decolonization and self-determination, this project equally took on a

political meaning. After attending the Sir J. J. School of Art in Bombay, Kanvinde was sent to the United States by the Indian government in 1947 in order to attend the Graduate School of Design at Harvard University, where he studied under Walter Gropius and mingled with several Bauhaus émigrés and fellow students, such as I. M. Pei and Paul Rudolph. This educational trajectory is somewhat typical of this pioneering generation of South Asian architects, many of whom studied in the West before returning home and starting their own careers. While a large number of notable architects continued to receive their education from British schools, the increasing appeal of US educational institutions not only exemplified the new world order after World War II but also was a state-sanctioned attempt at emancipation from British dominance.[62]

Operating from his New Delhi office, Kanvinde designed a great number of significant institutional and educational buildings across the country, often resorting to overt tectonic expression based on exposed concrete in dialogue with other materials. Among the outstanding projects of the early phase of his career were the campus for the newly founded Indian Institute of Technology (IIT) Kanpur (1959–66) and the University of Agricultural Sciences (UAS) Bangalore (1967–73)—two among many newly founded institutions of higher learning that speak to the educational aspirations of the post-Independence nation (fig. 14; see Pieris, pp. 35–60). Both institutions are organized as decentralized groupings of formally rigorous buildings on open, landscaped campuses.[63] Kanvinde's conceptualization of the campus as an organism was communicated through the choice of materials: the structural skeleton of IIT Kanpur is articulated as a modular system of reinforced concrete, whereas the infill walls, forming a kind of membrane or skin, are built in local brick.[64] This overt expression of tectonic system versus infill, with its easy structural legibility even for a lay audience, was widely applied in post–World War II construction across the globe.

59   For an interesting discussion of the relationship between gender and Brutalist architecture, see Timothy M. Rohan, "Rendering the Surface: Paul Rudolph's Art and Architecture Building at Yale," *Grey Room*, no. 1 (2000): 84–107.

60   Yasmeen Lari, quoted in Mariyam Nizam, "Lari House," in Elser, Kurz, and Cachola Schmal, *SOS Brutalism*, 323.

61   For a discussion of the term "translation" in the context of decolonizing architecture, see Esra Akcan, *Architecture in Translation: Germany, Turkey, and the Modern House* (Durham, NC: Duke University Press, 2012).

62   Muzharul Islam should be mentioned in this regard. He came to the United States in 1950 from East Bengal (the future East Pakistan/ Bangladesh) to study at the University of Oregon and later completed his studies at Yale University under Paul Rudolph. See Adnan Morshed, "Modernism as Postnationalist Politics: Muzharul Islam's Faculty of Fine Arts (1953–56)," *Journal of the Society of Architectural Historians* 76, no. 4 (December 2017): 543–49.

63   Besides the strong built evidence, the intention behind these designs is further underscored by a publication on this topic: Achyut Kanvinde and H. James Miller, *Campus Design in India: Experience of a Developing Nation* (Topeka, KS: Jostens, 1969). See also Prajakta Sane, "Negotiating the International and the Local: A Reading of Achyut Kanvinde's Indian Institute of Technology Campus, Kanpur (1960–1967) and *Campus Design in India* (1969)," in *Architecture, Institutions and Change*, ed. Paul Hogben and Judith O'Callaghan, Proceedings of the Society of Architectural Historians Australia and New Zealand 32 (Sydney: SAHANZ, 2015), 536–47.

64   See Kanvinde and Miller, *Campus Design*, 70.

Fig. 14   Indian Institute of Technology (IIT) Kanpur, India. 1959–66. Architect: Achyut Kanvinde (1916–2002). Engineer: Shaukat Rai (1922–2003). View of the complex. Kanvinde Archives

Fig. 15   University of Agricultural Sciences (UAS) Bangalore (Bengaluru), India. 1967–73. Architect: Achyut Kanvinde (1916–2002). Engineer: Shaukat Rai (1922–2003). Exterior view of the administration block with the library in the foreground. Kanvinde Archives

Likewise, while the preference for local brick echoes the economic realities of a postcolonial nation, the overall approach was nevertheless aligned with the ethical and aesthetic tenets of Brutalism.[65] Conversely, the UAS of a decade later takes up the exposed concrete frameworks of the earlier building but uses local gray granite for the infills, not only hinting at the country's economic development in the interim through the choice of a more expensive material but also anticipating the proliferation of stone-clad facades in the regionalist turn in South Asian architecture from the 1980s onward (fig. 15).

Among Kanvinde's most significant buildings are those he designed—making extensive use of exposed concrete—for the National Dairy Development Board (NDDB) in several locations across India. These projects were all part of what became known as the "White Revolution"—the ambitious transformation of India into one of the world's largest producers of milk.[66] Specifically, the NDDB was responsible for promoting the dairy cooperative movement that had started in the state of Gujarat in the mid-1960s across the entire country in what became known as "Operation Flood." The White Revolution exemplified Nehru's vision of a massive industrialization of the country's economy. However, by supporting the establishment of cooperatives of individual farmers, the undertaking sought to retain the traditional livelihoods of small producers in a manner that related more to Gandhi's "village" approach for how to transform India into an independent and self-sufficient country.

Kanvinde's Dudhsagar ("sea of milk") Dairy (1970–73) is a monument to the remarkable socioeconomic shift accompanying the White Revolution (fig. 16; see Portfolio, no. 26).[67] Situated in the open countryside near the village of Mehsana in Gujarat, this cathedral of industrial production has an imposing presence. The building's layout is the result of an ingenious spatialization of the production process from the delivery of raw milk to the packaging of

dairy products that harnesses gravity in order for the milk to flow through the plant (fig. 17). Kanvinde used concrete's formal potential in this instance for a powerful expression of the underlying socioeconomic ambitions. This is most evident in the regular grid of ventilation shafts that allow the heat released in the production process to dissipate merely by means of convection currents. As architecture, these shafts form the building's crown and lend the building's profane function a highly evocative and expressive form.

PREFABRICATION AND CLIMATE

As we have seen in the case of the Hall of Nations and its elaborate concrete space frame, the abundant availability of cheap unskilled labor meant that prefabrication in post-Independence South Asia remained largely aspirational and elusive, and a large part of concrete construction continued to be based on in situ practices. An early and less well-known project by the Sri Lankan architect Geoffrey Bawa (1919–2003) is an exception to the rule. Bawa is recognized as an architect who synthesized his modernist training at the Architectural Association School of Architecture in London with cues taken from traditional and vernacular Sri Lankan building traditions.[68] However, several of his early buildings—many of them designed in partnership with the Danish architect Ulrik Plesner (1930–2016)—are aligned with the international modernism of the period, among them a classroom block at Bishop's College (1960–63) in Colombo. This project—for which he did not yet use prefabricated elements—features a modular grid of concrete frames poured in situ and projecting beam ends, which lend the facade a consistent rhythm and transform it into a diaphragm moderating light and shadow (fig. 18). The building's structural system is in many ways reminiscent of Kenzō Tange's celebrated Kagawa Prefectural Office (1954–58), which translated traditional Japanese wood construction into a modern structure using concrete.[69] The project for which Bawa most extensively experimented with prefabrication was the Ceylon Steel Corporation

65 See Sane, "Negotiating the International and the Local," 543–44; and Banham, *New Brutalism*.
66 See Bruce A. Scholten, *India's White Revolution: Operation Flood, Food Aid and Development* (London: I. B. Tauris, 2010).
67 For a brief discussion of the project see Prajakta Sane, "Dudhsagar Dairy Complex," in Elser, Kurz, and Cachola Schmal, *SOS Brutalism*, 324–25; see also Sane, "Dudhsagar Dairy at Mehsana, India (1970–73): Achyut Kanvinde and the Architecture of White Revolution," in *Open*, ed. Alexandra Brown and Andrew Leach, Proceedings of the Society of Architectural Historians Australia and New Zealand 30 (Sydney: SAHANZ, 2013), 1:355–64.
68 Shanti Jayewardene has recently attempted to demonstrate to what degree Bawa was inspired by anticolonial thinkers in order to break with the hegemony of Western thought and precedent in modern architecture. See Jayewardene, *Geoffrey Manning Bawa: Decolonizing Architecture* (Colombo: National Trust Sri Lanka, 2017).
69 Anoma Pieris argues persuasively that Valentine Gunasekara, a partner of Bawa's in the Colombo office of Edwards Reid & Begg from the late 1950s to the mid-1960s, was inspired by Kenzō Tange's work. We can assume the two principal designers in the office would have been in constant exchange about current architecture, including the Asian version of postwar modernism proposed by the Japanese Metabolists. See Pieris's contribution to this volume, p. 43.

Fig. 16 Dudhsagar Dairy, Mehsana, India. 1970–73. Architect: Achyut Kanvinde (1916–2002). Engineer: Shaukat Rai (1922–2003). Exterior view. Kanvinde Archives

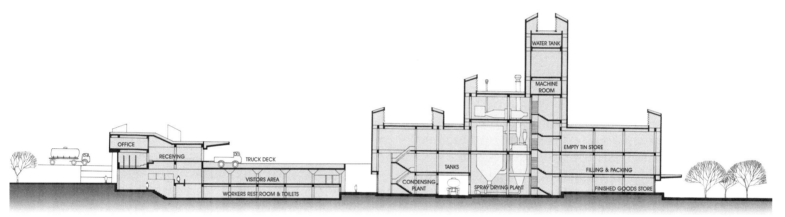

SECTION AA

Fig. 17 Dudhsagar Dairy, Mehsana, India. 1970–73. Architect: Achyut Kanvinde (1916–2002). Engineer: Shaukat Rai (1922–2003). Section. Kanvinde Archives

Fig. 18 Bishop's College, Colombo, Ceylon (Sri Lanka). 1960–63. Geoffrey Bawa (1919–2003) and Ulrik Plesner (1930–2016)/Edwards Reid & Begg. Exterior view. The Lunuganga Trust

Office Building in Oruwala (1966–69; fig. 19). The office building is situated perpendicular to the steel rolling mill on the same compound. Featuring a simple rectangular scheme based on a concrete grid that allows for an open floor plan, the building protrudes dramatically over an artificial water basin. The frame structure with its infills of precast concrete panels is counterbalanced by the outward cantilevering third floor, which is inspired by temple buildings in the Indian state of Kerala and in Nepal. (This solution echoes Bawa's concurrent design for the iconic Bentota Beach Hotel [1967–69] on Ceylon's southwestern coast.) The cantilever offers protection from the sun and the monsoon and allows for the use of breathing walls, which provide natural air circulation and make air-conditioning unnecessary.[70] Another feature through which Bawa sought to synthesize the modernist grid with vernacular references was the pitched tiled roof. This feature was anathema to modernist dogma, but it became a frequent presence in many of Bawa's buildings.[71]

In terms of the construction process, Bawa's Steel Corporation office building was in fact a hybrid between the in situ poured concrete of the grid structure and the prefabricated panel infills with precast rectangular openings. While it appears ironic that the administrative center of a steel factory would be built in (reinforced) concrete, as opposed to steel, the choice was predicated on the shortage of a wide variety of materials under Ceylon's restrictive "import substitution policy" aimed at fostering domestic production.[72] Bawa's project was built with the assistance of the Soviet Union and in line with a number of "aid and trade" agreements that the Ceylonese government signed during the 1960s with several countries of the Eastern Bloc. Ceylon had joined the Non-Aligned Movement in 1961, seeking to position itself within a Cold War world order bifurcated between the capitalist West and the communist East, alongside

an increasing number of so-called Third World countries, many of which had only recently reached independence from colonial rule. In reality, joining the Non-Aligned Movement often went hand in hand with a strong socialist leaning. The Soviet Union and its Eastern European satellite states relied heavily on prefabrication in their construction economy, and hence it was consequential that similar building technologies would be tested out in an industrial project funded by the USSR.[73]

While Bawa's office building for the Steel Corporation played out the long-standing association of exposed concrete with leftist politics and the working class on a site of industrial production,[74] another urban project of Bawa's, from roughly a decade later, sought to translate these connotations to the country's administrative complex. The twelve-story State Mortgage Bank (now known as the Mahaweli Building) of 1976–78 is Bawa's only realized high-rise and was one of the first of its kind on Colombo's skyline, anticipating the subsequent development of the city's downtown business district (fig. 20). Like the Steel Corporation building, this office tower was erected in a hybrid construction technique consisting of a concrete frame poured in situ and precast concrete elements for the ventilation grilles on the facade. The irregular, open floor plan, which is interrupted only by a handful of columns, responds to the aerodynamics of the local prevailing winds while minimizing direct sun exposure. With its highly innovative and intricate natural ventilation system, the building has been retroactively lauded as a prototype of a bioclimatic high-rise.[75] In terms of developing a modern idiom suitable to the tropical climate, Bawa may have taken cues from Minnette de Silva (1918–1998) and her Karunaratne House in Kandy (1947–51), which served as a touchstone for her manifesto-like discussion of climatic considerations as a key aspect of design within the context of

---

70 See David Robson, *Geoffrey Bawa: The Complete Works* (London: Thames & Hudson, 2002), 106; and David Robson and Channa Daswatte, "Serendib Serendipity: The Architecture of Geoffrey Bawa," *AA Files*, no. 35 (Spring 1998): 32–33.

71 For a detailed account of this story, see Pieris, *Imagining Modernity*, 114–15; and Pieris's contribution to this volume, pp. 41–43.

72 This policy was only reversed in 1977 with the turn to a liberalized economy. See Ronald J. Herring, "Economic Liberalization Policies in Sri Lanka: International Pressures, Constraints and Supports," *Economic and Political Weekly* 22, no. 8 (February 21, 1987), 325–33.

73 In embracing prefabricated concrete construction, the Soviet Union and subsequently its global allies responded to massive housing shortages after World War II and the need to build on an industrial scale. The technology became official state doctrine following a speech Nikita Khrushchev delivered to the All-Union Conference of Builders, Architects, and Workers in the Building Material Industry in December 1954. See Forty, *Concrete and Culture*, 150. While prefabricated reinforced-concrete construction came to dominate the landscape across the Eastern Bloc in the following decades, comparable systems were also developed and implemented at large scale in Western social democracies.

74 For a discussion of the (leftist) politics of concrete, see Forty, "Politics," chap. 5 in *Concrete and Culture*.

75 For a consideration of the building along these lines, see Tan Beng Kiang and David Robson, "Bioclimatic Skyscraper—Learning from Bawa" (conference paper, PLEA2006: The 23rd Conference on Passive and Low Energy Architecture, Geneva, Switzerland, September 6–8, 2006), http://web5.arch.cuhk.edu.hk/server1/staff1/edward/www/plea2018/plea/2006/Vol1/PLEA2006_PAPER134.pdf.

Fig. 19   Ceylon Steel Corporation Office Building, Oruwala, Ceylon (Sri Lanka). 1966–69. Geoffrey Bawa (1919–2003) and Ulrik Plesner (1930–2016)/Edwards Reid & Begg. Exterior view from the water. 2015. Photograph: Sebastian Posingis

Fig. 20   State Mortgage Bank (Mahaweli Building), Colombo, Ceylon (Sri Lanka). 1976–78. Geoffrey Bawa (1919–2003)/Edwards Reid & Begg. Exterior view

Fig. 21   Limestone Mining and Cement Works Housing, Joypurhat, Bangladesh. 1978–84. Muzharul Islam (1923–2012). Exterior view. Muzharul Islam Archives

Fig. 22   Loyola Chapel and Auditorium, Trivandrum (Thiruvananthapuram), India. 1971. Laurie Baker (1917–2007). Interior view. The Laurie Baker Centre for Habitat Studies

Fig. 23   Jatiya Sangsad Bhaban (National Parliament House), Sher-e-Bangla Nagar, Dhaka, East Pakistan (Bangladesh). 1962–82.
Louis I. Kahn (1901–1974); completed by David Wisdom & Associates. Photographic collage showing the building under
construction. c. January–February 1969. Gelatin silver prints with staples and tape, approx. 11 ft. 2½ in. × 37 in. (341.6 × 94 cm).
Henry Wilcots Collection, The Architectural Archives, University of Pennsylvania

South Asian modernism.[76] Ultimately, however, the Mahaweli Building's sculptural form and bold concrete expressiveness came to mark the end of an interventionist and idealist government policy, which would be substituted by a shift to an era of neoliberal laissez-faire and a subsequent turn in architectural sensibility toward regionalism—of which Bawa would eventually be the leading figure in this part of the world. The ascendance of regionalist approaches was mirrored in the 1980s on a global scale, bringing to an end a remarkable chapter in exposed concrete's international history.

CEMENTLESSNESS

While major architects widely regarded concrete to be the material of choice that allowed them to address both the universalist aspirations and the specificity of modernization in South Asia, it was by no means uncontested. The Limestone Mining and Cement Works Housing (1978–84; fig. 21), designed by Muzharul Islam (1923–2012) in Joypurhat, Bangladesh, is a noteworthy counterexample. The discovery of extensive limestone holdings in the vicinity of the town led to the construction of a large compound including housing, a hospital, a school, sports fields, a bazaar, and a mosque for two thousand workers and their families.[77] Islam's design was heavily influenced by the stereotomic monumentality of the nearby ruins of the famous Paharpur Buddhist monastery. Disregarding the factory's raison d'être, Islam favored the use of load-bearing exposed brick walls instead of concrete for the scheme, in keeping with the region's traditions, but also as a counterpoint to Louis I. Kahn's iconic parliament building in Dhaka, and its use of concrete to build a vision of modernity at monumental scale (fig. 23).[78]

The leading voice in the formulation of an alternative to concrete construction, however, was the British-born Indian architect Laurie Baker (1917–2007), whose advocacy of brick construction was part of a radical model of self-reliance and self-empowerment.[79] Acting from his base in

Trivandrum in southern India, Baker's approach harnessed the skills of local craftspeople and was informed by vernacular traditions. By embracing a do-it-yourself, low-tech approach based on brick and the recycling of waste materials for the construction of hundreds if not thousands of low-cost homes, Baker provided an inexpensive alternative to top-down government housing schemes (see Mehrotra, pp. 122–28). Through his radically democratizing approach, he also redefined the architect's profession. Instead of being an "armchair architect" absorbed in design, rather than the practice of construction, Baker pursued a hands-on approach that blurred the (Western) distinction between the conceptual/artistic role of the architect and that of the builder. Rather than an act of planning and designing, in his model of practice architecture was an act of creative improvisation.[80]

Baker's work was not limited to housing alone; he also designed a number of exceptional large-scale institutional buildings in Trivandrum, including the Loyola Chapel and Auditorium (1971; fig. 22; see Portfolio, no. 23), the iconic Indian Coffee House (c. 1980; see Portfolio, no. 38), and, perhaps most importantly, the campus of the Centre for Development Studies (1967–71; see pp. 214–17). For the last of these, Baker deployed permeable, latticed brick walls in order to create a natural cooling system, while at the same time giving the buildings a strong visual identity.[81]

Throughout his career, Baker advocated for lime as a cheap, readily available, and reliable alternative to cement. The stark contrast between the high-tech industrial fabrication of cement (as the basis for concrete construction) and the low-tech, economical, and ecological alternative of lime is strikingly illustrated in one of Baker's charming yet polemical drawings (fig. 24). The larger macroeconomic considerations that were at stake in Baker's fundamental critique of the industrialization of India's construction sector are expressed in an article published in 1974 in the *Hindustan Times*, tellingly titled

76   See Minnette de Silva, "A House at Kandy, Ceylon," *Marg* 6, no. 3 (June 1953): 4–11. The essay is discussed more extensively on pp. 178–81 of this volume.

77   See Kazi Khaleed Ashraf and James Belluardo, eds., *An Architecture of Independence: The Making of Modern South Asia; Charles Correa, Balkrishna Doshi, Muzharul Islam, Achyut Kanvinde* (New York: Princeton Architectural Press, 1998), 64.

78   For the Indian Institute of Management Ahmedabad (1962–74; see figs. 14, 15 on p. 50), Kahn had originally also intended to use exposed concrete, following Le Corbusier's example, but was convinced by local students, practitioners, and artisans to use brick instead, the long-standing material of choice of the local construction industry. See Scriver and Srivastava, "South and Southeast Asia," 301.

79   See Gautam Bhatia, *Laurie Baker: Life, Works & Writings* (New Delhi: Penguin, 1991).

80   This of course brings to mind Claude Lévi-Strauss's famous distinction between the engineer and the bricoleur. See Lévi-Strauss, *Wild Thought*, trans. John Leavitt (Chicago: University of Chicago Press, 2021), 21–24.

81   See Jayesh S. Pillai, ed., *Masterpiece of a Master Architect: Centre for Development Studies* (Thrissur, India: COSTFORD, 2014).

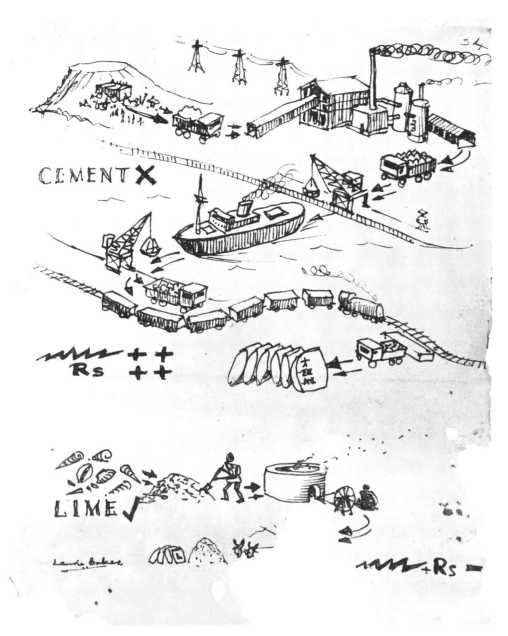

Fig. 24   Laurie Baker (1917–2007). Original of drawing featured on p. 30 of Baker's *Houses: How to Reduce Building Costs* (Thrissur, India: COSTFORD, 1986)

Fig. 25   The Hall of Nations Complex following its demolition, Pragati Maidan, New Delhi. April 2017. Photograph: Abhilash Mallick

"Cementlessness."[82] The author here pointed not only to the short supply of raw materials, but also to "fuel and power problems, difficulties of transport and distribution, labour troubles, and so on" that affected the production of cement and its application in India's construction sector.

Baker's critique of concrete construction—and, by extension, of a progressivist, Nehruvian approach to modernity premised on industrialization—and his advocacy for an alternative path for India's future, which was clearly modeled on Gandhi's elevation of village life, invite a concluding remark on the question to what degree the universalist aspirations of modernism and decolonializing nationalisms can be reconciled. Whereas these two categories have often been perceived as antagonistic and exclusive of each other,[83] the various concrete buildings discussed in this essay point to the ways in which architects melded modern materials such as concrete with the ideological tenets of postcolonial nationhood. By acknowledging and embracing the economics of scarcity and the reality of manual labor, they invented an architecture that spoke to these ambitions of the political elites as well as to the life conditions of the people on the ground. That both groups could identify with these buildings made them powerful symbols of a shared civic vision. Concrete construction not only reflected the hopes for progress and prosperity in the newly independent nation-states of the postcolonial period; they also signaled in powerful architectural gestures the politics of decolonization and self-determination. In retrospect, the gap between these ambitions and the conditions on the ground remained too large to bridge, and the "love affair with concrete" came to an end with what historian Ian Talbot calls "the clash between the 'optimistic promises' of a liberating modernism and the realities of entrenched interests, continuing poverty, and disparities of power."[84]

A POSTSCRIPT FROM THE PRESENT

The ambitious project of political and societal transformation that concrete construction stood for in the foundational years of post-Independence South Asia is presently under acute distress. Despite protests and petitions from leading architects and architectural historians across the world, New Delhi's Hall of Nations Complex was surreptitiously demolished overnight on April 23–24, 2017 (fig. 25; see Rajagopalan, pp. 165–66). India's Heritage Conservation Committee took the fatal legalistic position that the building could not be protected because it was less than sixty years old.[85] The rationale for this act of vandalism against modern cultural heritage was to make way for a grandiose redevelopment scheme of the Pragati Maidan fairgrounds that will allegedly be more suitable to the contemporary needs of exhibitions and conventions. It is all too evident that one of the most symbolic representations of the Nehruvian vision of a progressive, cosmopolitan India is fundamentally at odds with the Hindu nationalist stance of the present government. The destruction of the Hall of Nations is perhaps the most visible indication that the modernist legacy of post-Independence India runs counter to the current political climate. Moreover, it also exemplifies, and not for the first time, how vulnerable even the most architecturally accomplished buildings are to changing tastes. The new and progressive architecture of yesteryear often fails to represent these values for the present. But if we return to the analogy between the now lost temple to Indian modernity and London's Crystal Palace invoked earlier, we might, in light of the latter's own destruction in a fire in 1936, maintain that powerful architectural images can be generated as much by actual buildings as by their mnemonic representations that continue to haunt us.

82   Laurie Baker, "Cementlessness," *Hindustan Times* (New Delhi), November 4, 1974.
83   See Prakash, *Le Corbusier's Chandigarh*, 32.
84   Ian Talbot, *A History of Modern South Asia: Politics, States, Diasporas* (New Haven, CT: Yale University Press, 2016), 151.
85   See, for instance, Sanjeev K. Ahuja, "Delhi: Pragati Maidan's Hall of Nations Demolition Triggers Outrage," *Hindustan Times* (New Delhi), May 1, 2017, https://www.hindustantimes.com/delhi/delhi-pragati-maidan-s-hall-of-nations-demolished-triggers-outrage/story-MBN29qKNgeXJ1PbCFb4pgO.html.

INSTITUTIONALIZING SOVEREIGNTY: DESIGNS FOR NEW UNIVERSITIES

Anoma Pieris

Fig. 1   Indian Institute of Technology (IIT) Kanpur, India. 1959–66. Architect: Achyut Kanvinde (1916–2002). Engineer: Shaukat Rai (1922–2003). Walkways linking major buildings. Kanvinde Archives

In the years following the end of British colonial rule, the governments of South Asia's newly independent countries harnessed postcolonial sentiment for advancing progressive development agendas, blending cultural specificity with cosmopolitanism and cultivating secular traditions linked to decolonizing goals.[1] Speaking at the opening of the Nangal Canal in 1954, India's first post-Independence prime minister, Jawaharlal Nehru, famously described hydroelectric dams as "temples of the new age"—characterizing them as constituent elements of nation-building programs alongside schools, universities, hospitals, and factories.[2] Governments, private patrons, and international donors commissioned and influenced the creation of a wide range of institutions that were previously colonial or ethno-religiously aligned. Charting their own paths through the ideals and formal languages of modernism, pioneering architectural professionals across South Asia contributing to these efforts interpreted aesthetic approaches learned through Western education or by working closely with Western experts as an intentional or effective tactic of decolonization. Modernism became the language through which a generation of architects sought individual agency and legitimacy for the profession, but equally the foundation from which they hoped to build a distinctive architectural culture for South Asia.

This approach was not without problems. Modernist architecture was sharply criticized for subscribing to Western ideals of universality and encouraging neocolonial relationships. Its reception was impacted by residual anticolonial sentiment, the desire for meaningful cultural representation, and suspicion of techno-science. The formal articulation of modernist designs was often perceived as derivative of alien cultural traditions with imperial pasts. Reservations and prejudices such as these continually modified modernism's signification, inhibiting recognition of its positive contribution to institutional change. This essay explores how a selection of South Asian architects negotiate these issues, focusing on designs for schools and higher-educational institutions as emblematic of decolonization as a social process. The intention is to reevaluate important architectural legacies as decentering modernism's origins and trajectories.

INSTITUTIONAL CHANGE

Reliance on Western models would always prove contentious in South Asia because modernization and colonization had been coconstitutive. After Independence, the architectural profession remained reliant on the West for its pedagogy, and the desire for progressive internationalization remained partly subservient to the authority of foreign expertise in other ways, too. Despite the involvement of local architects, deference shown to pedigreed European or American professionals won these new arrivals significant political commissions, most notably for the new government-building complexes at Chandigarh, Dhaka, and Islamabad, through which modernist architecture gained firm regional footholds. Due to the convergence of this expertise and the nascent profession, and through the influential patronage of progressive elites—politicians, civil servants, and private industrialists—modernism was the preferred aesthetic for mid-twentieth-century institutional architecture.

This category included several designs for higher-education facilities. A nation of twenty institutions of higher education at Independence, India created a further forty during the 1960s, with industrialization and agriculture as new pedagogical priorities (fig. 1).[3] The few universities and many smaller colleges of arts, law, or medicine established before Independence in Ceylon and Pakistan similarly expanded or multiplied during the mid-twentieth century. The political leaders of South Asia saw such institutions as enabling their simultaneously cosmopolitan and liberal nationalist visions of self-reliance, as universal access to public education freed a rising generation from the entrenched social divisions created by British curricula and denominational private schools. Many colleges and university campuses of this early period were designed to reflect distinctive interpretations of sovereignty.[4] Their formal layouts and aesthetic and material choices were conceived with the intention of augmenting their users' newfound agency, and they are fondly remembered by members of the generation in question as integral to their respective nations' own coming-of-age. Placement quotas ensured greater inclusivity of socially marginalized caste

I would like to thank Peter Scriver and Sanjay Kanvinde for comments on the draft, Prajakta Sane for sharing sources, and Amit Srivastava, Madhavi Desai, and Gauri Bharat for responding to my queries.

1   See Peter Scriver and Amit Srivastava, "Nation Building: Architecture in the Service of the Postcolonial State, 1947–1960s," in *India, Modern Architectures in History* (London: Reaktion, 2015), 127–69.
2   Jawaharlal Nehru, "Temples of the New Age," *Jawaharlal Nehru's Speeches*, vol. 3, *March 1953–August 1957* (New Delhi: Ministry of Information and Broadcasting, 1960), 3.
3   Achyut Kanvinde and H. James Miller, *Campus Design in India: Experience of a Developing Nation*, (Topeka, KS: Jostens, 1969), 15–17.
4   See Kazi Khaleed Ashraf and James Belluardo, eds., *An Architecture of Independence: The Making of Modern South Asia; Charles Correa, Balkrishna Doshi, Muzharul Islam, Achyut Kanvinde* (New York: Princeton Architectural Press, 1998).

and tribal groups in India, although high-caste groups who had benefited from colonial educational pathways still dominated the student population.[5] And the enrollment of women was encouraged: notwithstanding cultural and familial pressures against coeducation, many residential colleges were adapted to accommodate them. Conservative nationalists' idealization of women as upholding domestic culture contrasted sharply with their increasing professionalization.

Inspired by the Indian *swaraj* (self-rule) movement of the late nineteenth century, whose political struggle for national independence and self-sufficiency was hugely influential throughout the region, a handful of emerging architects conceived of ideal learning environments in novel architectural idioms within which architectural agency, national consciousness, and developmental goals were closely entwined. Wary of colonial monumental traditions as symbolizing the oppression they contested, they produced a genre of institutional architectures unique to South Asia's decolonizing processes, not simply because their designs were modernist but rather because they utilized this novel aesthetic tradition to express emancipation as a vital force. Owing to their Western-centric professional education and mentorship by influential international experts, these architects' buildings were viewed by their critics as derivative of the so-called masters,[6] and their stylistic dependency lamented as arising from a sense of inferiority.[7] A more complex reading of such work, however, suggests aesthetic itineraries that can be understood as negotiating diverse motivations— indigenized self-consciousness, drives for political self-determination, and resistance to certain kinds of religious or ethnic nationalism. This generation of post-Independence architects cultivated a distinctive South Asian version of international architectural modernism that held sway until it was superseded by explicit cultural markers of regionalism in the 1980s.

INDIGENIZED MODERN SELF-CONSCIOUSNESS

The worldview of South Asia's post-Independence architects can be traced back not only to anticolonial struggles of the Indian *swadeshi* movement but also, more specifically, to the creative endeavors of the Bengali Renaissance since the nineteenth

century. The liberal humanist tradition this movement produced, culminating in the towering intellect of Rabindranath Tagore, had given rise to a unique model for tertiary education. Tagore's Visva-Bharati University, a "world university" established in 1919 in an immersive rural setting outside Calcutta at Santiniketan, had curricula patterned on indigenous ways of learning and was open to men and women. The institution's buildings— hybrid compositions of regional, religious, and vernacular references—were designed largely by Surendranath Kar (1892–1970) in collaboration with Tagore, and embodied the latter's vision of an organic cosmopolitanism rooted in a cultural context. The institution's symbiosis with its natural surroundings was achieved partly through the orientation of individual buildings outward toward the landscape, and partly through classes held informally out in the open, denying the inherited university model its colonial pomposity.[8]

Santiniketan's rustic eclecticism was, however, too like the late-colonial Indo-Saracenic styles to be pioneering.[9] The by-then widespread British colonial use of nominally Islamic or Hindu architectural forms and motifs had trivialized these references as part of an Orientalist tradition, thus making the exemplary monumental heritage of South Asia unavailable to post-Independence architects. This partly explains the embrace of modernism as an alternative to indigenous traditions by the mid-twentieth century, when it had also been established as an architectural embodiment of progressive politics, not least through the meetings of the Congrès Internationaux d'Architecture Moderne (CIAM) from 1928 to 1959. Inspired by the secular spirit of internationalism that emerged out of the devastating human and political failures of World War II, many Western and non-Western architects regarded the techno-science that underpinned their faith in modern architecture as universally applicable.

Internationalism also offered a way of rejecting the communal religio-cultural values that had proved politically divisive during Partition in 1947, when an estimated half-million people died and millions more became refugees in the violence that followed the hasty implementation of the decision to separate

5   See Ajantha Subramanian, *The Caste of Merit: Engineering Education in India* (Cambridge, MA: Harvard University Press, 2019).
6   Vikram Bhatt and Peter Scriver, *After the Masters: Contemporary Indian Architecture* (Ahmedabad: Mapin, 1990), 11.
7   Ibid., 13.
8   See Mousumi Mukherjee, "Tagore's 'Rooted Cosmopolitanism' and International-Mindedness against Institutional Sustainability," *Asia Pacific Journal of Education* 40, no. 1 (March 2020): 49–60.
9   Samit Das, *Architecture of Santiniketan: Tagore's Concept of Space* (New Delhi: Niyogi, 2003), 30.

India and the Muslim-dominated East and West extremities of the subcontinent, which formed Pakistan (see Datta, pp. 110–15). Tropes of indigenization dignified and unified emancipated national populations, but risked dividing them along ethno-religious lines. Wary of adopting references invoking the feudal heritage of princely states or the symbols used by Hindu nationalists inimical to the pluralism of Mohandas Gandhi, India advocated secularism in government building, reaffirming this stand through an amendment to the constitution in 1976. Although Pakistan was identified as an Islamic Republic from 1956 and the religion was encoded in its constitution in 1972, many architects in East and West Pakistan, including Muzharul Islam (1923–2012) and Anwar Said (b. 1940), consciously repudiated monumental Islamic motifs. Also in 1972, when the official name "Sri Lanka" replaced "Ceylon," the protection of Buddhism as the religion of the Sinhala majority was included in the country's republican constitution, marginalizing its Tamil and Muslim minorities. Such preferences were already features of the island's public architecture, most notably its Independence Hall (1953), which was modeled on the Royal Audience Hall in Kandy. Sri Lankan architects such as Minnette de Silva (1918–1998) and Geoffrey Bawa (1919–2003) deliberately rejected these monumental religious traditions, favoring forms and motifs from ordinary vernacular buildings. Throughout South Asia, architects did not straightforwardly adopt internationalism but synthesized modernist designs with a situated place-consciousness that would anchor their architecture in its respective geographical context.

Several South Asian architects who established careers after independence were mentored by luminaries of architectural modernism—Achyut Kanvinde (1916–2002) and Habib Rahman (1915–1995) by émigré architect Walter Gropius at Harvard University, Muzharul Islam by Paul Rudolph at Yale University, and Balkrishna V. Doshi (b. 1927) by Le Corbusier in his Paris office in the early 1950s. Maxwell Fry (1899–1987) and Jane Drew (1911–1996), both also designing at Chandigarh, were equally instrumental in guiding students in the program in tropical architecture established at the Architectural Association School of Architecture (AA) in London in 1954. The ambitious modernist government-building complexes at Chandigarh, Dhaka, and Islamabad—where Le Corbusier, Louis I. Kahn, and Constantinos A. Doxiadis, respectively, conceived the master plans—were profoundly influential. German-Jewish architect and town planner Otto Koenigsberger (1908–1999) was also a key figure: he had moved to India in 1939 and stayed until 1951, assuming many development-planning roles, not least as Federal Director of Housing for Nehru's government. Upon returning to London after fourteen years in India, he would take over as head of the AA's Department of Tropical Architecture and later established University College London's Development Planning Unit, both attracting international students from postcolonies. Several South Asian architecture students of that generation were educated in Australia along similar lines under the Colombo Plan scheme during the 1950s and 1960s.

Women's careers were equally shaped by education at overseas institutions and exposure to eminent Western architects. Both Minnette de Silva, who worked for Koenigsberger before attending the AA in London, and the Indian architect Urmila Eulie Chowdhury (1923–1995), who studied at the University of Sydney, were deeply influenced by Le Corbusier, the former as a close friend and the latter as a senior architect on the design team for Chandigarh from 1951 to 1963.[10] Gira Sarabhai (1923–2021) was a student apprentice at Frank Lloyd Wright's Taliesin West studio from 1947 to 1951.[11] Pravina Mehta (1923–1992), who with Charles Correa (1930–2015) and Shirish Patel (b. 1932) proposed and developed the New Bombay Plan in 1965, studied at the Chicago Institute of Design under the Russian-born British architect Serge Chermayeff. Minakshi Jain (b. 1943), a pioneer of the architectural conservation movement, studied under Kahn at the University of Pennsylvania.[12] Many women architects also worked in New Delhi at the office of the Nebraska-born Joseph Allen Stein (1912–2001), which was established in 1955.[13]

As with their male compatriots, international training and social mobility identified certain women as elites among their contemporaries. Wealthy, educated women were increasingly instrumental in commissioning and collaborating with male architects, as was the case with textile designer Ena de Silva (1922–2015) and artist and writer (and also textile designer) Barbara Sansoni (b. 1928) and their

10   Madhavi Desai, *Women Architects and Modernism in India: Narratives and Contemporary Practices* (London: Routledge, 2017), 54. De Silva also apprenticed with Bombay firm Khedwar and Mistry, and briefly attended the Sir J. J. School of Art in the same city.
11   Ibid., 59. Gira's brother Gautam Sarabhai also attended the school.
12   "Minakshi Jain," CEPT Archives, accessed July 15, 2021, http://www.ceptarchives.org/Peoples/minakshi-jain.
13   Mary N. Woods, *Women Architects in India: Histories of Practice in Mumbai and Delhi* (London: Routledge, 2017).

Fig. 2   Minnette de Silva climbing a ladder to inspect concrete pillars and slab work at Nedra de Saram's house, Colombo, Ceylon (Sri Lanka). 1951

Fig. 3   Loyola Graduate Women's Hostel, Trivandrum (Thiruvananthapuram), India. 1970. Laurie Baker (1917–2007). View from internal courtyard. The Laurie Baker Centre for Habitat Studies

support of the partnership of Geoffrey Bawa and Danish architect Ulrik Plesner (1930–2016) in Ceylon. Urban conservationist and architect Brinda Somaya (b. 1949), from the second generation of post-Independence women architects, has noted the importance of women's patronage in her career.[14] Nevertheless, women were conspicuously absent from major architectural commissions, often relegated to the sidelines as assistants to men, or confined to domestic and commercial design spheres dependent on familial networks. Although the 1950s push to expand technical education had created a pathway for women's professionalization,[15] women students were underrepresented in nascent architecture programs until the 1970s.[16] Design curricula typically referred to architects as "he," even when the Indian nation was feminized—as in Charles and Ray Eames's 1958 *India Report*, which led to the establishment of the National Institute of Design (NID) in Ahmedabad.[17] A photograph of a sari-clad de Silva climbing a ladder at Nedra de Saram's house in Colombo in the early 1950s captures both her agency and her objectification through the camera's lens (fig. 2).

Many women architects engaged in direct forms of political activism; indeed, the will to indigenize their sources and methods frequently politicized their career pathways. Gandhi's advocacy of gender equality proved consequential for this change, as did the activism of family members for some women. Gira Sarabhai, who with her brother Gautam helped set up and designed the aforementioned NID, was the daughter of a prominent industrialist and supporter of Gandhi.[18] Her aunt Anasuya Sarabhai was a pioneer in India's women's labor movement, and her sister, Mridula, participated in the famous Salt March Gandhi organized in 1930.[19] Minnette de Silva's mother, Agnes, championed women's suffrage in Ceylon. Their families' politicization influenced de Silva's and Pravina Mehta's nonviolent civil disobedience actions. Mehta was imprisoned in 1942 after being arrested at a protest organized by the anticolonial Quit India Movement, the same year that de Silva was expelled from the colonial Sir J. J. School of Art in Bombay

for participating in a student rally over Gandhi's arrest.[20] These women embodied the anticolonial struggle, de Silva famously pursuing self-determination through international advocacy of a regionally rooted architectural practice.

DEFUSING CHRISTIAN AUTHORITY

The distinctive regional history produced by modernism's intended programmatic and aesthetic autonomy in South Asia included the aesthetic revision of many colonial institutions, foremost among them those associated with traditions of Christian proselytization. As postcolonial institutions advanced their secular pedagogies, the favorable status Christian religious education had enjoyed in the colonial era was subject to greater scrutiny. In Ceylon, the state took over Catholic schools in 1960. Some religious institutions adapted indigenous architectural forms and motifs, among them the Cathedral of Christ the Living Saviour (1968–73)—the Protestant mother church in Ceylon's capital city—which was designed by government buildings department architects Tom Neville Wynne-Jones and P. H. Wilson Peiris in the octagonal form of a Buddhist prayer hall. Christian institutions also frequently turned to experiments with the language of modernism. And architects practicing in the 1950s and 1960s judiciously used modernist aesthetics to defuse the authority of the Church, striving to humanize the architectural presence of its buildings and integrate them with their surroundings. In the process, the universality of the modernist aesthetic was called into question, and situational characteristics were emphasized.

For example, at the campus of the Jesuit institution Loyola College in Trivandrum, Kerala, the British-born Indian architect Laurie Baker (1917–2007) domesticated the barrack dormitory model for his Loyola Graduate Women's Hostel (1970; fig. 3), turning it into a familial configuration of cottages, gardens, and pools that would soften the inhabitants' separation from home. Avoiding an expensive, monolithic structure for the Loyola

14   Ibid., 68.
15   Scriver and Srivastava, *India*, 215–16.
16   When Bombay-based architect Hema Sankalia (1934–2015) studied at the Sir J. J. School of Art in 1951, there were only three women in a class of sixty. Desai, *Women Architects*, 71.
17   Thanks to Gauri Bharat for information on the curricula of the Centre for Environmental Planning and Technology in Ahmedabad. Charles and Ray Eames, *The India Report* (April 1958) (Ahmedabad: National Institute of Design, 1997), 7, 11, http://echo.iat.sfu.ca/library/eames_58_india_report.pdf.
18   Desai, *Women Architects*, 59.
19   The Salt March was a nonviolent rally of civil disobedience protesting the British salt monopoly.
20   Desai, *Women Architects*, 65, 399.

Chapel and Auditorium (1971; see fig. 22 on p. 29; Portfolio, no. 23), Baker placed two smaller buildings side by side. An ingenious double-wall, supported with brick cross-bracing, created a lofty interior beneath a roof that sloped downward on wooden trusses from the nave along the entire building's length.[21] Baker's simple, craft-based approach, honed through private residential commissions, gave his institutional designs a disarming humility and allowed them to blend successfully into the landscape. A material palette of exposed brick and tile, with the rare functional use of concrete, patterned or molded in fanciful details, tempered the austerity of the modernist geometries. Baker's biographer, Gautam Bhatia, traces the architect's committed moral economy to the austere simplicity of his Quaker upbringing, which was augmented by Gandhian values.[22]

A comparable talent for softening modernist contours was evident in the work of Geoffrey Bawa, who would gain an international reputation as a regionalist architect following his celebrated indigenous formal plan and aesthetic for Sri Lanka's 1982 parliamentary complex. His early efforts—in collaboration with Ulrik Plesner from 1958 to 1967— at adapting modernist architectural forms by introducing elements drawn from rural vernacular architecture suggest that he was already questioning the relevance of the borrowed style. Bawa's buildings for elite missionary schools in Colombo, designed in the Architectural Association's Tropical Modernist idiom, are what architecture scholar David Robson describes as "part of a series of experiments to develop an effective system of breathing walls . . . using local materials and traditional forms."[23] The Montessori School for St. Bridget's Convent (1963–64), in Colombo, features a first-floor slab on mushroom-top *pilotis* with a cavernous textured undercroft, contrasted with a high roof canopy on the airy upper floor (fig. 4). Robson characterizes it as "a witty reworking of a traditional wattle-and-daub village school,"[24] while architectural historian Shanti Jayewardene, who attributes Bawa's intellectual break with modernist thought to his growing sensitivity to the island's indigenous past, interprets his introduction of overhanging, pitched vernacular roof forms as an act of decolonization, continuing similar endeavors

by de Silva in a wattle-and-daub reception center at Sigiriya in 1954 and a proposal for a seaside resort at Kalkudah in 1959.[25] Incrementally, across a number of projects, both de Silva and Bawa (with Plesner) introduced vernacular architectural features to their modernist designs. "The umbrella country-tile on asbestos roof and lattice timber window boxes became signature motifs of the Plesner-Bawa architecture," Jayewardene writes.[26] The sweeping gabled roof perched on its Brutalist base at St. Bridget's Montessori School can thus be seen as marking an aesthetic turning point in an established colonial institution—the alma mater of Sirimavo Bandaranaike, incumbent prime minister of Ceylon at the time. In this building, two aesthetic traditions, one modernist and the other derived from the country's vernacular building tradition, were in counterpoint.

Beyond its formal expression, which marked an early phase in Bawa's aesthetic of decolonization, Bawa and Plesner's playful design, further articulated through collaboration with artists Laki Senanayake (1937–2021) and Barbara Sansoni, has the capacity to delight its juvenile occupants. The low walls and freestanding concrete cavelike cubicles, balconies, and spiral staircases fashion an adobe-style environment that mimics the curve of the human hand (fig. 5). A differentiated space for the playful intrigues of childhood, distinct from the rectilinear orthodoxy of the institution's colonial buildings, the project draws out the phenomenological qualities of darkness and light, curvature and texture, as key to the architects' decolonizing praxis. Given that the flat, urban site imparts no clues to its geographical context, they created their own internal topography, opening up vistas to the sky. Decades later, when regionalist architectures (influenced in part by his example) held sway, Bawa was commissioned to design campus buildings for the University of Ruhuna in Matara, on Sri Lanka's southern coast. For this project (1980–88), he envisioned an expanded indigenized institutional complex of urban-scale vernacular architecture. Colonnaded passages and towering hipped roof structures cascading down the site's sharp inclines suggest an architectural outgrowth from the island's culture and terrain. De Silva conceived of a similar pavilion hall structure in her 1984 design for the

21   Gautam Bhatia, *Laurie Baker: Life, Works & Writings* (New Delhi: Penguin, 1991), 174–78.
22   Ibid., 16.
23   David Robson, *Geoffrey Bawa: The Complete Works* (London: Thames & Hudson, 2002), 66.
24   Ibid., 68
25   Shanti Jayewardene, *Geoffrey Manning Bawa: Decolonizing Architecture* (Colombo: National Trust Sri Lanka, 2017), 82, 84, 123.
26   Ibid., 88.

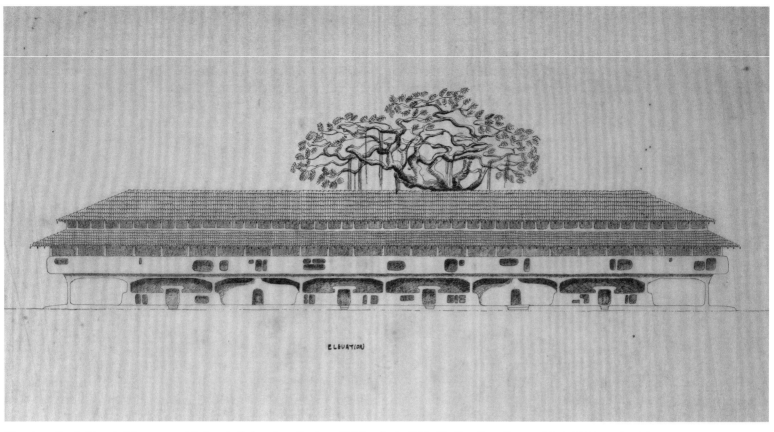

Fig. 4 St. Bridget's Montessori School, Colombo, Ceylon (Sri Lanka). 1963–64. Geoffrey Bawa (1919–2003) and Ulrik Plesner (1930–2016)/ Edwards Reid & Begg. 1963. Elevation. Ink on tracing paper, 16 9/16 x 39 3/8 in. (42 x 100 cm). The Lunuganga Trust

Fig. 5 St. Bridget's Montessori School, Colombo, Ceylon (Sri Lanka). 1963–64. Geoffrey Bawa (1919–2003) and Ulrik Plesner (1930–2016)/ Edwards Reid & Begg. Interior view. The Lunuganga Trust

Kandyan Art Association's Centenary Cultural Centre, whose building profile echoed Kandy's mountainous setting and whose many changing levels captured the configuration of space through terracing typical of a hillside village. The modernist legacies of these buildings were effectively masked.

A quite different strategy was pursued by Sri Lankan architect Valentine Gunasekara (1931–2017), who was a onetime partner with Bawa at the Edwards Reid & Begg practice in Colombo and in the 1960s was designing similarly curvaceous forms to those of Bawa and Plesner's Montessori School, for example at the Convent of Our Lady of the Cenacle at Hiniduma (1964–65). He cited Kenzō Tange's Yoyogi National Gymnasium in Tokyo (1961–64) as informing his own efforts at aesthetic and cultural synthesis, which he explored in close collaboration with engineer Jayati Weerakoon (1928–2021).[27] For Gunasekara—whose commitment to modernism was strengthened by conversations with Kahn, Richard Neutra, and the Eameses about their work in South Asia during a trip to the United States in 1966—the introduction of a skirt roof at the Roman Catholic Chapel of Our Lady of Providence at Tewatte (1969) combined a negotiation of the formal demands of a modern chapel with aspects that integrated the building with its village setting. The spiral plan, with a conversation pit for the congregation, responded to the liturgical reforms of the Second Vatican Council a few years prior.[28] The walls peel back to let in slivers of light along the interior perimeter, and the skylight at the apex of the roof illuminates the center of the building. The floating, asymmetrically placed roof form is supported on four columns designed by Gunasekara to represent the four evangelists bearing the sheltering tent of God (figs. 6, 7).

Whereas Bawa sidestepped the teleology of modernization, reinstating a familiar vernacular tradition as timeless and continuous, Gunasekara was captivated by the possibility of creative autonomy, testing many unique and daring structural innovations as yet alien to Ceylon. He was inspired by a regionally inflected California modernism, which he saw as aligned with a more self-conscious modernity. His Jesuit Chapel in Colombo ((1960; fig. 8) responds to its modern urban setting with a hybrid composition reminiscent of Le Corbusier's Notre-Dame du Haut

(1954–55) and Mexican vernacular forms. Like many Indian architects of the era, Gunasekara saw Continental and American stylistic inspirations as liberating architecture from reference to both a feudal caste-bound past and oppressive British colonial legacies.

EMBODIED CAMPUS PLANNING

Bawa's and Gunasekara's radical departures from colonial institutional typologies contrasted with buildings constructed by Ceylon's government architects during the late 1940s and 1950s. As mentioned above with regard to Colombo's Independence Hall, the emphasis on Buddhism, the religion of the Sinhala majority, marginalized minority ethnic identities. Bawa's aforementioned University of Ruhuna campus was preceded more than thirty years earlier by an equally celebrated University of Ceylon campus at Peradeniya (1949–52; now named University of Peradeniya), on which work had begun in the early 1940s. The building designs combined Deco-style modernism with Buddhist architectural features in a manner reminiscent of Surendranath Kar's eclectic application of religious and cultural motifs at Santiniketan. The Public Works Department's "university architect," Shirley D'Alwis (1925–2017), the only non-Briton on a team including architects/town planners Patrick Abercrombie (1879–1957) and Clifford Holliday (1897–1960), channeled his Sinhalese heritage through references to the landscaping strategies used at the ancient Buddhist monasteries in Anuradhapura, in north-central Ceylon. Decorative facade elements and building features amplified this connection. While the institution encouraged greater gender equality and vastly expanded educational opportunities in a country that had granted women suffrage as early as 1931, formal hall rituals based on the Oxbridge model persisted as a colonial norm. *Marg*, the Bombay-based progressive magazine of art and architecture, whose architectural editors included de Silva, criticized the design as having "lost the opportunity of creating a modern local tradition in architecture."[29]

Whereas Ceylon's government architects favored Buddhist revivalist aesthetics even after Independence, Indians, by contrast, were emboldened— not least through the example of Le Corbusier at Chandigarh—to explore other more or less related

27   Anoma Pieris, *Imagining Modernity: The Architecture of Valentine Gunasekara* (Colombo: Stamford Lake, 2007), 114.
28   A circular plan was likewise introduced in Laurie Baker's conical St. John's Cathedral in Kerala (1972–74), reflecting a global reevaluation of entrenched institutional forms and hierarchies.
29   "Ceylon's First University," *Marg* 3, no. 1 (1949): 12–19.

Fig. 6   Chapel of Our Lady of Providence, Tewatte, Ceylon (Sri Lanka). 1969. Valentine Gunasekara (1931–2017). Section drawing by Milinda Pathiraja, 2004

Fig. 7   Chapel of Our Lady of Providence, Tewatte, Ceylon (Sri Lanka). 1969. Valentine Gunasekara (1931–2017). Plan drawing by Milinda Pathiraja, 2004

Fig. 8   Jesuit Chapel, Colombo, Ceylon (Sri Lanka). 1960. Valentine Gunasekara (1931–2017). Exterior view. Valentine Gunasekara Archive

strains of Continental modernism. Following his training at the Sir J. J. School of Art in Bombay and then in the United States under Walter Gropius at Harvard University, Achyut Kanvinde pursued functionalist modernism in his early institutional projects. The first aspect of this to emerge took the form of a modernist national style stripped of the eclectic ornamentation that marked colonial architecture in the past. This proposition was endorsed by Nehru at the Seminar on Architecture convened by Kanvinde at the Lalit Kala Akademi, New Delhi, in 1959.[30] The "unanimous opinion" of seminar participants was summarized thus: "the present architecture in India can be evolved by rationally expressing . . . solutions connected with materials, technological and climatic considerations within the social and economic objectives in a harmonious way satisfying the visual demands and not by applying fragments and adornments of past styles of architecture."[31]

The second dimension of US professional practice that Kanvinde advocated for was the elaboration of the architect's role to include social planning. This entailed a new, expanded function for the profession that had historically played second fiddle to engineers on large government projects. The belated recognition of the autonomy of architecture, as Kanvinde saw it, was due to the paucity of training programs under the colonial administration and the subservient role of indigenous practitioners in the past. Appointed to the government council responsible for setting up national scientific and industrial research institutions and laboratories, Kanvinde put his advocacy into practice.[32]

Established with the intention of narrowing developmental disparities both within India and between India and Western nations, five Indian Institutes of Technology (IITs) and seven State Agricultural Universities were built from 1951 to 1964.[33] In consultation with Harvard Business School and the MIT Sloan School of Management, the first two

Indian Institutes of Management (IIMs) were also established, in Ahmedabad and Calcutta, in 1961. The focus on professional courses in technology and science was based on that of the American land-grant universities that had been set up in the second half of the nineteenth century. The first of the IITs was planned by Swiss architect Werner Moser (1896–1970) and built in 1951–52 in Kharagpur (outside Calcutta), on the grounds of the infamous Hijli Detention Camp, where many anticolonial protestors were once detained, creating a link between the campus designs and the colonial cantonment spaces that preceded them.[34] The early IITs were funded variously by the USA, the Soviet Union, West Germany, and the UK, reflecting the consequences of India's position as a leading member of the Non-Aligned Movement with respect to international aid.

Secular scientific education was a key nation-building strategy in Nehru's model of centralized economic planning. As both colonial and feudal systems had been dependent on labor-intensive economies, the new goal was the expansion of "a highly trained and powerfully motivated educated class."[35] Less than 2 percent of college-age Indians were enrolled in higher education in 1965, compared with 40 percent in the United States.[36] In their retroactive design manifesto, *Campus Design in India*, Kanvinde and H. James Miller (an American consultant on campus planning) highlighted these disparities while inserting Indian institutions into a global survey of campus designs that also accounted for regional precursors: Buddhist centers of learning at Taxila (in today's Pakistan) and Nalanda and Ajanta (in today's India).[37] The fourteenth-century Islamic Madrasa-e-Feroz Shahi in New Delhi, significant for India's Muslim minority, was additionally used to historicize an indigenous typology. Unlike in Ceylon, such precedents did not influence a revivalist aesthetic; in fact, Kanvinde's preference for functional modernism accorded with Nehru's vision of the secular "temples" of modern India, an analogy Prajakta Sane has applied in her study of Kanvinde's career.[38]

30 Achyut Kanvinde, ed., *Seminar on Architecture* (New Delhi: Lalit Kala Akademi, 1959).
31 "Report of the Seminar on Architecture," in ibid., 10.
32 See Ashok B. Lall, "Kanvinde and His Times," in *Achyut Kanvinde: Ākār*, ed. Tanuja Kanvinde and Sanjay Kanvinde (New Delhi: Niyogi, 2017), 28–37.
33 Kanvinde and Miller, *Campus Design*, 3.
34 Sabil Francis, "The IITs in India: Symbols of an Emerging Nation," *Südasien-Chronik/South Asia-Chronicle*, no. 1 (2011): 311.
35 *A Report of the Education Commission, 1964–66: Education and National Development* (New Delhi: Ministry of Education, 1966), as quoted in Kanvinde and Miller, *Campus Design*, 15.
36 Ibid., 18.
37 Ibid., 75.
38 Prajakta Sane, "Modern Temples for Post-Independence India: Institutional Architecture of Achyut Kanvinde" (PhD thesis, University of New South Wales, 2016), 12, http://unsworks.unsw.edu.au/fapi/datastream/unsworks/40403/SOURCE02.

Santiniketan, not a planned campus but an accretion of aesthetically eclectic buildings, was absent from this genealogy.

One of the book's model campuses was IIT Kanpur (1959–66; see Portfolio, nos. 5, 6),[39] for which Kanvinde (with the engineer Shaukat Rai) showcased an elegant and articulated modernism in the functionalist multimodular design tradition he learned from his mentor Gropius, expressing its clean lines and material integrity in a concrete-frame-and-brick-infill architecture. Envisioning a staged program of works, they elaborated on and extended their design to fill the entire campus master plan. A networked system of elevated and internal pedestrian walkways linking various buildings produced an integrated organism with a discernible hierarchy (fig. 9), where, as Kanvinde and Miller put it:

> The "structural skeleton" is the framework of buildings. The "muscles" are the ordered sequence of linked spaces, classed as static or dynamic, collector, focal, intimate or monumental. The services provide the networks of "nerves" and the "circulation system" consists of pedestrian ways and roads. There is an administrative "brain center" that should be convenient and easily identified from the campus entrance. And finally, it is important for a campus to have a "heart" or core of centralized activity around which the whole campus grows and functions. . . . In India the heart of the campus is the ideal location for a Gandhi Bhavan [a commemorative hall].[40]

Anthropomorphic analogies were a familiar architectural currency in India, both in the geomantic *vāstu* tradition and in its translation in Le Corbusier's urban plan for Chandigarh. But while in both of these cases the diagrammatic axiality of the prostrate human body reinforced programmatic hierarchies and thus shared this at least with Edwin Lutyens and Herbert Baker's colonial-era designs for New Delhi, Kanvinde's layout was structured around the distance between central core and periphery, calculated on the basis of the ten-minute walk from dormitory to classroom typical for smaller US residential campus plans.[41] The integral role of this embodied practice and the related pedestrian network is evocatively captured in his graphite perspectives (fig. 10).

Unlike the much more grandiose visions of democratic institutions idealized at Chandigarh, Kanvinde focused on the rights and freedoms that Independence had brought with it. In his thinking, these translated into greater educational opportunities, higher standards of living, and better civic amenities.[42] Such egalitarian sentiments guided his designs for residential campuses where, while referencing the traditional *gurukul* system (in which the pupil lives in the sage's house), he refused to organize staff quarters by rank.[43] Kanvinde was also eager to make these environments gender-inclusive, despite the male-dominated environment and technical focus of the IITs. Indeed, *Campus Design in India* features many images of women in various educational settings. Advocating for the engagement of privately practicing architects in development programs, a section of the report framed an organizational structure involving the appointment of a "director or university architect who coordinates all university physical development activities."[44] According to this model, a role that had previously been reserved for government engineers and architects would be freed from the pressures of the government bureaucracy. Kanvinde adapted the campus model for many research institutions linked to India's major industries, most notably for the National Dairy Development Board at Anand (1967–72). Here, too, his designed embodiment of human experiences expressed a more democratic decolonization than the anthropomorphized hierarchies of the geomantic tradition referenced at Chandigarh.

COSMOPOLITAN COLLABORATIONS

The Indian federation, organized as fourteen states and seven union territories between 1950 and 1956, gave rise to a number of new state capitals, most notably at Chandigarh for the eastern, Indian part of Punjab, but also, for example, at Gandhinagar and

39   See Prajakta Sane, "Negotiating the International and the Local: A Reading of Achyut Kanvinde's Indian Institute of Technology Campus, Kanpur (1960–1967) and *Campus Design in India* (1969)," in *Architecture, Institutions and Change*, ed. Paul Hogben and Judith O'Callaghan, Proceedings of the Society of Architectural Historians Australia and New Zealand 32 (Sydney: SAHANZ, 2015), 536–47.
40   Kanvinde and Miller, *Campus Design*, 38.
41   Ibid., 30.
42   Ibid., 10.
43   Ibid., 9, 43.
44   Ibid., 45.

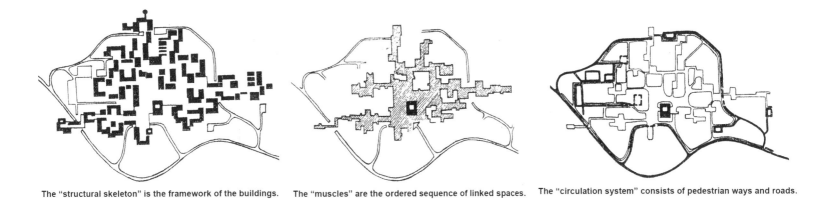

The "structural skeleton" is the framework of the buildings.   The "muscles" are the ordered sequence of linked spaces.   The "circulation system" consists of pedestrian ways and roads.

Fig. 9   Indian Institute of Technology (IIT) Kanpur, India. 1959–66. Architect: Achyut Kanvinde (1916–2002). Engineer: Shaukat Rai (1922–2003). Master plan showing the campus as an integrated organism. Kanvinde Archives

Fig. 10   Indian Institute of Technology (IIT) Kanpur, India. 1959–66. Architect: Achyut Kanvinde (1916–2002). Engineer: Shaukat Rai (1922–2003). Perspective drawing by Kanvinde. Kanvinde Archives

Fig. 11   Calico Dome (Calico-shop Dome), Ahmedabad, India. 1963. Collapsed in 2001; restoration planned. Gira Sarabhai (1923–2021) and Gautam Sarabhai (1917–1995). Exterior view. Sarabhai Foundation, Calico Museum of Textiles

Fig. 12   Ahmedabad Textile Industry's Research Association (ATIRA) Building, Ahmedabad, India. 1950–54. Achyut Kanvinde (1916–2002). Exterior view. Kanvinde Archives

Fig. 13   Ahmedabad Textile Mill Owners' Association (ATMA) Building, Ahmedabad, India. 1951–56. Le Corbusier (Charles-Édouard Jeanneret, 1887–1965). Exterior view. c. 1965

Bhubaneswar. In addition to state governments and foreign donor agencies, private patrons influenced and came to define the program and goals of these newly defined spaces, seizing the many opportunities they presented for post-Independence institution-building. Such collaborations were not entirely unusual: even before Independence, the Bombay-based Parsi industrialists running the conglomerate Tata Sons advanced the career of Otto Koenigsberger by offering him numerous commissions, no doubt easing his transition from government architect of Mysore State to post-Independence India's Federal Director of Housing.[45] Preeti Chopra writes of collaboration between elite entrepreneurial communities and the colonial government of British Bombay as a "joint enterprise."[46] Similar alliances gave unique expression to the institutions of Ahmedabad, reclaimed as the temporary capital of the new state of Gujarat from 1960 to 1970, where the patronage of Jain industrialists afforded plentiful opportunities for architectural experimentation. The groundwork for them was shaped in part through commissions awarded to Le Corbusier and Louis I. Kahn, whose work incubated an indigenized strain of modernist architecture with regional characteristics.

Although not a prominent colonial entrepôt like Bombay, Ahmedabad had been linked to global networks of capital and industry since the nineteenth century, largely through the enlightened calico mill–owning Lalbhai and Sarabhai families.[47] In the 1920s and 1930s, these families supported Gandhi, whose association with Ahmedabad augmented its virtues. The Sabarmati Ashram, where he and his followers lived between 1917 and 1930—and from which he led the famous Salt March—was named after and located on the banks of the river that flows through the city. The state capital that replaced Ahmedabad in 1970 would be named Gandhinagar, literally "City of Gandhi."[48] The mill owners appeared not to see a contradiction between their capitalist outlook and Gandhian values. Rather, as Daniel Williamson observes, in the buildings they commissioned, the "use of an architectural language rooted in industrial forms and materials . . . helped naturalize their industry as a

legitimate manifestation of modern Indian identity," even if their capitalist worldview clearly contrasted with Nehru's socialist ethos as much as with Gandhi's asceticism. Indeed, their transformation of commercial capital into cultural capital was founded on the moral obligation that Jain merchants had felt toward shaping their city over generations and an attempt to make the city a rival to its great competitor, Bombay.[49] Ahmedabad's new institutions were dispersed in the more exclusive western section of the city and involved many collaborators: the Ahmedabad Education Society's elite patrons, the Gujarat state government, the Ford Foundation, and, most significantly, the siblings Vikram, Gautam, and Gira Sarabhai, the first a physicist and the last two a brother-and-sister team of architects.

Surendranath Kar, Tagore's architect at Santiniketan, had renovated and redesigned the Sarabhai house in the 1930s, inspiring Gira to join Santiniketan before she pursued an architecture apprenticeship under Frank Lloyd Wright.[50] The two architect siblings' 1949 Calico Museum of Textiles and a new office building Wright designed for the Sarabhais before Independence were forerunners to the geodesic Calico Dome, also known as the Calico-shop Dome, built by Gira and Gautam in 1963 (fig. 11). The Sarabhais invited the Eameses, R. Buckminster Fuller, Frei Otto, Kahn, and other prominent Western architects and thinkers to the city.[51] The family commissioned an early effort at testing the Bauhaus-via-Harvard aesthetic in Achyut Kanvinde's ATIRA Building (1950–54) for the Ahmedabad Textile Industry's Research Association (fig. 12; see Portfolio, no. 10). Le Corbusier was invited to build villas for the Sarabhai and Shodhan families as well as the Ahmedabad Textile Mill Owners' Association (ATMA) Building (1951–56; fig. 13), and Sanskar Kendra (1956), a museum for the city. These were followed by Kahn's influential Indian Institute of Management Ahmedabad (IIMA) building (1962–74; figs. 14, 15), which experimented with a more homogeneous exposed-brick architecture, and was designed with the assistance of Doshi and architect Anant D. Raje (1929–2009), NID students, and junior faculty.

45   Rachel Lee mentions Koenigsberger's designs for the dining hall/auditorium and the Departments of Aeronautical Engineering and Metallurgy at the Indian Institute of Science in Bangalore, as well as the Tata Institute of Fundamental Research in Bombay, in "Constructing a Shared Vision: Otto Koenigsberger and Tata & Sons," *ABE Journal*, no. 2 (2012), https://doi.org/10.4000/abe.356.
46   Preeti Chopra, *A Joint Enterprise: Indian Elites and the Making of British Bombay* (Minneapolis: University of Minnesota Press, 2011).
47   See Daniel Williamson, "Modern Architecture and Capitalist Patronage in Ahmedabad, India 1947–1969," PhD thesis, New York University, 2016.
48   Ravi Kalia, *Gandhinagar: Building National Identity in Postcolonial India* (Columbia: University of South Carolina Press, 2004).
49   Ibid., 19.
50   Ibid., 40.
51   Desai, *Women Architects*, 60.

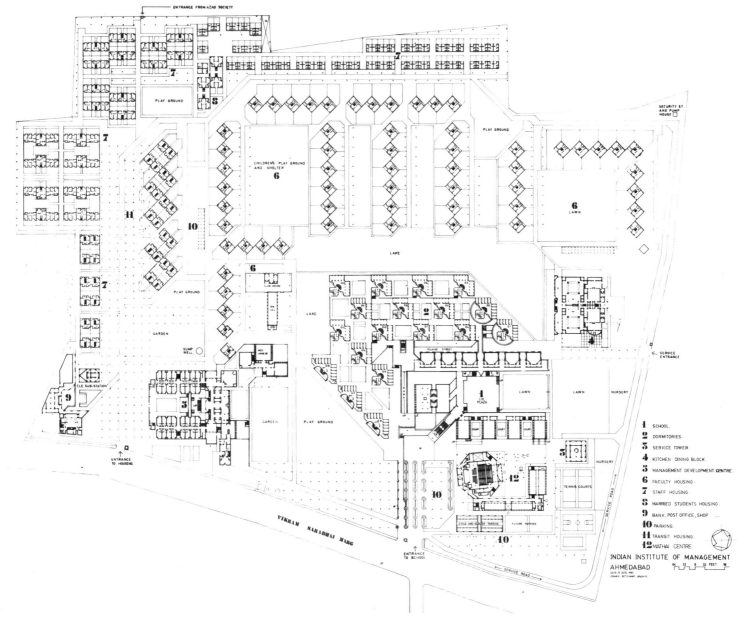

Fig. 14   Indian Institute of Management Ahmedabad (IIMA), Ahmedabad, India. 1962–74. Architects: Louis I. Kahn (1901–1974) with
Balkrishna V. Doshi (b. 1927) and Anant D. Raje (1929–2009). Engineer: Mahendra Raj (b. 1924). Site plan. Ink on paper, 9¹/₂ x 12 in.
(24.1 x 30.4 cm). Anant D. Raje Collection, The Architectural Archives, University of Pennsylvania

Fig. 15   Indian Institute of Management Ahmedabad (IIMA), Ahmedabad, India. 1962–74. Architects: Louis I. Kahn (1901–1974)
with Balkrishna V. Doshi (b. 1927) and Anant D. Raje (1929–2009). Engineer: Mahendra Raj (b. 1924). View of one of the
dormitory buildings under construction. IIMA Archives

Conceived by their clients as architectural symbioses of a capitalist model of modernity and a self-conscious negotiation of postcolonial identities, prominent cultural institutions built in Ahmedabad over the following decades undertook novel cosmopolitan interpretations of cultural sovereignty that departed from modernist formulas. As time went on, expanded architectural education produced a generation of practitioners and teachers anchored in the region—most prominently Doshi, a native Gujarati speaker who settled in Ahmedabad in 1955, and later became well known for his distinctive atelier, a center for discussion and debate named Sangath (1978–80; fig. 16), which translates, roughly, to "in fellowship." Doshi also designed Ahmedabad's Lalbhai Dalpatbhai Institute of Indology (1957–62; fig. 17; see Portfolio, no. 1), and, in collaboration with the structural engineer Mahendra Raj (b. 1924), Tagore Memorial Hall (1963–67; see fig. 7 on p. 18) and Premabhai Hall (1956–74; see fig. 10 on p. 20; Portfolio, no. 3). Charles Correa's Gandhi Memorial Museum (1958–63) at the Sabarmati Ashram (see fig. 6 on p. 152), meanwhile, even as it was influenced by the formal geometry of Kahn's Trenton Bath House (1955–57), in Ewing, New Jersey, reinterpreted the grid of pavilions and courtyards to signify attributes of the Indian vernacular expressive of Gandhian ethics.

The new institutional architecture of this period in Ahmedabad reflected an experimental approach to the creation of total environments (with accommodation facilities) for new educational programs in industrial or scientific research or management education. Gira and Gautam Sarabhai's flagship campus for the National Institute of Design (NID) (1959–67) introduced students to the professional-practice model, where they addressed design problems that their professors were currently engaged in, "blurring the line between school and apprenticeship."[52] Doshi's School of Architecture (1962–68), a kind of rival to NID that evolved into the Centre for Environmental Planning and Technology (CEPT)—cultivated an ethos of social responsibility through curricula engaging with broader local concerns (see pp. 198–201). The building's architectural language reciprocated its pedagogical orientation: the openness and interconnectivity of its educational approach was echoed in the site layout, with corner entry-points maximizing pedestrian flows. Using repetitive bays of concrete beams supported on load-bearing brick walls, Doshi hollowed out the interiors of the School of Architecture building like a

sculptor excavating a hillock, incorporating covered streets, shaded passages, and outdoor rooms (see Portfolio, no. 24).[53] Both schools attracted students from across India, and, maintaining close connections to a wider international circle of architects, sent many of them to the United States for further studies. Anant D. Raje, who had worked with Kahn in Philadelphia and completed Ahmedabad's IIM building after his untimely death, taught (like Doshi) at CEPT and many institutions in North America. Correa, similarly, helped export the Ahmedabad outlook he had explored in the Gandhi Memorial Museum and the Tube House he designed for the Gujarat Housing Board (1961–62; see figs. 4, 5 on p. 123) to the practice he established concurrently in Bombay.

DIVIDING SOVEREIGNTY

This congruence of institutional expansion with postcolonial nation-building in India and Ceylon, nominally secular nation-states with dominant religious majorities, initially seemed to apply equally to the newly fashioned Muslim constituencies of East and West Pakistan. These two Muslim-majority areas of former British India were now on either side of the northern Indian states. The division of power between these territorial segments proved contentious, as West Pakistan's Urdu-speaking population exerted political and economic dominance over the more numerous Pakistani Bengalis in the East. Provoked by these inequalities, Bangladeshi nationalists challenged national Pan-Islamic unity in an internecine conflict culminating in the short but bitter 1971 Indo-Pakistan War. Indian forces intervened to secure East Pakistan's independence as the newly formed nation of Bangladesh, souring Indo-American relations as the US sought regional footholds against Soviet influence through strategic relations with Pakistan.

During the politically turbulent early decades after the end of British rule, Pakistan swung between democratic and military government and periods of martial law. In the early years, at least from 1947 to 1956, Pakistan operated as a secular Muslim state. Two years later, the Army general Ayub Khan forcibly seized power in a coup. His elaborate modernizing schemes continued the experimentation with secular aesthetic traditions, most notably for the new capital Islamabad and the National

52 Ibid., 193.
53 James Steele, *The Complete Architecture of Balkrishna Doshi: Rethinking Modernism for the Developing World* (London: Thames & Hudson, 1998), 44, caption.

Fig. 16   Balkrishna V. Doshi (b. 1927) in his studio, Sangath (1978–80), Ahmedabad, India. Photograph: Edmund Sumner. Vāstu Shilpā Foundation Archives

Fig. 17   Lalbhai Dalpatbhai Institute of Indology, Ahmedabad, India. 1957–62. Balkrishna V. Doshi (b. 1927)/Vāstu Shilpā. Exterior view. Photograph: Vinay Panjwani. Vāstu Shilpā Foundation Archives

Assembly complex in Dhaka. Making clever use of the aid investments of UN and US technical assistance programs, Khan's military government embarked on elaborate social and physical planning programs, channeling systems of patronage and foreign expertise into the country. While India and Ceylon were among the founding members of the Non-Aligned Movement (NAM), and Bangladesh joined soon after its independence in 1973, Pakistan joined only in 1979. During Khan's rule, interventions and alliances inimical to the tenets of the NAM sensitized the region to broader global events and, as Farhan Karim argues, while expanding Pakistan's institutional landscape, aligned the country with the United States, introducing decentralization, deregulation, and reduced state control, which led to a weakened civil society.[54] This US-led developmental model contrasted with India's, which was was influenced by Soviet-style economic planning. Given the paucity of private architectural practices, many leading Western architects were invited to design the nation's new institutions, among them Americans including Edward Durell Stone, Richard Neutra, Stanley Tigerman, Richard E. Vrooman, Daniel C. Dunham, Paul Rudolph, and Louis I. Kahn, as well as the Greek architect Constantinos A. Doxiadis.

Before working on his most prominent commission in the region, the master plan for Islamabad (1958–67), Doxiadis (1913–1975) had been a consultant for the Ford Foundation and the government of Pakistan, designing the Korangi Township in West Pakistan (1958–63) for refugees displaced by Partition. His firm, Doxiadis Associates (DA), had developed an approach they named *ekistics*, the "science of human settlements," a method referencing late 1950s "systems thinking" based on systematic investigation of the factors needed for preserving human-scale local activities as part of a global system. Applying this approach to institutional architecture, DA designed a standardized system and rationale for the East Pakistan School Building Program (1961–66), introducing modular prototypes for over eight thousand schools.[55] As part of the Ford Foundation's programs in

transnational cultural diplomacy, school buildings, colleges, and institutes were established in both East and West Pakistan.[56]

Many of DA's institutional designs were small colleges: polytechnics, home-economics colleges, teacher-training centers, and academies for village development in rural areas. These contrasted with the urban scale of DA's planning at Korangi and in the new town for the University of the Punjab on the outskirts of Lahore (1959–73; figs. 18, 19). For the latter, West Pakistan's past urban traditions were invoked, encompassing the Mughal palace architecture of Lahore and the urban formations of the ancient Buddhist city of Taxila, but avoiding British colonial institutional styles typified, for example, by the Mayo School of Arts in Lahore.[57] Unlike the anthropomorphic layout of Kanvinde's Kanpur campus, DA's design for the university used Lahore's Bari Doab canal as an organizing axis that divided student housing from staff residences and academic blocks, and would allow for expansion to the north and south. A second axis—a linear, partially covered, central spine along the length of the administrative complex—echoed the esplanade along the canal. Intricately interwoven open courts and patios culminated in a central pedestrian square, offering a range of spatial experiences complemented by surrounding green areas referencing the rural hinterland.[58] This accretion of spaces was, in fact, suggestive of the vernacular urban morphologies to which Doxiadis referred in design analyses juxtaposing the palace and the ancient city.[59] His preferences were partly inflected by his own regard for the urban monumental traditions of his homeland, Greece.[60] But, despite such occasional references to the past, his vision was firmly focused on "the city of the future" produced by systemic design.[61] Two major principles of 1960s planning, the dynamics of growth and the mechanism of circulation, guided the campus layout.[62] DA's model of designing something not fixed but always with an eye to potential future growth saw its ultimate expression in the Dynapolis (or dynamic city) described in the firm's master plan for Islamabad (see pp. 186–89).[63]

54   Farhan Karim, "Between Self and Citizenship: Doxiadis Associates in Postcolonial Pakistan, 1958–1968," *International Journal of Islamic Architecture* 5, no. 1 (March 2016): 137.
55   Government of Pakistan, "Primary Schools Programme, East Pakistan," *Ekistics* 16, no. 94 (September 1963): 185.
56   Karim, "Between Self and Citizenship," 138.
57   Ahmed Zaib K. Mahsud, "Doxiadis' Legacy of Urban Design: Adjusting and Amending the Modern," *Ekistics* 73, nos. 436–41 (2006): 249.
58   Ahmed Zaib Khan Mahsud, "Rethinking Doxiadis' Ekistical Urbanism," *Positions*, no. 1 (Spring 2010): 22.
59   Mahsud, "Doxiadis' Legacy," 247.
60   "The University of the Panjab," *DA Bulletin*, no. 56 (July 1963).
61   "Islamabad: The New Capital of Pakistan," *DA Bulletin*, no. 64 (March 1965).
62   Mahsud, "Doxiadis' Legacy," 245.
63   "Islamabad: The New Capital of Pakistan," 2.

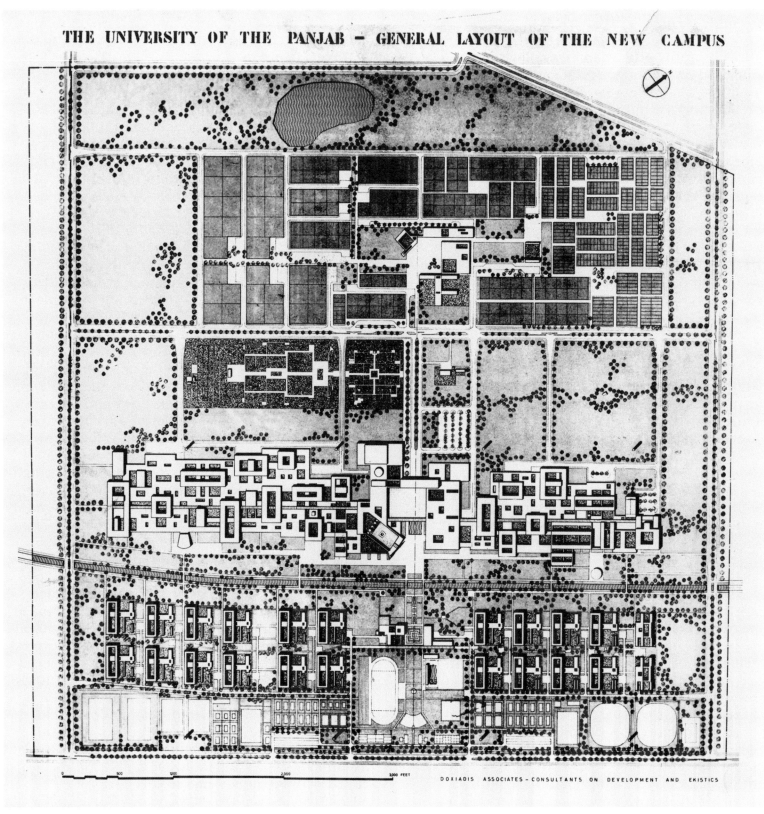

Fig. 18   The University of the Panjab (Punjab), Lahore, Pakistan. 1959–73. Doxiadis Associates (est. 1951). General layout of the new campus. Constantinos A. Doxiadis Archives

Fig. 19   The University of the Panjab (Punjab), Lahore, Pakistan. 1959–73. Doxiadis Associates (est. 1951). Exterior view. Constantinos A. Doxiadis Archives

Fig. 20   Home Economics College for Women, University of Dhaka, East Pakistan (Bangladesh). 1959–61. Doxiadis Associates (est. 1951). Photograph of site model. 1959. Constantinos A. Doxiadis Archives

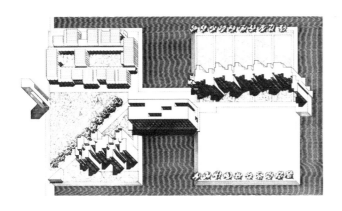

Fig. 21   Five Polytechnic Institutes, East Pakistan (Bangladesh). 1965–71. Muzharul Islam (1923–2012)/Vastukalabid and Stanley Tigerman (1930–2019). Plan oblique drawing. Ryerson and Burnham Art and Architecture Archives, The Art Institute of Chicago

DA turned to rural inspirations for the Village Development Academies, which were established to train village workers and disseminate new farming practices. Village-like formal and spatial configurations, with accommodation clusters for different grades of employees, characterized the academies in Comilla, East Pakistan, and Peshawar, West Pakistan, both commissioned by the Ford Foundation in 1957.[64] In East Pakistan, Doxiadis somewhat unfairly concluded that life on a flood plain prevented an urban monumental tradition comparable to that of the British colonial or Mughal eras, and his designs for urban educational institutions emulated rural settlements, breaking up discrete functions into scattered pavilion units.[65] On flat urban sites such as those of the Education Extension Centre and Home Economics College for Women at the University of Dhaka, pavilions were linked by sheltered walkways.[66] Doxiadis also introduced certain iconic features to differentiate the architecture of East Pakistan from West.[67] The *dochala* roof, the curvilinear roof typical of Bengali vernacular architecture, for example, was a dominant feature in all of his projects in East Pakistan, although, as Farhan Karim notes, the form had also been used by the Mughal Empire, notably as a canopy over the throne room—and thus served as evidence of the centralization of power even in its far-flung provinces.[68] Doxiadis applied his scientific method to justify regional variations, invoking climatic and topographical features, although his formal aesthetic references disclosed his biases toward what he considered to be an urban civilization in West Pakistan and an agrarian culture in the East.

At DA's Home Economics College for Women, completed in 1961, the mosque and assembly hall are the only standalone elements in a spatially integrated pavilion complex (fig. 20). The master plan was rationalized using three interconnected elements: closed rooms, semiclosed verandas, and open courtyards,[69] with each type reflecting the accommodations that traditional Bengali

architecture made to the tropical climate.[70] The pavilion-like classrooms linked to formal laboratory spaces create a contrast to the barrack-like hostel building, capturing the intended education of women through "house-keeping and citizenship."[71] By dignifying household activities as a means of emancipation, these much-lauded institutional programs unwittingly reinforced patriarchal divisions of labor and the affiliation of women with the domestic sphere. This may have been reflected in the architecture, too: Doxiadis described the cluster morphology of traditional Bengali villages as an expression of fundamental patriarchal relations, which "should be looked at if we want to avoid big upsets of the pattern of life overnight."[72] It was hardly surprising that the consultant promoted its formal adaptation, along with these embedded values: even South Asian architects who recognized a need to overcome social hierarchies persistently failed to recognize the discriminatory gendered subtexts encoded in the spatial organization of traditional dwelling types.

The approach adopted by Bangladeshi modernist Muzharul Islam (1923–2012) was different from that of Doxiadis, if equally sensitized to territorial distinctions. Deeply influenced by Bengali resistance to the imposition of Urdu under West Pakistan's political leadership, he experienced Pakistan's bifurcated nationalism as a visceral anxiety. In his work, as with others in a similar position, self-awareness inspired by the anticolonial independence movement was complemented by his Marxist social consciousness. However, unlike Doxiadis, Islam adopted a distinctively modernist urban formalism in his designs for East Pakistan's institutions, beginning with the highly acclaimed Institute of Fine Arts (1953–56; see Portfolio, no. 11) and Public Library (1953–54; see Portfolio, nos. 21, 22) at the University of Dhaka. This was not surprising considering his eclectic education, which consisted of engineering studies in Calcutta and later, from 1952 to 1961, architecture studies overseas—at the University of Oregon, in the AA's

64 Doxiadis Associates, "Village Development Academies in Pakistan," *Monthly Bulletin*, no. 12 (April 1960).
65 Constantinos A. Doxiadis, Pakistan Diary, October–November 1954, 2:18–23, DOX-PP 20, Constantinos A. Doxiadis Archives, Benaki Museum, Athens.
66 Doxiadis Associates, "Education Extension Center at Dacca, East Pakistan," *Monthly Bulletin*, no. 16 (August 1960); and Doxiadis Associates, "Home Economic College at Dacca, Pakistan," *Monthly Bulletin*, no. 17 (September 1960).
67 Karim, "Between Self and Citizenship," 149.
68 Ibid., 150.
69 Doxiadis Associates, "Home Economics College at Dacca, Pakistan," *Monthly Bulletin*, no. 17 (September 1960).
70 Doxiadis Associates, "Two Educational Buildings at Dacca," *Ekistics* 7, no. 42 (April 1959): 347.
71 Ibid.
72 Constantinos A. Doxiadis, Pakistan Diary, January 20–February 24, 1955, as quoted in Markus Daechsel, *Islamabad and the Politics of International Development in Pakistan* (Cambridge, UK: Cambridge University Press, 2015), 88.

program in tropical architecture in London, and under Paul Rudolph at Yale. Islam and American architect Stanley Tigerman (1930–2019) collaborated on five polytechnic institutes between 1965 and 1971 that were featured as framing new approaches to tropical architecture in a 1968 issue of *Architectural Record*.[73] Modular prototypes were developed using a systemic, kit-of-parts approach, with buildings arranged as a contiguous urban morphology. But in contrast to Doxiadis's preference for rural pavilion forms, and unlike Islam's own purpose-designed Jahangirnagar University (1967–70), and Chittagong University (1965 71; see pp. 206–209; Portfolio, no. 25), Islam and Tigerman adapted their system (fig. 21) uniquely to the setting of each institute, rejecting tabula rasa site-creation.

Extensive data collection on a range of environmental and social factors preceded their designs. The architects drew cues from topographical variations of familial housing clusters and the climatic orientation and porosity of village buildings across Bengal—arguably the same formations that Doxiadis observed.[74] Modular brick and concrete envelopes wrapped the various strata of university housing in a homogenizing formal aesthetic, disguising the persistent rank and gender distinctions within them. North-south-oriented exposed-brick fins laid out in a staggered, repeating fashion produced narrow, undulating formal components of up to five levels that gave village artisans opportunities to build in a familiar language at an institutional scale (fig. 22). Islam's landmark water towers were almost classically Brutalist, reminiscent of aspects of Rudolph's Yale Art and Architecture Building (1963), while the abstract volumetric geometries emulated the inspirational modernism of architects such as Kahn, who was invited on Islam's recommendation to build the Dhaka Capitol Complex (1962–82). Corridors weaving between and around the varied spatial containments of the institutes created thoroughfares and lobby spaces porous to the buildings' surroundings, while the louvered facades acted like perforated screens.[75]

Funded by the International Bank for Reconstruction and Development as a government initiative to expand technical education in South Asia, the institutes were symbols equally of East Pakistani modernism and of the internationalization of Pakistan. In conversations recorded by Kazi Khaleed Ashraf, Islam describes the necessity of being both "world man" and "Bengali,"[76] synthesizing culture, religion, and environment with modernist thinking in ways that bring to mind his spiritual mentor, Tagore.[77] By the late twentieth century, however, modernism itself seemed on the retreat as regionalism became an ever more powerful force, spearheaded internationally by the Geneva-based Aga Khan Foundation, a transnational NGO with a non-Western focus, launched in 1977. Although focused largely on rural development, the foundation also set up architecture education programs at Harvard University and the Massachusetts Institute of Technology. At the Aga Khan Award's seminar on "Regionalism in Architecture," held in Dhaka in 1985, Suha Özkan rejected the division between modernism and regionalism, describing how the former could itself provide the tools to achieve the goals of the latter.[78] On the same occasion, Islam, with Ashraf and Saif Ul Haque, made the case for regionalism, identifying the key issues as: recognizing the role of topography and climate, historicizing Bengali roots that had been disrupted by Mughal and British imperialism, sustaining the vitality of material and spiritual aspirations, and resisting Western dominance in global architectural culture.[79] Rather than modernism itself, it was "internationalism" that came to be vilified as the lineage of modernism most profoundly antithetical to regionalist ideals.

CONCLUSION

Through their radical innovations in the design of educational institutions, many local architects across South Asia domesticated modernist antecedents, inventing new aesthetic approaches for ever more confident expressions of decolonization. These have been interpreted as masking Christian

73   Raymond Lifchez, "Master Plan Study Gives East Pakistan New Approaches for Tropical Architecture," *Architectural Record*, September 1968, 153–60.
74   Kazi Khaleed Ashraf ed., *An Architect in Bangladesh: Conversations with Muzharul Islam* (Dhaka: Loka, 2014), 129.
75   Zainab F. Ali and Fuad H. Mallick, *Muzharul Islam, Architect* (Dhaka: Brac University Press, 2011), 93–104.
76   Ashraf, *Architect in Bangladesh*, 45.
77   Ibid., 171; and Adnan Morshed, "Modernism as Postnationalist Politics: Muzharul Islam's Faculty of Fine Arts (1953–56)," *Journal of the Society of Architectural Historians* 76, no. 4 (December 2017): 545.
78   Suha Özkan, "Introduction: Regionalism Within Modernism," in *Regionalism in Architecture*, ed. Robert Powell (Geneva: Aga Khan Award for Architecture, 1985), 12.
79   Muzharul Islam, Kazi Khaleed Ashraf, and Saif Ul Haque, "Background: Introducing Bangladesh—A Case for Regionalism," in Powell, *Regionalism in Architecture*, 23–26.

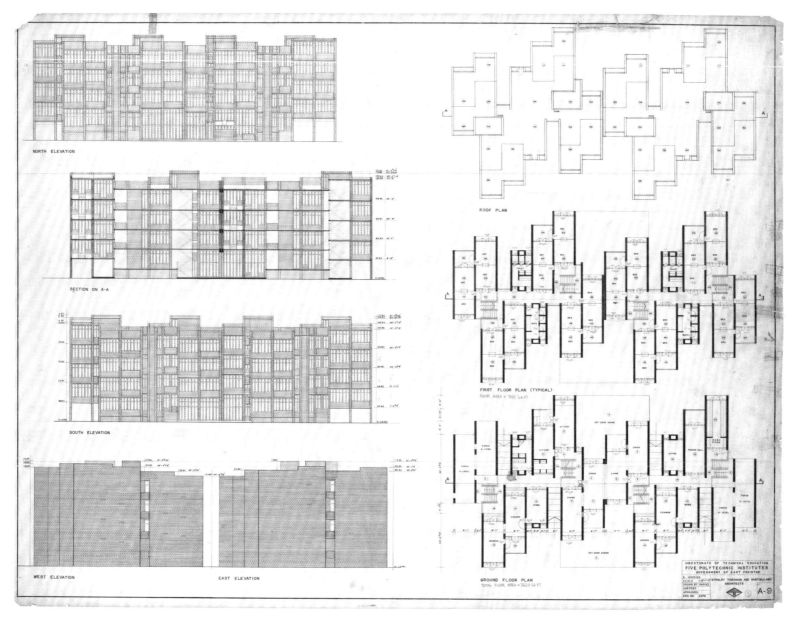

Fig. 22   Five Polytechnic Institutes, East Pakistan (Bangladesh). 1965–71. Muzharul Islam (1923–2012)/Vastukalabid and Stanley Tigerman (1930–2019). Plans and elevations. ⅛″ = 1′-0″. Muzharul Islam Archives

programs, embodying and anthropomorphizing decolonized subjectivities, and synthesizing the dynamic political and economic transformations of post-Independence sovereignty. Maintaining an openness to exogenous—which is to say, primarily Western—influences throughout these key nation-building decades, architects were energized and supported by state-sanctioned commissions and, at least in India, the patronage of influential industrialists. In conjunction with the anticipation of informality and the engagement with and orientation toward local landscapes in building layouts, the widespread denial of axiality—which seemed redolent of colonial urban planning, not least because of the broad, straight avenues of colonial New Delhi—and of overtly religious symbolism convincingly demonstrates how internal social forces were beginning to shape the practices of architects across South Asia. The freedoms and opportunities of political sovereignty were encoded in their designs, and this humanistic impulse was also expressed through materials that softened the aesthetic homogeneity of archetypally modernist exposed-concrete frames and incorporated South Asia's masonry craft traditions. Because of their introduction via neocolonial channels, patronizing aid programs, and foreign expertise, however, the many innovations of the time were overlooked in subsequent decades, when publics demanding more culturally specific aesthetics greeted modernist legacies with misgivings.

A certain elitism based on the traditional architectural display of symbolic caste and class markers affected the reception of the modernist aesthetic outside the world of architects educated into its vocabulary. Unplastered brickwork or exposed concrete was perplexing to many as indicative of impoverishment rather than taste.[80] International modernism was also associated with a period of austerity and economic stagnation for the urban upper-middle classes across South Asia during the 1970s, inflecting modernist architecture with biases of reception unrelated to its design intentions. The legacy of modernism was also associated with the many hastily built and badly designed boxlike concrete structures that proliferated in South Asia's cities. The incipient profession was insufficiently visible, and architectural training had not yet produced a wider educated public culture that could engage with these issues beyond the mutually respectful client-architect relationships that supported their concentration in certain times and

places, as in the somewhat unique case of Ahmedabad. Modernism's novel cosmopolitan ideals and restrained aesthetic formalism were best conveyed and sometimes best appreciated where several modernist institutional complexes in proximity to one another produced immersive, publicly accessible urban landscapes. Arguably, that is why the Capitol Complexes at Chandigarh and Dhaka had a greater impact—if not an uncontroversial one—than the many university campuses that were built across the subcontinent.

Global critiques of technoscientific rationalism and of policies of import substitution (by which governments applied high tariffs to goods from abroad in order to encourage domestic industrialization) reinforced these reservations throughout the 1970s. The antipathy toward Western cultural domination and intolerance of seemingly foreign aesthetic approaches were inflamed by the residual anticolonial sentiment that the legacy of British rule still provoked, while a sense of political autonomy and influence was accentuated through membership of the Non-Aligned Movement. A determined turn toward vernacular approaches and the oil crises of 1973 and 1979 triggered a reorientation among South Asian architects toward craft-based technologies and an emphasis on cultural rootedness as a core value. The Aga Khan Award seminars in 1983 and 1985, focused on identity and regionalism, respectively, were watershed moments in this shift, and, along with the emergence of the South Asian Association for Regional Cooperation (SAARC), established in Dhaka in 1985, seemingly marked the end of the post-Independence era. In the architecture of the time, formerly buried or implicit aesthetic gestures of indigenization became visible, expressive interpretations of cultural sovereignty. Nonetheless, "culture" proved to be a slippery categorization that shifted between an essentializing primitivism, an acultural humanism, and an autonomous—in many respects undeniably "Western"—eclecticism. Many architects who participated in the Aga Khan seminars negotiated between two perspectives—one informed by the indigenous identities that made their voices authentic and the the other by Western education that legitimized them and often led them to modify their design vocabulary to gain international recognition.[81] Earlier cosmopolitan modes of self-expression were suppressed and superseded, awaiting belated reflective scrutiny alongside comparable modernist legacies.

80   Balkrishna Doshi, *Paths Uncharted* (Ahmedabad: Mapin 2019), 272–73.
81   Samer Akkach, "Identity in Exile: The Aga Khan's Search for Excellence in Islamic Architecture," in *On What Grounds? Conference Proceedings*, ed. Sean Pickersgill and Peter Scriver (Adelaide: SAHANZ, 1997), 1 8.

Building on the work of the Aga Khan Program in the previous decade through the journal *Mimar* (1981–1992) and its Architects of the Third World series of monographs, a generation of scholars, many of them South Asian, advanced critiques of architectural production that questioned the profession's ongoing Western bias. These were corroborated during the early 2000s by numerous analyses of colonialism, social modernity, and nationalism as social and political processes manifested in urban built form.[82] Recognition of shared postcolonial sensibilities increasingly inspired comparative studies not limited to a nation or a city. Duanfang Lu's 2011 anthology of essays, *Third World Modernism*, claimed an autonomous trajectory for modernism in non-Western geographies, as did another collection from that year, William Siew Wai Lim and Jiat-Hwee Chang's *Non West Modernist Past*.[83] The award of the Pritzker Architecture Prize to Doshi in 2018 illuminated a career that has negotiated the transition from modernism to regionalism during the latter half of the twentieth century. The project *SOS Brutalism: Save the Concrete Monsters!*—a global survey of the 1950s–70s aesthetic that began as an exhibition at the Deutsches Architekturmuseum in Frankfurt in 2017 and was accompanied by a book and an online platform—incorporated examples from across Asia.[84] Although sometimes still burdened by the epistemic limitations of Western definitions of universality, such retrospective reflections offered a broader framing than that afforded by architectural scholarship's dominant Euro-American focus, not least through the attention paid to the Global South. Regionalism, too, has been increasingly critiqued— for its artifice of authenticity, and its descent, at times, into sentimental nostalgia, ripe to be exploited by the tourism and real-estate industries. The culturally explicit, decolonized regionalist aesthetic nevertheless repositioned South Asia's bold modernist legacies as foils to its own agenda, ultimately making it possible to look at them anew.

82 See Nihal Perera, *Society and Space: Colonialism, Nationalism, and Postcolonial Identity in Sri Lanka* (Boulder, CO: Westview, 1998); Swati Chattopadhyay, *Representing Calcutta: Modernity, Nationalism, and the Colonial Uncanny* (London: Routledge, 2005); Jyoti Hosagrahar, *Indigenous Modernities: Negotiating Architecture and Urbanism* (London: Routledge, 2005); Peter Scriver and Vikramaditya Prakash, eds., *Colonial Modernities: Building, Dwelling and Architecture in British India and Ceylon* (London: Routledge, 2007); William J. Glover, *Making Lahore Modern: Constructing and Imagining a Colonial City* (Minneapolis: University of Minnesota Press, 2008); and Anoma Pieris, *Architecture and Nationalism in Sri Lanka: The Trouser under the Cloth* (London: Routledge, 2012).
83 Duanfang Lu, ed., *Third World Modernism: Architecture, Development and Identity* (London: Routledge, 2011); and William Siew Wai Lim and Jiat-Hwee Chang, eds., *Non West Modernist Past: On Architecture & Modernities* (Singapore: World Scientific, 2011).
84 See Oliver Elser, Philip Kurz, and Peter Cachola Schmal, eds., *SOS Brutalism: A Global Survey* (Zurich: Park Books, 2017).

PORTFOLIO

Randhir Singh

Editors' note: The portfolio that follows was commissioned for this book from New Delhi–based photographer Randhir Singh. Due to travel restrictions connected to the ongoing coronavirus pandemic, it could not be completed as originally conceived. It features fewer projects from Pakistan and Sri Lanka than originally intended, and incorporates a small number of images from the photographer's archive. Nevertheless, the portfolio captures the curatorial vision and the afterlives of modern architecture in South Asia in the post-Independence period.

1   Lalbhai Dalpatbhai Institute of Indology, Ahmedabad, India. 1957–62. Balkrishna V. Doshi (b. 1927)/
Vāstu Shilpā. Exterior view

2   Shri Ram Centre for Art and Culture, New Delhi, India. 1968–72. Architect: Shiv Nath Prasad (1922–2002).
Engineer: Mahendra Raj (b. 1924). Exterior view

3　Premabhai Hall, Ahmedabad, India. 1956–74. Architect: Balkrishna V. Doshi (b. 1927)/Vāstu Shilpā.
Engineer: Mahendra Raj (b. 1924). Exterior view

4   Sardar Vallabhbhai Patel Municipal Stadium, Ahmedabad, India. 1959–66. Architect: Charles Correa (1930–2015). Engineer: Mahendra Raj (b. 1924). Exterior view

5   Indian Institute of Technology (IIT) Kanpur, India. 1959–66. Architect: Achyut Kanvinde (1916–2002).
Engineer: Shaukat Rai (1922–2003). Exterior view

6   Indian Institute of Technology (IIT) Kanpur, India. 1959–66. Architect: Achyut Kanvinde (1916–2002).
    Engineer: Shaukat Rai (1922–2003). View of walkway

7   Indian Institute of Management (IIM) Bangalore (Bengaluru), India. 1977–92. Balkrishna V. Doshi
(b. 1927)/Vāstu Shilpā. View of walkway

8   Lunuganga Estate, Bentota, Ceylon (Sri Lanka). 1948–98. Geoffrey Bawa (1919–2003). 2019. Exterior view

9   National Institute of Design (NID), Ahmedabad, India. 1959–67. Gira Sarabhai (1923–2021) and
Gautam Sarabhai (1917–1995). Exterior view

10 Ahmedabad Textile Industry's Research Association (ATIRA) Building, Ahmedabad, India. 1950–54. Achyut Kanvinde (1916–2002). View of entrance

11 College of Arts and Crafts (Institute of Fine Arts), University of Dhaka, East Pakistan (Bangladesh).
    1953–56. Muzharul Islam (1923–2012). Exterior view

12 India International Centre (IIC), New Delhi, India. 1958–62. Joseph Allen Stein (1912–2001). Exterior view of roof and facade details

13 India International Centre (IIC), New Delhi, India. 1958–62. Joseph Allen Stein (1912–2001). Interior view of
C. D. Desmukh Auditorium

14 Golconde guesthouse, Pondicherry (Puducherry), French India (India). 1937–42. Antonin Raymond
(1888–1976), George Nakashima (1905–1990), François (František) Sammer (1907–1973), and
Chandulal Shah (d. 1945). Exterior view

15 Triveni Kala Sangam, New Delhi, India. 1957–63. Joseph Allen Stein (1912–2001). Exterior view

16 St. Xavier's Primary School, Ahmedabad, India. 1967. Hasmukh C. Patel (1933–2018). View from one of the terraces

17 Lalit Kala Akademi (LKA), New Delhi, India. 1961. Habib Rahman (1915–1995). Exterior view

18 Type II Flats, Netaji Nagar, New Delhi, India. 1954–56. Habib Rahman (1915–1995). Exterior view

19 Kamala House, Ahmedabad, India. 1963–86. Balkrishna V. Doshi (b. 1927)/Vāstu Shilpā. Interior view

20　Lunuganga Estate, Bentota, Ceylon (Sri Lanka). 1948–98. Geoffrey Bawa (1919–2003). 2019. Interior view

21 Public Library (University of Dhaka Library), Dhaka, East Pakistan (Bangladesh). 1953–54.
Muzharul Islam (1923–2012). Interior view

22   Public Library (University of Dhaka Library), Dhaka, East Pakistan (Bangladesh). 1953–54.
Muzharul Islam (1923–2012). Interior view

23 Loyola Chapel and Auditorium, Trivandrum (Thiruvananthapuram), India. 1971. Laurie Baker (1917–2007). Interior view

24   School of Architecture, Centre for Environmental Planning and Technology (CEPT), Ahmedabad, India. 1962–68. Balkrishna V. Doshi (b. 1927)/Vāstu Shilpā. Exterior view

25 Chittagong University, Chittagong, East Pakistan (Bangladesh). 1965–71. Muzharul Islam (1923–2012)/ Vastukalabid. Exterior view

26 Dudhsagar Dairy, Mehsana, India. 1970–73. Architect: Achyut Kanvinde (1916–2002).
Engineer: Shaukat Rai (1922–2003). Exterior view

27 Shell House, Karachi, Pakistan. 1978. Habib Fida Ali (1935–2017). Exterior view

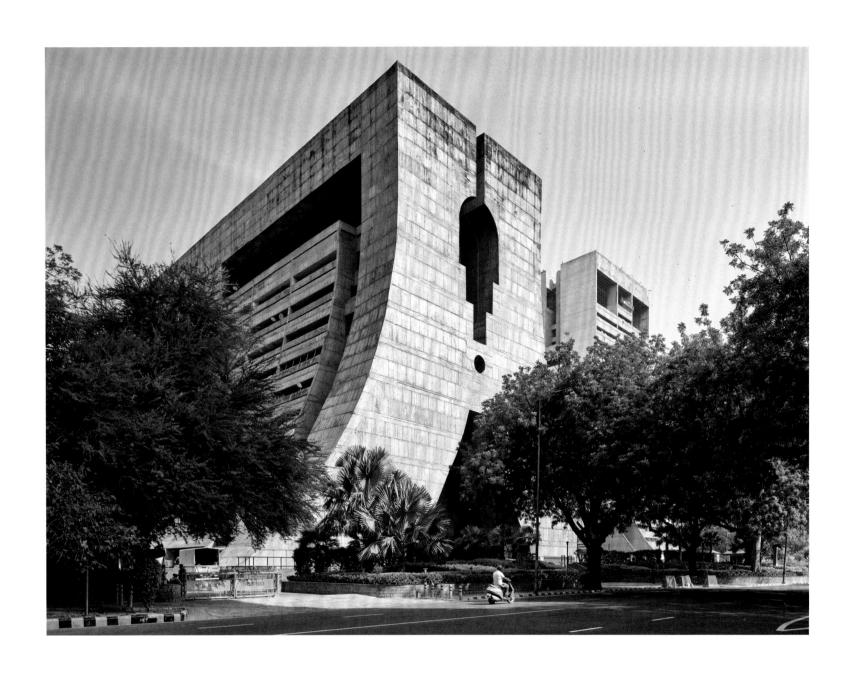

28 New Delhi Municipal Corporation (NDMC) Headquarters (Palika Kendra), New Delhi, India. 1973–83.
Architect: Kuldip Singh (1934–2020). Engineer: Mahendra Raj (b. 1924). Exterior view

29 Halls of Industries, Pragati Maidan, New Delhi, India. 1970–72. Demolished 2017. Architect: Raj Rewal (b. 1934). Engineer: Mahendra Raj (b. 1924). Exterior view. 2015

30 Kamalapur Railway Station, Dhaka, East Pakistan (Bangladesh). 1968. Daniel C. Dunham (1929–2000) and
Robert G. Boughey (b. 1940)/Louis Berger and Consulting Engineers. Exterior view

31 "C" Type Mosque (Ahle-Hadith Mosque), Islamabad, Pakistan. 1969–73/1975–77. Anwar Said (b. 1940).
Interior view

32 "B" Type Mosque (Al Mustafa Mosque), Islamabad, Pakistan. 1973–75. Anwar Said (b. 1940). Exterior view

33 Gandhi Ghat, Barrackpore, Calcutta (Kolkata), India. 1947–49. Habib Rahman (1915–1995). Exterior view

34 New Secretariat Building, Calcutta (Kolkata), India. 1949–54. Habib Rahman (1915–1995). Exterior view

35   Flower Market, Koyambedu, Madras (Chennai), India. 1988–96. Architect: Kuldip Singh (1934–2020).
Engineer: Mahendra Raj (b. 1924). Exterior view

36 National Cooperative Development Corporation (NCDC) Office Building, New Delhi, India. 1978–80.
    Architect: Kuldip Singh (1934–2020). Engineer: Mahendra Raj (b. 1924). Exterior view

37 Kanchanjunga Apartments at Cumbala Hill, Bombay (Mumbai), India. 1970–83. Charles Correa (1930–2015). Exterior view

38 Indian Coffee House (Maveli Café), Trivandrum (Thiruvananthapuram), India. c. 1980. Laurie Baker (1917–2007). Exterior view

IN FOCUS

CITIES AND REHABILITATION FOLLOWING PARTITION IN 1947

Nonica Datta

The Partition of India was the most violent legacy of British imperialism; it resulted in about half a million fatalities and the displacement of thirteen million people.[1] The division of the subcontinent into India and Pakistan was the outcome of the politics of the Muslim League, the Indian National Congress, and the British imperial state in the 1940s. The Radcliffe Line, declared on August 17, 1947, two days after Partition itself, created the international border between India and Pakistan. This arbitrarily drawn boundary divided the provinces of Punjab and Bengal along religious lines, making them into border states where people were totally unprepared for the impending calamity.

India and Pakistan faced a complete collapse of the social fabric in the border regions as thousands of people found themselves on the "wrong" side and attempted to flee horrific violence; many were killed as they fled. The enormity of these atrocities continues to haunt intergenerational memories, which are laden with narratives of abduction, rape, and murder. When the immediate crisis subsided, newly formed governments were initially preoccupied with accommodating the flood of refugees, after which they turned to rebuilding and expanding cities and planning new modern state and national capitals. Initially, colonial bodies such as Improvement Trusts and Public Works Departments (PWDs) undertook rehabilitation and reconstruction programs, and the measures they and the national and international agencies that succeeded them carried out became inseparable from the broader, interconnected processes of decolonization, nation-building, modernization, and development. Though India and Pakistan followed different trajectories, there were certain overlapping features relating to the legacies of colonial landscapes, citizenship, governance, and refugee settlements that arose from the fractured histories of South Asia as a whole. Both local and international architects were engaged to design some of the era's most significant projects—ranging from housing schemes to master plans for entire cities—as iconic expressions of post-Partition democratic secular India and the nascent Islamic state of Pakistan. These formations had to anticipate how recently disenfranchised and uprooted populations would identify as citizens of their new countries (fig. 1).

Fig. 1   Margaret Bourke-White (1904–1971). *Exodus, Pakistan.* 1947. Gelatin silver print, 11 × 10¾ in. (27.9 × 27.3 cm). The Museum of Modern Art, New York

Following Partition, in Delhi alone, some 329,000 Muslims moved out of the city while 495,000 Hindus and Sikhs from the Pakistani state of West Punjab entered it, congregating in pockets in and around old and New Delhi and creating a larger conurbation.[2] Indian Prime Minister Jawaharlal Nehru viewed refugee resettlement as part of the independent nation's urban, industrial, liberal, and, importantly, secular vision. He created a new Ministry of Relief and Rehabilitation, which was tasked with, among other things, protecting the Muslims who had decided to stay in India, though it was not always successful at doing so. (fig. 2).

Fig. 2   Margaret Bourke-White (1904–1971). *Purana Qila Refugee Camp*. 1947. Muslim refugees, many of them preparing to leave for Pakistan, at the Purana Qila (old fort) refugee camp, New Delhi, India, October 1947. Gelatin silver print, 10 5/16 × 13 3/8 in. (26.2 × 34 cm)

Initially, the government provided three types of settlements to the incoming Hindu and Sikh refugees in Delhi: first, the camps (some of which had previously sheltered Muslim refugees); second, evacuee properties left by Muslims; and finally plots for building shops and houses in new self-contained neighborhoods, colloquially called "colonies." Here, the Delhi Improvement Trust (DIT), Central Public Works Department (CPWD), Delhi Development Authority (DDA), as well as cooperatives and private investors, constructed administrative, commercial, and residential buildings.[3] The collective initiatives of refugees from West Pakistan contributed to the rehabilitation process in the city, while many Muslims who remained ended up living in specially designated "Muslim zones" considered to be "safe areas."[4]

In the initial years, planners such as the German Otto Koenigsberger and the American Albert Mayer shaped independent India's vision of refugee towns.[5] Under Koenigsberger's direction, the government set up the Hindustan Housing Factory in Delhi in 1950 "for the manufacture of prefabricated houses to rehabilitate displaced persons."[6] Although this project was abandoned, Koenigsberger's experiment with building new towns such as Nilokheri and Rajpura in Punjab and the satellite settlement of Faridabad, outside Delhi, proved a success.[7] At Nilokheri, which was supported by the Ford Foundation, Koenigsberger and the CPWD planner S. N. Joglekar planned to accommodate approximately six thousand refugees, mainly from the Pakistani province of Sindh.[8]

India's larger vision of rehabilitation was influenced by foreign networks. For Delhi's master plan of 1961, advisers from the Ford Foundation, which was headed by Mayer, worked with the Indian Town and Country Planning Organization.[9] The plan was funded by the Ford Foundation, whose policies were, as Ravi Sundaram writes, "mediated through the lens of modernization theory and development rhetoric."[10] According to D. E. Goodfriend, Mayer saw "India as a 'laboratory' for testing western planning theory in a developing nation."[11] The Delhi master plan was an all-encompassing urban community development program that focused on industry, housing, transportation, sewage, zoning, and, above all, the creation of an urban community within a modern, democratic setup.[12]

In Pakistan, the port city of Karachi—the country's capital from 1948 to 1958—faced the challenge of accommodating Mohajirs (Urdu-speaking Muslim immigrants). Around eighty thousand arrived from Delhi alone, and by 1951, 28 percent of Karachi's population was migrant.[13] With a large number of properties vacated by Hindu residents fleeing to India, the city became a center for Muslim refugee resettlement.

In 1958, the Pakistani government hired Doxiadis Associates (DA), the firm of the Greek architect-planner Constantinos A. Doxiadis, to develop the township of Korangi, about ten miles outside Karachi, in a project funded by the Ford Foundation and USAID (figs. 3–5).[14] The endeavor was part of the Greater Karachi Resettlement Plan, a slum clearance project for the crowded inner city of the Pakistani capital, and entailed the marathon task of housing thirty to forty thousand displaced poor families.[15] DA proposed the development of self-sufficient towns "with the provision of employment through industries and commercial areas along with residential settlement."[16] Amazingly, the Ministry for Reconstruction and Refugee Rehabilitation kept its promise of completing fifteen thousand housing units ahead of schedule.[17] Cut off from Karachi, the project eventually failed, however, because it did not provide business and industrial opportunities and other employment-generating activities.

Fig. 3   Cover of Doxiadis Associates' *Monthly Bulletin*, no. 25 (March 1961). Special issue, "Korangi Township." Constantinos A. Doxiadis Archives

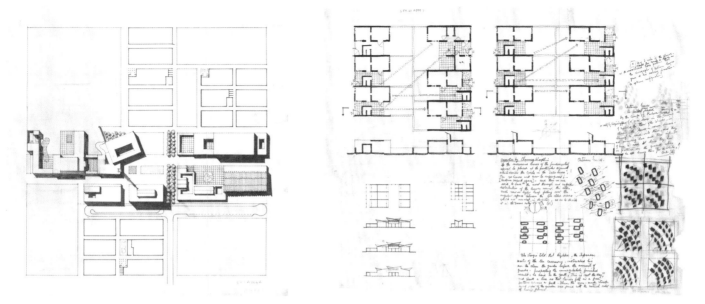

Fig. 4   Korangi Housing Project, Korangi, Pakistan. 1959. Doxiadis Associates (est. 1951). Hassan Fathy (1900–1989). Plan of a
          settlement center with mosque and public buildings. 1959. Ink and pencil on calque tracing paper, 18 1/8 × 18 1/8 in. (46 × 46 cm).
          Rare Books & Special Collections Library, American University in Cairo
Fig. 5   Korangi Housing Project, Korangi, Pakistan. 1959. Doxiadis Associates (est. 1951). Hassan Fathy (1900–1989). Plan, section and
          elevation sketches. 1959. Ink and pencil on calque tracing paper, 14 3/16 × 18 7/8 in. (36 × 48 cm). Rare Books & Special Collections
          Library, American University in Cairo

That same year, the government of Pakistan decided to plan a new national capital,
Islamabad, which was envisaged as a symbol of national pride, identity, and security
(see pp. 186–89).[18] President Ayub Khan said, "Islamabad has been my dream always. . . .
With the two provinces of Pakistan, separated as they are from each other, you want to
bring the people on a common platform. The thing to do was to take them to a new place
altogether."[19] It was thus hoped that the capital would elicit the loyalty of the entire population of East and West Pakistan (fig. 6). Designed by Doxiadis Associates, and backed
by the Ford Foundation and the American International Cooperation Administration,[20]
Islamabad was based on the theory of the Dynapolis—a dynamic city with an organic and
unidirectional growth pattern.[21]

Fig. 6   President Ayub Khan and the cabinet of Pakistan at the meeting where the Islamabad master plan was approved, Shakarparian
          Hills, Islamabad, Pakistan. May 24, 1960. Constantinos A. Doxiadis Archives

Pakistan's new capital city was set amid a picturesque landscape at the foot of the
Margalla Hills and near the existing city of Rawalpindi, which became the temporary seat of
government during Islamabad's construction. With its wide avenues, Islamabad was hailed
as a "unique" example of a large new city "planned for the future and built for the present."[22]
In Doxiadis's words, "A green belt is provided between Islamabad and Rawalpindi in order

to form a physical barrier between them."[23] As Matthew Hull writes, the urban design conformed to "a rationalised form of the neighbourhood unit," contrasting with the "old cities" of Lahore and Rawalpindi.[24] Inspiration for the geometrical order came from the architecture of the Mohenjo-daro archaeological site, the Mughal Lahore Fort, and, above all, what Hull calls the "rationalism of European modernist planning."[25] Local architects were few, but Zaheer ud-Din Khwaja was the chief engineer on the project.[26] The site of the city was determined in part with a view to the national capital's future security vis-à-vis India, which was provided by the Army Headquarters in Rawalpindi.

In an altogether different context, the central government of India allocated funds for building new state capitals.[27] Chandigarh was one result of this endeavor; its plan was ultimately produced by the Swiss-French architect Le Corbusier and a team that included Jane Drew, Maxwell Fry, and Pierre Jeanneret.[28] Prominent Indian architects, bureaucrats, political leaders, engineers, artists, and citizens played a significant role in planning the city. Chandigarh gave a new administrative center to a truncated Punjab that had lost Lahore as its capital. It was envisaged as a city for the future, freed from the state's traumatic past. Nehru wanted Chandigarh to be "an expression of the nation's faith in the future."[29] For him, it would also be a "soothing balm on the wounded spirit of the Punjab" (fig. 7).[30]

Fig. 7   Le Corbusier (Charles-Édouard Jeanneret, 1887–1965) with a scale figure of the Modulor man and a plan of Chandigarh, India. 1951. Fondation Le Corbusier

Built around a rectangular grid plan and surrounded by agricultural land and forest, with views onto the foothills of the Himalayas, Chandigarh was influenced by the idea of the "garden city," which drew on the colonial image of an ordered landscape with uniform tree-lined avenues, green open spaces, parks, and lakes. Le Corbusier was, as the political scientist Sunil Khilnani has written, "insistent that it must be solely a seat of government, not of industry and manufacture."[31] Ironically, the rational spatial ordering turned out to be an amalgam of the modern and the traditional. The architect Balkrishna V. Doshi, who worked with Le Corbusier, averred (in Nabaparna Ghosh's paraphrase) that the latter's plans for the city had "preserved Indian tradition by invoking the concept of the sacred in Hindu religion."[32] Chandigarh's architecture, according to Vikramaditya Prakash, "can be understood as the adoption of a non-Western, or non-Eurocentric, modernism."[33] Above all, however, Chandigarh represented optimism, freedom, and a new life for modern India.

Liberation from colonial rule created competing urban visions of resettlement and new cities in South Asia. Most of these projects depended on foreign aid and expertise, while the central governments, in different ways, exercised bureaucratic, political, and, at times, military control. The unmistakable continuity of the colonial spatial order after 1947 became enmeshed with futuristic perspectives that were largely shaped by American, British, and European models and experts. Indigenous forms were enmeshed with rational and scientific principles of urban ordering. The differentiated, yet overlapping, projects of planning, resettlement, and development acquired many meanings and contradictions in the aftermath of Partition. The refugee question was central to the new political dispensations, but so was a vision of new capital cities. The two ideas were fundamentally different: the immediate need of settling refugees drove the expansion of old cities, while the new capitals were symbols of national identity, as exemplified in their modernist architecture, which catered to the aspirations of officials, politicians, and "privileged" citizens. The two competing projects—of refugee resettlement and of establishing national or regional capitals—were never reconciled or harmonized with the larger visions of decolonization in India and Pakistan. Indeed, the problem of being a refugee *and* a citizen remains one of the most critical questions in the postcolonial imagination. In spite of distinct approaches toward urban planning and administration in the two countries, under democratic and military governments, respectively, neither the new cities nor the rehabilitation settlements in old cities fully addressed the pains of dislocation and loss, and the trauma of building a new life.

1   Since there was no official head count of fatalities, this is only one of the estimated figures, which range from two hundred thousand to (as in one relatively recent estimate) more than one million. See Patrick French, *Liberty or Death: India's Journey to Independence and Division* (London: Flamingo, 1998), 349.

2   V. N. Datta, "Panjabi Refugees and the Urban Development of Greater Delhi," in *Delhi Through the Ages: Selected Essays in Urban History, Culture and Society*, ed. R. E. Frykenberg (New Delhi: Oxford University Press, 1983).

3   Pillar Maria Guerrieri, *Negotiating Cultures: Delhi's Architecture and Planning from 1912 to 1962* (New Delhi: Oxford University Press, 2018), 10.

4   Vazira Fazila-Yacoobali Zamindar, *The Long Partition and the Making of South Asia: Refugees, Boundaries, Histories* (New York: Columbia University Press, 2010), 29.

5   Ashok Kumar, Sanjeev Vidyarthi, and Poonam Prakash, *City Planning in India, 1947–2017* (London: Routledge, 2021), 112–13.

6   "Matters of Administration: VII. Housing," in *Selected Works of Jawaharlal Nehru*, second series, ed. S. Gopal, vol. 6 (New Delhi: Oxford University Press, 1987), 410n4.

7   Peter Scriver and Amit Srivastava, *India*, Modern Architectures in History (Chicago: University of Chicago Press, 2016), 141.

8   Kumar, Vidyarthi, and Prakash, *City Planning*, 125.

9   Maria Guerrieri, *Negotiating Cultures*, 7–10.

10 Ravi Sundaram, *Pirate Modernity: Delhi's Media Urbanism* (London: Routledge, 2010), 38.

11 D. E. Goodfriend, "The Delhi Master Plan of 1962: An Anthropological Analysis" (unpublished holding of the Ford Foundation archives, New York), 2, as quoted in Tridib Banerjee, "US Planning Expeditions to Postcolonial India: From Ideology to Innovation in Technical Assistance," *Journal of the American Planning Association* 75, no. 2 (August 2013): 199.

12 Matthew S. Hull, "Communities of Place, Not Kind: American Technologies of Neighbourhood in Postcolonial Delhi," *Comparative Studies in Society and History* 53, no. 4 (October 2011): 757–90.

13 Prashant Bhardwaj, Asim Khawaja, and Atif Mian, "The Partition of India: Demographic Consequences," *International Migration*, June 2009, 4.

14 Markus Daechsel, "Islam and Development in Urban Space: Planning 'Official' Karachi in the 1950s," in *Cities in South Asia*, ed. Crispin Bates and Minoru Mio (New York: Routledge, 2015), 76.

15 Markus Daechsel, "Sovereignty, Governmentality and Development in Ayub's Pakistan: The Case of Korangi Township," *Modern Asian Studies* 45, no. 1 (January 2011): 131–57.

16 Tania Soomro and Mohsin Ali Soomro, "Planning Failure of Satellite Town: A Case Study of Korangi, Karachi-Pakistan," *Mehran University Research Journal of Engineering & Technology* 37, no. 1 (January 2018): 209.

17 Daechsel, "Islam and Development in Urban Space," 76.

18 Hermann Kreutzmann, "Islamabad—Living with the Plan," *Südasien-Chronik/South Asia Chronicle*, no. 3 (2013): 135–60.

19 Ayub Khan, preface to *Islamabad Takes Shape* (Islamabad: Capital Development Authority, 1965), as quoted in Glenn V. Stephenson, "Two Newly-Created Capitals: Islamabad and Brasilia," *The Town Planning Review* 41, no. 4 (October 1970): 323.

20 Markus Daechsel, *Islamabad and the Politics of International Development in Pakistan* (Cambridge, UK: Cambridge University Press, 2015), 200.

21 Stephenson, "Two Newly-Created Capitals," 326.

22 J. M. Frantzeskakis, "Islamabad: A Town Planning Example for a Sustainable City," *Sustainable Development and Planning* IV, vol. 1 (2009): 75.

23 Constantinos A. Doxiadis, "Rawalpindi: A Part of the Metropolitan Area" (September 30, 1960), DOX-PA 92, Capital Development Authority, Islamabad, CDA 36, as quoted in Matthew Hull, "Uncivil Politics and the Appropriation of Planning in Islamabad," in *Crisis and Beyond: Re-evaluating Pakistan*, ed. Naveeda Khan (London: Routledge, 2009), 448.

24 Hull, "Uncivil Politics," 459.

25 Ibid., 450.

26 Daechsel, *Islamabad*, 119.

27 Kreutzmann, "Islamabad," 137.

28 Maxwell Fry, "Le Corbusier at Chandigarh," in *The Open Hand: Essays on Le Corbusier*, ed. Russell Walden (Cambridge, MA: MIT Press, 1977).

29 Nehru in an article in the *Hindustan Times* (New Delhi), July 8, 1950, as quoted in Ravi Kalia, *Chandigarh: The Making of an Indian City* (1987; repr., Delhi: Oxford University Press, 1998), 21.

30 Nehru in a speech in 1950, as quoted in Nabaparna Ghosh, "Modern Designs: History and Memory in Le Corbusier's Chandigarh," *Journal of Architecture and Urbanism* 40, no. 3 (September 2016): 221.

31 Sunil Khilnani, *The Idea of India* (1997; repr., New Delhi: Penguin Books India, 2004), 130.

32 Doshi as paraphrased in Ghosh, "Modern Designs," 225.

33 Vikramaditya Prakash, "Epilogue: Third World Modernism, or Just Modernism: Towards a Cosmopolitan Reading of Modernism," in *Third World Modernism: Architecture, Development and Identity*, ed. Duanfang Lu (London: Routledge, 2011), 262.

INFRASTRUCTURE AND INDUSTRY

Peter Scriver and Amit Srivastava

Monumental works of modern infrastructure and industry furnished some of the most inspirational images of nation-building to emerge from South Asia in the decades that followed independence from colonial rule. Colossal dam-building schemes such as India's iconic Nagarjuna Sagar project (1955–67; fig. 1) and the new power plants and factories that they would serve were the "temples" of the modern age, as Indian Prime Minister Jawaharlal Nehru memorably described them.[1] Comparable megaprojects to harness the hydrological potential of the subcontinent for electricity and irrigation would be corner-stones of development programs and nation-building narratives across the region.

Fig. 1   Workers on scaffolding during the construction of the Nagarjuna Sagar Dam, Telangana, India. May 1963.
Photograph: John Scofield

New industries were also a focus of hope and renewal for the poor and downtrodden of these emerging ex-colonial states, including the millions of refugees who had been uprooted by the 1947 Partition of the subcontinent (see Datta, pp. 110–15). In addition to new jobs (fig. 2), industry was creating new homes, often in the context of neatly planned industrial townships built with replicable and rapidly implementable construction systems that were repatterning the spatial practices of everyday life, along with work.

Fig. 2   Sunil Janah (1918–2012). Untitled, from the series Industrial Documents. 1940s–60s. Gelatin silver print, 14 3/16 × 11 1/4 in.
           (36 × 28.5 cm). Swaraj Art Archive

In the larger project of decolonization, however, these industrial developments were not
a clear rupture with the past as much as a dramatic escalation in the scale and scope of the
economic and social engineering in which the new states aspired to engage. Industry and
infrastructure had been intimately intertwined in South Asia's prior colonial-modern development as well as in the political struggle to transcend it. The distinctive and increasingly
diverse industrial architectures that emerged by the 1970s were a reflection of an ongoing
dialectic between the rhetoric of progress and its formal expression, on the one hand,
and underlying continuities in the building cultures of modern South Asia, on the other.

Development under British administration had been extensive. Beginning in the mid-nine-
teenth century, colonial Public Works Departments (PWDs) had built the networks of
technical and institutional infrastructure—from irrigation, railways, and communications
to military and civil buildings—that sutured together British-controlled territories across
the subcontinent. Equally consequential were the new modes and means of production
that had been introduced. In the building trades in particular, the PWD system effectively
industrialized previous craft methods through a paper-based system of standardized
designs and costing and construction procedures that would thereafter be carried out by
an increasingly specialized and hierarchical division of manual and technical labor, dominated by engineers.[2]
    The scope and broader benefit of these developments were limited, however, by the
extractive nature of the colonial economy, prompting enterprising indigenous industrialists to exploit neglected opportunities. Pioneering manufacturing ventures in textiles and
steel consciously challenged the prevailing political economy in solidarity with the anticolonial struggle and its affiliation with *swadeshi*, a turn-of-the-century political movement

focused on indigenous self-sufficiency.[3] Political independence brought new freedom for private-sector industrialists to accelerate and expand significantly on colonial-era initiatives. Meanwhile, each of the new South Asian nation-states sought to restore government leadership in industrial development. Under centralized economic-planning strategies—embraced by both left-leaning and military administrations in the immediate postcolonial decades—large state-owned enterprises would compete with private industrialists to develop substantial new productive capacity.

Early factories by emerging design leaders such as Achyut Kanvinde and Geoffrey Bawa aspired to a rationalism directly informed by graduate studies and work experience abroad (figs. 3, 4). That aesthetic proved difficult to realize with the intended finesse and precision, however, especially in public-sector projects where the construction norms and practices of the colonial PWD remained an enduring legacy. But long-span industrial buildings also presented opportunities for progressive collaborating engineers, such as Mahendra Raj (see Stierli, pp. 17–21), to experiment with new structural systems and fabrication methods, and with ways to implement them locally (fig. 5).[4]

Fig. 3   Suhrid Geigy Factory, Vadodara, India. 1958. Achyut Kanvinde (1916–2002). Perspective drawing. c. 1958. Ink and pencil on paper. Kanvinde Archives

Fig. 4   Ekala Industrial Estate, Jaela, Ceylon (Sri Lanka). 1959–65. Geoffrey Bawa (1919–2003) and Ulrik Plesner (1930–2016)/Edwards Reid & Begg. Exterior view. c. 1965. Photograph: Ulrik Plesner. Plesner Archives

Fig. 5   Hindon River Mills, Ghaziabad, India. 1969–73. Architect: Achyut Kanvinde (1916–2002). Engineer: Mahendra Raj (b. 1924). View of suspension-arch roof structure. c. 1973. Photograph: Stella Snead. Mahendra Raj Archives

Fig. 6   Escorts Factory, Faridabad, India. 1958–62. Joseph Allen Stein (1912–2001). Interior view. 1964. Photograph: Madan Mahatta

Townships, meanwhile, presented a broad spectrum of additional design challenges, from low-cost solutions (fig. 6) to individual unit layouts and construction to planning and community-building at the scale of small cities. Such schemes, for example those by American émigré Joseph Allen Stein for industrial new towns at Durgapur and Rourkela in northeast India (1955–59)—the latter designed in collaboration with Benjamin Polk and engineer Binoy Chatterjee—exhibited minimalist detailing and clever clustering, privileging communal green spaces, reflecting progressive town-planning theory and exemplary precedents from around the globe. Neatly articulated into housing sectors and differentiated dwelling types for managers and workers of different grades, however, these idyllic enclaves also reverberated with the sense of order of the prevailing caste system as well as the paternalist/socialist character of other planned settlements, such as railway colonies and military cantonments, that were still familiar to many South Asians from their colonial-modern experiences.[5]

By the 1970s the architecture of industry had become more diverse and less predictable. South Asian architects had also situated themselves more comfortably in their respective postcolonial identities and were more confident in exploring the creative tensions and contradictions between the international and regional registers of their work.

In Muzharul Islam's industrial housing at Joypurhat (see fig. 21 on p. 29 and fig. 9 on p. 126), designed in 1978, seven years after the traumatic rebirth of his nation as Bangladesh, austere walls of unadorned brick erupted directly from the rice paddies at their base as if literally grounded in the muddy soil and the agrarian culture of the place. Yet the crystalline abstraction of the cluster geometry and planning prescribed reconfigured and culturally detached new lifestyles for their residents, on the model of the modern nuclear family.

Bawa's astonishingly picturesque approach to the design of the Ceylon Steel Corporation offices and housing (1966–69; see fig. 19 on p. 28) represented a comparable disjunction between content and form. Belying the gritty reality of the adjacent Soviet-built steel-rolling works, the architecture alluded to the gentler and regionally acclimatized tectonic culture of colonial-modern industrial buildings such as tea factories and rubber mills, reimagining the industrial enclave as a designed landscape with offices, bungalows, and rest houses deployed poetically around the factory cooling pond.

A suite of industrial dairy complexes and associated housing and training facilities designed by Kanvinde and partners (fig. 7; see also figs. 16, 17 on p. 26) articulated further challenging realities that were becoming creatively productive in the work of postcolonial Indian architects in this same period. Eschewing the aspirational rationalism of this architect's earlier industrial work in a neo-Bauhaus vein, these towering dairy buildings almost literally embodied Nehru's notion of "temples" of industry as key infrastructure in the so-called White Revolution that was securing India's agricultural self-sufficiency by simultaneously industrializing and socializing its milk production (see Stierli, p. 25). The brute medium-tech expressionism of the built forms and finishes struck a balance between the rhetoric of industrial transformation and the reality—particularly in the technically underequipped construction industry—of an overabundance of labor with limited skills, where all hands needed to be engaged above and before the rationalizing prerogatives of industrial efficiency.

Fig. 7   Dudhsagar Dairy, Mehsana, India. 1970–73. Architect: Achyut Kanvinde (1916–2002). Engineer: Shaukat Rai (1922–2003). Perspective of extension to the administration building. Drawing: Shrikar Garde. c. 1975. Pencil on paper, 19⅞ × 30 in. (50.5 × 76.3 cm). Kanvinde Archives

The dialectical contradictions of decolonization were particularly telling in the architecture of tourism, another industry that was rapidly becoming a key driver of economic development across postcolonial South Asia. Following Independence, privately developed luxury hotels such as New Delhi's Oberoi Intercontinental (1958–62) had initially sufficed to supplement colonial-era hotels and clubs as cosmopolitan new venues for the elite to mix with foreign visitors. By the later 1960s, however, affordable commercial air travel encouraged governments to develop substantial new capacity to receive the fast-growing volume of foreign-exchange-bearing budget travelers from overseas, along with the increasingly mobile South Asian middle classes. Alongside new transportation hubs and terminals, new hotel architecture was conceived as integral to the infrastructure of the developing tourism industry.

Architects Valentine Gunasekara, working in Ceylon (see pp. 210–13 for a discussion of his Tangalle Bay Hotel), and Shiv Nath Prasad, working in New Delhi with engineer Mahendra Raj (fig. 8), embraced such commissions such commissions as opportunities to depart from the formulaic norms of the International Style and address local building contexts and sites more directly. Despite their expressive hubris, the hotels they designed were not destinations as such, but purposeful, typologically innovative, and socially porous facilities, accessible to a broad class of visitors and guests—due not least to their new cost-saving construction methods and potential for expansion.[6]

Fig. 8   Akbar Hotel, New Delhi, India. 1967–69. Architect: Shiv Nath Prasad (1922–2002). Engineer: Mahendra Raj (b. 1924). Exterior view. 1970. RIBA

Bawa's Bentota Beach Hotel (1967–69), on Ceylon's southern coast, posed a distinct alternative. Designed in parallel with his Ceylon Steel Corporation offices, this paradigm-shifting prototype for the next generation of South Asian resort development made the architecture itself the primary object of consumption. For all its picturesque informality, grace, and good taste, however, the success of this hybrid neocolonial/vernacular idiom depended above all on the compound walls, verandas, and inward-turning courtyards that secured the views and comfort of the privileged few who could afford it.[7]

The contest between modernist and colonial-modern inspirations in the architecture of the South Asian tourism industry underscores the particular tensions between progress and precedent that persisted more generally in South Asia's postcolonial development. Design and construction processes inherited from colonial-modern practice continued to mediate the development of industrial architecture and infrastructure in the region, resulting in an approach to modernity characterized by "comfort and caution rather than revolutionary disjunctions."[8] Ironically, industrial estates and townships could be compared in this regard with hotels and later IT campuses, each of which offered cautiously walled enclaves of order, productivity, and/or repose removed from the chaos of increasingly crowded and informally structured societies still struggling to achieve full, equitable economic progress and cultural self-determination.

1   Jawaharlal Nehru, "Temples of the New Age," *Jawaharlal Nehru's Speeches*, vol. 3, *March 1953–August 1957* (New Delhi: Ministry of Information and Broadcasting, 1960), 3.
2   See Peter Scriver, "Empire-Building and Thinking in the Public Works Department of British India," in *Colonial Modernities: Building, Dwelling and Architecture in British India and Ceylon*, ed. Scriver and Vikramaditya Prakash (London: Routledge, 2007), 69–92.
3   See Sumit Sarkar, *The Swadeshi Movement in Bengal, 1903–1908* (New Delhi: People's Publishing House, 1973).
4   Vandini Mehta, Rohit Raj Mehndiratta, and Ariel Huber, eds., *The Structure: Works of Mahendra Raj* (Berlin: Park Books, 2016).
5   Peter Scriver and Amit Srivastava, *India*, Modern Architectures in History (London: Reaktion, 2015) 23–69, 171–221.
6   Anoma Pieris, *Imagining Modernity: The Architecture of Valentine Gunasekara* (Colombo: Stamford Lake, 2007), 130–46.
7   Ibid., 130–32.
8   Amit Srivastava, "The Struggle with Modernity," in *A Work of Beauty: The Architecture & Landscape of Rashtrapati Bhavan*, ed. Narayani Gupta (New Delhi: Sahapedia, 2016), 59.

HOUSING IN A TIME OF DECOLONIZATION: ARCHITECTS AND STATE PATRONAGE

Rahul Mehrotra

The newly independent countries of South Asia made significant investments in housing in the 1950s. The Partition of 1947 had made the need for new institutional infrastructures for the delivery of mass housing critical for the millions of refugees who found themselves looking for shelter in their new homelands (see Datta, pp. 110–15).[1] In India, the German-Jewish architect Otto Koenigsberger, then housing adviser to the government, started the process of setting up the Government Housing Factory—later the Hindustan Housing Factory—in 1948, in an at least initially ill-starred attempt to mass-produce the prefab housing that he believed was the solution to India's chronic housing shortage.[2] The government's Ministry of Works, Housing and Supply was set up in 1952 and organized the International Exhibition on Low-Cost Housing in New Delhi (fig. 1) two years later—a milestone project in which eighty houses were built to serve as a demonstration of what "aided self-help" could do to overcome the housing crisis.[3] As opposed to the government itself delivering housing, this model proposed that it could instead assist with technical knowhow to encourage people to build their own homes.

Simultaneously, the Indian government began channeling its efforts toward the creation of new planned towns. In 1950, Prime Minister Jawaharlal Nehru invited Le Corbusier to design Chandigarh, which opened up a debate about how the constraints of space allocations and building costs could be turned into innovations in spatial as well as site-planning approaches. Because each sector of the new state capital of the Indian Punjab was designed for a different economic stratum, however, the architect's attempt to reinvent how a modern society could be spatially organized ultimately reinforced economic segregation. This would lead to typological inventions such as the categories of Low-Income Group (LIG), Middle-Income Group (MIG), and High-Income Group (HIG) housing that are still ubiquitous in India today.

Subsequent noteworthy housing projects that responded to the Chandigarh experiment were those by Balkrishna V. Doshi for Ahmedabad Textile Industry's Research Association (ATIRA) staff (1958–65; fig. 2), a low-cost housing scheme that used traditional materials and forms (such as brick vaults), and Habib Rahman's Multi-storeyed Flats (1965–69; fig. 3),

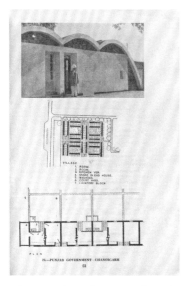

Fig. 1   Page from *Designs for Low Cost Housing* (New Delhi: Ministry of Works, Housing and Supply, 1954), showing a concrete-vaulted standard design for low-cost workers' quarters by the Punjab State Government PWD, Chandigarh, India

Fig. 2   Staff Housing and Guest House for the Ahmedabad Textile Industry's Research Association (ATIRA), Ahmedabad, India. 1958–65. Balkrishna V. Doshi (b. 1927)/Vāstu Shilpā. Exterior view. c. 1960. William J. R. Curtis and Vāstu Shilpā Foundation Archives in Ramakrishnapuram, New Delhi. Also in Ahmedabad, the Gujarat Housing Board hosted the National Competition for Low-Cost Housing in 1961,[4] which led to one of the most seminal projects of the time: the Tube House (1961–62; figs. 4, 5), by Charles Correa, whose design incorporated both natural ventilation and "open-to-sky" spaces, while the structure's height allowed for a mezzanine, enlarging the usable area within the stipulated footprint. Most importantly, Correa proposed a low-rise, high-density paradigm that led to a significant shift in the Indian state's reimagination of housing design.

Fig. 3   Multi-storeyed Flats in Ramakrishnapuram, New Delhi, India. 1965–69. Habib Rahman (1915–1995). Exterior view. 1965. Habib Rahman Archives

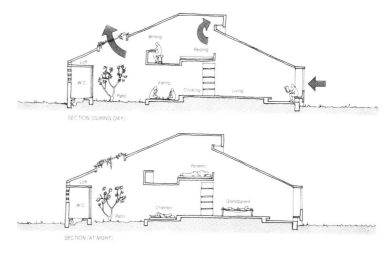

Fig. 4   Tube House, Ahmedabad, India. 1961–62. Prototype unit, demolished 1995. Charles Correa (1930–2015). Exterior view. c. 1962. Charles Correa Foundation
Fig. 5   Tube House, Ahmedabad, India. 1961–62. Charles Correa (1930–2015). Section by day and by night. Charles Correa Foundation

Pakistan too, right at its inception, faced the extremely daunting task of resettling and housing the massive wave of refugees, as well as establishing a new seat of government. The country's leaders secured the consultancy services of some of the most talented Western architects of the time: taking a cue from Chandigarh, Pakistan's second president, General Ayub Khan, invited Constantinos A. Doxiadis and Louis I. Kahn to design a new capital city in West Pakistan and a new government district in East Pakistan, respectively.[5] Doxiadis's design for Islamabad (1958–67; see pp. 186–89) was inextricably linked to the Korangi resettlement project he had started working on in 1958 at the edge of Karachi.[6] While the new capital was reserved primarily for the military and bureaucratic elite, the relocation of refugees and the poor to Korangi divided the country's planning ambitions across similar lines, leading Pakistan into what Tariq L. Rahman has called a "new era of functional inequality."[7]

The Pakistani military, which had brought Khan to power in 1958, went on to become the country's largest cooperative housing developer, with the creation of the Army Welfare Trust in 1971 and the navy-run Bahria Foundation in 1982.[8]

In East Pakistan, initiatives supported by foreign-aid packages also produced notable schemes to house people who had been displaced by Partition, among them Mohammadpur (1959–64), on the outskirts of the capital Dhaka, and Mirpur (1959–68), a satellite town to the north of the city.[9] Bengali architect Muzharul Islam, himself displaced by Partition, designed the modernist blocks of the Azimpur Government Quarters (1962).

In the 1970s, it became increasingly clear to many in South Asia that the abject poverty seen in informal settlements was a visible manifestation of the failure of the state to deliver adequate housing. The Indian government had established the national-level Housing and Urban Development Corporation (HUDCO) in 1970 with the intent of addressing broad urbanization challenges, such as the supply of land for affordable housing.[10] Yet the decade became a period of demolition and destruction rather than constructive efforts by the state. The massive slum clearance drives carried out in India under Indira Gandhi's government during the Emergency of 1975–77 rendered thousands of people homeless.

During these same years, architecture across South Asia turned or evolved from its modernist imaginaries toward a more decentralized approach rooted in privately financed initiatives and using local practices and resources. Exemplary among them is the Tara Group Housing (1975–78; fig. 6) in New Delhi, designed by Charles Correa, Jasbir Sawhney, and Ravindra Bhan. Characterized by high-density, low-rise structures with traditional regional elements such as courtyards arranged in a seemingly organic aggregation of units evoking traditional *mohallas* (or clusters of dwellings around semipublic open spaces), this development would serve as an inspiration for housing design for the next decade.[11] In contrast, the housing projects sponsored by the state at the time typically took the form of mundane concrete frame structures in mid-rise buildings that used the grid as an organizational structure and were invariably segregated into low-, middle-, and high-income zones. An exception was Raj Rewal's Asian Games Village (1980–82; figs. 7, 8) in New Delhi, which was perhaps the only major government housing project in India that followed a neotraditional vocabulary. Here, the units were stacked in a manner that created multiple terraces for living and sleeping, resonating with traditional forms but also providing an armature to support social gatherings in semipublic configurations.

Fig. 6   Tara Group Housing, Delhi, India. 1975–78. Charles Correa (1930–2015), Jasbir Sawhney (b. 1939), and Ravindra Bhan (1931–2020). Exterior view of terraced apartments. 1978. Photograph: Dinesh Sareen. Charles Correa Foundation

Fig. 7   Asian Games Village, New Delhi, India. 1980–82. Raj Rewal (b. 1934). Perspective. c. 1980. Pencil on tracing paper, 35 7/16 × 49 5/8 in. (90 × 126 cm). The Museum of Modern Art, New York

Fig. 8   Asian Games Village, New Delhi, India. 1980–82. Raj Rewal (b. 1934). Exterior view. 1985. Photograph: Madan Mahatta

In Pakistan, Yasmeen Lari pioneered the way for regional and participatory architecture. Her Anguri Bagh Housing in Lahore (1972–75; see pp. 222–25) was the first large-scale public housing scheme undertaken by the government of Pakistan to involve the marginalized communities themselves in the building of housing at scale.[12] Lari's Lines Area Resettlement Project (1980), a comprehensive plan for resettling thirteen thousand households in Karachi's largest slum, was designed to allow people to add to their homes over time in an incremental manner, rather than insisting they build a complete housing unit at the outset.[13] Both projects were structured around pedestrian streets as well as a spectrum of semipublic spaces such as courtyards. Further significant examples of this approach are Kamil Khan Mumtaz's Kot Karamat Village in Lahore (1968–70) and Muzharul Islam's Limestone Mining and Cement Works Housing project (1978–84; fig. 9) in Joypurhat, Bangladesh.

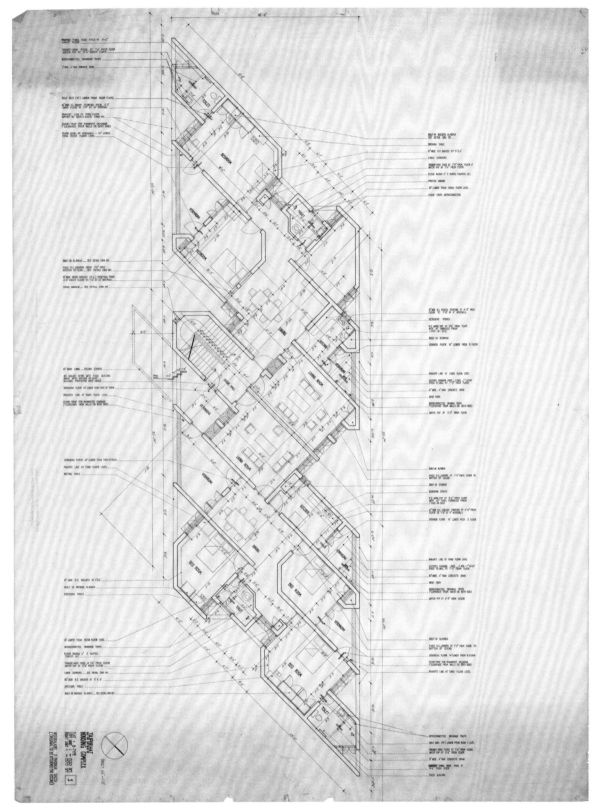

Fig. 9   Limestone Mining and Cement Works Housing, Joypurhat, Bangladesh. 1978–84. Muzharul Islam (1923–2012)/Vastukalabid.
Plan of B-type quarters. c. 1980. Muzharul Islam Archives

While South Asian governments sought to contribute to the provision of housing, too often they failed to include those at the lowest end socioeconomic scale. Not only privately sponsored housing projects but also many public or government housing schemes typically remained beyond the reach of the poorest sections of society, who continued to live in slums and other informal housing. In response, governments began adopting a "sites and services" paradigm,[14] where they provided only land and infrastructure such as plumbing connections. An early example of such a project was the Integrated Urban Development Project (1975) in Ahmedabad, by Kirtee Shah.

Realizing the limitations of solving housing problems through the design of buildings alone, several architects focused on redistributing resources and providing better employment opportunities, as well as on extensive research and experimentation in low-cost and low-technology solutions. In Pakistan, architects such as Arif Hasan carried out extensive research on sanitation models and affordable building materials. Meanwhile, in India, Laurie Baker championed local and cost-effective construction techniques before founding the Centre of Science and Technology for Rural Development (COSTFORD) in Trivandrum in 1985.[15]

Fig. 10   Belapur Incremental Housing (Artists' Village), New Bombay (Navi Mumbai), India. 1983–86. Charles Correa (1930–2015). A cluster of seven houses around a courtyard. 1986. Photograph: Joseph St. Anne. Charles Correa Foundation

In the 1980s, public authorities in India made one further major effort in the delivery of low-cost, high-density housing. The projects commissioned by the Indore Development Authority, on the one hand, and the City & Industrial Development Corporation (CIDCO) in New Bombay (now Navi Mumbai), on the other, were exemplary. Among the former, Doshi's Aranya Community Housing project (1983–89) near Indore was a sites-and-services scheme designed explicitly for low-income groups, but crucially it involved a demonstration cluster of about eighty houses that set the tone and architectural vocabulary for an additional construction of allocated plots by the families, whose adaptations of the prototype brought an incredible variety to the ensemble as they individualized their homes. In New Bombay, CIDCO was charged with constructing new housing for the city's expected three million inhabitants. Charles Correa's housing in the Belapur district (1983–86; fig. 10)—known as the Artists' Village—became an ambitious illustration of his theoretical position on equitable housing in the "developing world."[16] This project demonstrated how low-cost, low-rise housing could achieve extremely high densities of two hundred persons per acre (five hundred persons per hectare) while still allowing for open spaces, community facilities, schools, and a range of other amenities. Conceived as an incremental self-built housing typology, Correa's design stood in stark contrast to all other housing projects undertaken by the state, as well as the Chandigarh model, in as much as it attempted to dissolve all class and economic segregation, which had become a norm within housing design and site-planning in India.

These two projects by Correa and Doshi are emblematic of the evolution of the role of state patronage in housing delivery after Independence, from an all-encompassing production system run by the government in the early 1950s to a more nuanced partnership between the state, architects, and occupants by the 1980s. By taking account of both the limitations on resources and socioeconomic inequities across South Asia, such projects point to a future in which the state could facilitate the supply of land and infrastructure, while the architect could yet play a crucial role in facilitating sustainable housing design and site-planning.

1   The absolute number of migrants into India was 7.3 million, into West Pakistan 6.5 million, and into East Bengal (East Pakistan) around 0.7 million, as measured in the 1951 census. Prashant Bharadwaj, Asim Ijaz Khwaja, and Atif Mian, "The Big March: Migratory Flows after the Partition of India." *Economic and Political Weekly* 43, no. 35 (August 30–September 5, 2008): 42.
2   Rahul Mehrotra and Kaiwan Mehta, *State of Housing*, vol. 1, *Aspirations, Imaginaries and Realities in India* (Mumbai: Spenta, 2018), 26.
3   The exhibition had proven that a satisfactory-quality house could be constructed at low cost, and inspired the state to sponsor a total of almost 400,000 housing units between 1954 and 1985. Mehrotra and Mehta, *State of Housing*, 27.
4   Ibid., 28.
5   Doxiadis first arrived in Pakistan as part of the Harvard Advisory Group, tasked with the act of creating Pakistan's first five-year plan (1955–60), but ended up being one of the most instrumental architects in East Pakistan, along with Louis I. Kahn, Edward Durell Stone, Paul Rudolph, Richard Neutra, and Stanley Tigerman, who shaped the nation with their work.
6   Markus Daechsel, "Misplaced Ekistics: Islamabad and the Politics of Urban Development in Pakistan," *South Asian History and Culture* 4, no. 1 (January 2013): 87–106.
7   Tariq L. Rahman, "Enabling Development: A Housing Scheme in Rural Pakistan" (master's thesis, University of Oregon, 2016), 11.
8   Rahman, "Enabling Development," 27.
9   See Aminul Haq Khan, "Two Core Housing Schemes in Dacca: Mohammedpur and Mirpur," in *Urban Housing*, ed. Margaret Bentley Ševčenko, Designing in Islamic Cultures 2 (Cambridge, MA: Aga Khan Program for Islamic Architecture, 1982), 28, 30.
10 Mehrotra and Mehta, *State of Housing*, 29.
11 See Swati Chattopadhyay, "India," in *Encyclopedia of Twentieth Century Architecture*, ed. R. Stephen Sennott, vol. 2, *G–O* (New York: Fitzroy Dearborn, 2004), 673–74.
12 Shanaz Ramzi, "Retrospective: Yasmeen Lari," *Architectural Review*, September 2019, 16–25.
13 Yasmeen Lari, "The Lines Area Resettlement Project, Karachi," in Ševčenko, *Urban Housing*, 56–64.
14 Chattopadhyay, "India," 674.
15 Mehrotra and Mehta, *State of Housing*, 33.
16 See Charles Correa, *Housing and Urbanization* (Mumbai: Urban Design Research Institute, 1999).

THE ESTABLISHMENT OF A FIELD: ARCHITECTURAL EDUCATION

Farhan Karim

South Asian architectural education in the years after Independence catalyzed a transformation of the role of architects. While architects from the region had often worked as surveyors or assistant engineers to British architects during the colonial period, after its end they became critical interlocutors who shaped the discourse of national development and helped forge postcolonial identities. In the context of rapid urbanization and burgeoning domestic industrialization, new architecture schools promoted the professional autonomy of the field and its inherent interdisciplinarity. Although most of the architecture programs initially followed Euro-American curricula and all courses were taught in English, questions of local context, regional history, indigenous culture,

Fig. 1   Page from an album with two photographs showing workshops at the Mayo School of Arts, Lahore, British India. 1908. RCS Photograph Collection, Fisher Collection, University of Cambridge

and the discipline's social responsibility soon became imperative. By the 1980s, the pedagogical focus of South Asian architectural training had evolved toward creating resistance against the hegemonic "Western" discourse of modernism, albeit without completely rejecting its narratives. Throughout the post-Independence period, the architect's self-image formulated in these schools was embedded in the changing perception of the "region" and its fluctuating relationship with the "world."

In the colonial period, the architecture courses offered at arts and crafts schools including the Sir J. J. School of Art in Bombay (est. 1857) and the Mayo School of Arts in Lahore (est. 1875; fig. 1) mimicked the programs of British institutions such as the Glasgow School of Art and the Architectural Association School of Architecture in London. After Independence, the postcolonial state's patronage of architectural education in tandem with a general enthusiasm for national development resulted in a new pedagogical ethics in which architects were seen (and saw themselves) as potential agents of social development. Consequently, a fundamental restructuring took place that paved new ways for institutionalizing architectural education.

In independent India, Prime Minister Jawaharlal Nehru set in motion a rapid expansion of technical education that resulted in the establishment of four technology-oriented architecture programs. The first was in 1950, at the Eastern Higher Technical Institute (later renamed IIT Kharagpur) in West Bengal; the second in 1955, as the School of Town and Country Planning, which was affiliated with the University of Delhi and integrated the architecture department of Delhi Polytechnic. These were followed by IIT Bombay in 1958 and IIT Madras in 1959.[1] The broader curricular focus at these institutions shifted from the old vocational model to a technology-based developmental model adopted from the Massachusetts Institute of Technology. The Nehruvian prioritization of an overarching technocracy supplanted both of the colonial models of education—architecture as engineering, and architecture as craft—in favor of a program of industrialization whose reach extended to construction techniques and the choice of materials.[2]

More educational facilities would open soon afterward. The National Institute of Design (NID), established in 1961, was initiated by Ahmedabad industrialists as a means for creating a modern India and training a new generation of designers to cater to the country's fast-growing industrial base (fig. 2; see Portfolio, no. 9). The philosophical blueprint for the NID came from the *India Report* drafted by US architects and designers Charles and

Fig. 2   National Institute of Design (NID), Ahmedabad, India. 1959–1967. Gira Sarabhai (1923–2021) and Gautam Sarabhai (1917–1995). Interior view of a workshop. 1967. Photograph: P. M. Dalwadi. NID Archives

Ray Eames.[3] The NID's innovative pedagogical model involved students and faculty collaborating with Western architects, such as with Louis I. Kahn on the Indian Institute of Management in Ahmedabad. Although architecture was dropped from NID's curriculum in 1969, the institution's unique approach to design as a holistic vehicle propelled national development and helped to situate architecture at the nexus of industrial design and visual culture.

Fig. 3   Students discussing the structure of a bridge at the Centre for Environmental Planning and Technology (CEPT), Ahmedabad, India. c. 1960s. CEPT Archives

Fig. 4   Students working on a structural installation at the Centre for Environmental Planning and Technology (CEPT), Ahmedabad, India. c. 1960s. CEPT Archives

Similarly hoping to establish at a synergistic ecology of design and environment, in 1962 the Ahmedabad Education Society, supported by various Ahmedabad industrialists, established a School of Architecture that in 1972 would become part of the Centre for Environmental Planning and Technology (CEPT) (see pp. 198–201). Spearheaded by architect Balkrishna V. Doshi, CEPT catalyzed a plurality of disciplines around the concept of the environment, facilitating the emergence of a new generation of experimental architects (figs. 3, 4), including figures such as Chitra Vishwanath (b. 1962), who incorporated vernacular materials and techniques into her work.

After Partition, Pakistan faced a severe shortage of professionals and architecture teachers. Lahore's Mayo School of Arts was the only educational center for art and architecture at the time and did not offer a degree program. A handful of architects who had been trained in colonial India migrated to Pakistan and settled mostly in Karachi, the first capital of the new country. Mehdi Ali Mirza, a former professor at Delhi Polytechnic's department of architecture, migrated to Pakistan in 1947 and joined the Karachi Public Works Department (PWD), going on to play a leading role in setting up the Institute of Architects, Pakistan (est. 1957), and the Government School of Architecture (GSA) in Karachi, (est. 1954), which provided the country's first diploma-level architecture course.[4] Mirza's interest in localized modernity was reflected in the GSA's curriculum, which strove to embody the idea of Pakistan as a progressive nation-state with an Islamic identity, and to define its architectural manifestation.[5]

The government of General Ayub Khan (president from 1958 to 1969) undertook massive education-reform projects in East and West Pakistan, from revamping the existing primary-school system to establishing several new universities and vocational training institutes. Architecture schools were also seen as important to the country's broader development goals. The Mayo School of Arts was renamed the National College of Arts (NCA) in 1958. After Kamil Khan Mumtaz, a graduate of the AA in London, was appointed chair of the NCA in 1966, he restructured the curriculum to address local traditions and the place of history in the profession.[6]

Modeled on American technology-oriented architectural education, and with help from the US Technical Assistance Program, two new architecture programs were established in 1962 within two new engineering universities—West Pakistan University of Engineering and Technology (WPUET) in Lahore and East Pakistan University of Engineering and Technology (EPUET) in Dhaka. EPUET, which became BUET following Bangladeshi independence in 1971, faced resistance from local architects such as Muzharul Islam, who advocated including the new architecture school within the University of Dhaka in order to draw on the humanities, fine arts, and applied sciences for its philosophy and methodology.[7] In the context of inadequate urban infrastructure and the absence of a national planning or housing policy, the first three professors, Richard E. Vrooman, James C. Walden, and Samuel T. Lanford—who all came from Texas A&M University—strove to create an architectural language for mass housing and pedagogical and cultural infrastructure with limited resources.[8]

Fig. 5   Students working on architecture models at Bangladesh University of Engineering and Technology (BUET), Dhaka, Bangladesh, c. 1980. Photograph: Anwar Hossain

Fig. 6   Students working on a geodesic dome at Bangladesh University of Engineering and Technology (BUET), Dhaka, Bangladesh. c. 1980. Photograph: Anwar Hossain

While the architecture course at EPUET was financed through the US Technical Assistance Program USAID and so hinged on Cold War strategic aims, and CEPT was conceived in the context of Ahmedabad's entrepreneurial critique of the Nehruvian technocratization of architectural education, both schools advocated a hybrid of Bauhaus pedagogy and an education grounded in local context and history. At each school, a close examination of the respective country's historic monuments was a key element of the syllabus, intended to enable students to develop their knowledge of local architectural history in the later years of their education, especially in the final-year thesis project (figs. 5, 6).

In Ceylon, thanks to substantial effort by architects Tom Neville Wynne-Jones and Herbert Gonsal to formalize architectural education, the Ceylon Institute of Architects was established in 1956 and paved the way for the creation of architecture schools in the coming decades. Fully fledged architecture programs were consolidated in the late 1950s, and were mainly initiated by individual architects who began to return from overseas and either established their private practices or joined the PWD. Justin Samarasekera—the chief architect of the Colombo PWD and a graduate of the J. J. School—championed the country's first full architecture degree program at the Institute of Practical Technology in Katubedda in 1961. The early curriculum, which was closely monitored by the Royal Institute of British Architects (RIBA), reflected the colonial hierarchy of center and periphery.[9] Architectural education initially continued to reproduce the colonial imagination of Ceylon as the exotic margin of the empire, most notably in an aesthetic of tropical fantasy centered on the antiurban image of secluded tropical bungalows. Hence, the pedagogical focus at first overlooked pressing issues such as affordable housing, although it was later revised to address practical issues grounded in local knowledge and a new aesthetic and ethic of social responsibility.

133

Architecture schools thus provided a basis for institutionalized identity and legal authority for architects. But, more importantly, they built the discipline's intellectual foundation through critical interventions and by problematizing some of the sharp binaries developed through colonial thinking processes, such as modernity and tradition, global and local, rural and urban. Despite these advances, academia in general had minimal sway over an individual government's development and planning policies. This was, on the one hand, because the Public Works Departments continued to operate as clients and architects at the same time, as in the colonial model, and, on the other, because increasing opportunities for private practice sidelined urgent social questions of housing and urbanization. The schools nevertheless offered a productive ambivalence that oscillated between contested ideas about the possible trajectories of post-Independence modernization and postcolonial self-consciousness.

1   Peter Scriver and Amit Srivastava, *India*, Modern Architectures in History (London: Reaktion, 2015), 216.
2   See Singanapalli Balaram, "Design Pedagogy in India: A Perspective," in "Indian Design and Design Education," special issue, *Design Issues* 21, no. 4 (Autumn 2005): 11–22; and Charles and Ray Eames, *The India Report* (1958) (Ahmedabad: National Institute of Design, 1997), http://echo.iat.sfu.ca/library/eames_58_india_report.pdf.
3   See Saloni Mathur, "Charles and Ray Eames in India," *Art Journal* 70, no. 1 (Spring 2011): 34–53; and Farhan Sirajul Karim, "MoMA, the Ulm and the Development of Design Pedagogy in India," in *Western Artists and India: Creative Inspirations in Art and Design*, ed. Shanay Jhaveri (London: Shoestring, 2013), 122–39.
4   Neelum Naz, "Development of Architectural Education in Pakistan: A Historical Perspective," *Global Built Environment Review* 7, no. 1 (2010): 31–42.
5   Zain Mankani, *Mehdi Ali Mirza: Pioneer of Architecture in Pakistan, 1910–1962* (Karachi: ARCH Press, 2012).
6   See Chris Moffat, "Building, Dwelling, Dying: Architecture and History in Pakistan," *Modern Intellectual History* 18, no. 2 (June 2021): 520–46.
7   Nurur Khan in conversation with the author, 2019. Khan is an architect and archivist at the Muzharul Islam Archive, University of Asia Pacific, Dhaka.
8   See "Laying the Foundation for Bangladesh's Architectural Future: An Interview with James Walden," *Frontlines*, November–December 2012, https://2012-2017.usaid.gov/news-information/frontlines/new-players-and-graduation/laying-foundation-bangladesh%E2%80%99s-architectural; Rafique Islam, *The First Faculty of Architecture in Dhaka* (self-pub., 2011), Google Play Books; and Adnan Zillur Morshed, "A Symbol of Architectural Education in Bangladesh," *The Daily Star* (Dhaka), October 1, 2018.
9   Anoma Pieris, *Architecture and Nationalism in Sri Lanka: The Trouser under the Cloth* (London: Routledge, 2012), 167.

"PLANNING AND DREAMING": ARCHITECTURE AND THE MEDIA

Devika Singh

During the post-Independence decades of nation-building in South Asia, media throughout the region understood architecture as both an aesthetic and a political project, presenting it as a crucial agent in the transformation of societies. Outlets ranging from generalist newspapers to specialized magazines captured and amplified the passions and ambitions of the architectural milieu and refracted new and ongoing societal challenges. Moreover, they acted as channels of transnational exchanges, strengthening existing connections and situating architectural discourses within international debates.

Some of the most significant writings appeared in the Bombay-based English-language journal *Marg: A Magazine of Architecture & Art* (fig. 1). The writer Mulk Raj Anand founded *Marg* (both the acronym of the Modern Architectural Research Group and a word meaning "pathway" in Sanskrit) in Bombay in 1946 with a close network of collaborators and the support of the visionary industrialist J. R. D. Tata.[1] Distinguished by the variation of typefaces, inclusion of tracing papers, and numerous full-page, high-quality reproductions,[2] *Marg*'s visual identity positioned it as a platform to experience modern design, while its engaged editorials sought to prescribe discourse among cultural elites. The journal subscribed to a Nehruvian idea of India as a secular and inclusive democracy, and fostered debates on models of modernization. It can therefore be seen as a prime example of the ways in which state-led modernization and the media in the post-Independence era sustained a mutually reinforcing relationship.

Fig. 1   Cover of the inaugural issue of *Marg* (October 1946)

135

From the beginning, *Marg* advocated the importance of architecture's function in the idealistic construction of a better society. The cover of the first issue was loosely modeled on an architectural blueprint. The inaugural editorial, "Planning and Dreaming," described the figure of the architect as symbolic of "resurgent India."[3] At a time when vernacular art and architecture—whether folk, Hindu, Buddhist, or Islamic—had long been belittled under colonialism, *Marg* sought to reclaim India's precolonial past while persistently defending a pro-modern, anti-revivalist agenda.[4] Building on the work of pre-Independence nationalist art and architecture periodicals, *Marg* embarked on a historical investigation of subjects as diverse as Mughal art and architecture,[5] Hindu erotic sculpture, Mexican contemporary painting, and architectural education. The range of its interests was not unlike that of the Karachi-based *Pakistan Quarterly* (1948–72), which sought to engage foreign art forms, to connect the art scenes of West and East Pakistan, and to define Pakistani art and architecture legacies.[6]

After Independence, the architectural profession across South Asia shifted from a shared culture centered in the major places of practice and training of Calcutta, Bombay, and London to an emphasis on nationally focused projects. Among them were the building or expansion of the national and regional capitals of Delhi, Chandigarh (figs. 2, 3), and Karachi, and finding solutions to the challenges raised by the massive flows of refugees that accompanied the violence of Partition and the fragmentation of the subcontinent. Yet *Marg*'s editors criticized parochial forms of nationalism and promoted the sense of a transnational community, both internationally and across South Asia.[7] The "Planning and Dreaming" editorial began by highlighting "a certain continuity in contemporary culture which is running through the world from Moscow to Paris, London to Bombay, Shanghai to Honolulu and New York to Buenos Aires."[8] The first article in that issue, characterized as a manifesto and titled "Architecture and You," explained, "it is meaningless for us to think in terms of an 'Indian Style of Architecture' or of 'Indian Traditional Architecture,'" and described the recourse to nationalism in architecture as "a form of escape in the absence of our ability to create a national character expressive of ourselves to-day, in the 20th century."[9] Echoing Nehru's vision, the article concluded that "modern science and the machine speak a common language, which, in breaking down the old regional and social barriers, gives an expression of life common to all the peoples of the world."[10] Technology, according to this arguably flawed but powerful vision, was considered progressive, socially unifying, and for the benefit of all.

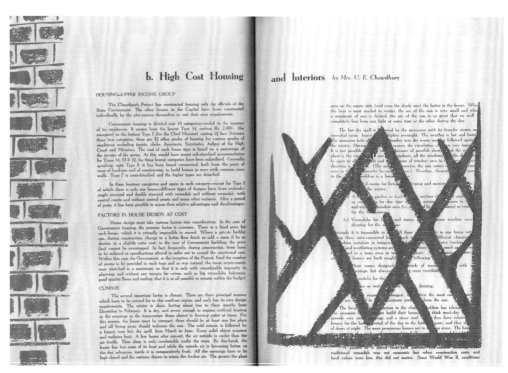

Fig. 2   Cover of *Marg* 15, no. 1 (December 1961). Special issue, "Chandigarh"

Fig. 3   Spread from *Marg* 15, no. 1, (December 1961). Special issue, "Chandigarh." Featuring the opening pages of Urmila Eulie Chowdhury's article "High Cost Housing and Interiors"

Among the figures who helped shape the early years of *Marg* were the Ceylonese architect Minnette de Silva (fig. 4) and the German-Jewish exile Otto Koenigsberger. De Silva had worked with him when he was serving as Government Architect of the Princely State of Mysore, after she had been expelled from the Sir J. J. School of Art in Bombay in 1944 for protesting Gandhi's arrest.[11] A few years later, she would participate, as the *Marg* delegate (and the only South Asian architect), in the CIAM conference in Bridgwater, UK.[12] Both Koenigsberger and de Silva influenced the journal's advocacy of a locally oriented synthesis of foreign styles and indigenous traditions, thus modulating the promotion of "modern science and the machine." Writing on her first completed project, the Karunaratne House (1947–51) in Kandy, Ceylon (see pp. 178–81), de Silva explained that "an attempt has been made to synthesize indigenous traditions with an architecture designed for a contemporary Buddhist Singhalese family and its way of living—using whatever materials and means were suitable—both modern and traditional."[13] This followed a logic that underpinned many practices after Independence, and one that de Silva maintained allegiance to for the rest of her career.

Fig. 4   From left: unidentified, Pablo Picasso, Minnette de Silva, Jo Davidson, and Mulk Raj Anand at the World Congress of Intellectuals in Defense of Peace, Wrocław University of Technology, Wrocław, Poland. August 27, 1948

While *Marg* would eventually pay less attention to architecture, *Design*, published from 1957 onward by Patwant Singh, a writer and publisher hailing from a contractor family, sustained a clear focus on the discipline (fig. 5). Launched in New Delhi, where architects from across India had relocated and where India's Central Public Works Department (CPWD) was based, *Design* was the successor to Singh's Bombay-based magazine, *The Indian Builder*. Like *Marg*, *Design* covered a variety of topics, from the work of textile designer Riten Mozumdar to the architectural inventions of French luminary Yona Friedman. During the building of Chandigarh in the 1950s and 1960s, both magazines looked back at the planned city of Jaipur (founded in 1727 in the Indian state of Rajasthan) and the Mughal complex of Fatehpur Sikri to anchor contemporary planning in an Indian genealogy.[14] However, by acknowledging the multiplication of unplanned dwellings in a rapidly urbanizing South Asia, the journals also tried to resolve the tensions between the need for planning and the desires of the state and of the architectural profession, on the one hand, and the informality of the urban habitat, on the other. The New Delhi–based magazine *Seminar*, founded in Bombay in 1959 by Raj and Romesh Thapar, would take a different stance, with architect and activist Jai Sen criticizing formal development and instead favoring "a hybrid rural-urban society with appropriate social structures and institutions which allows [the poor] to be part of both city and village."[15]

137

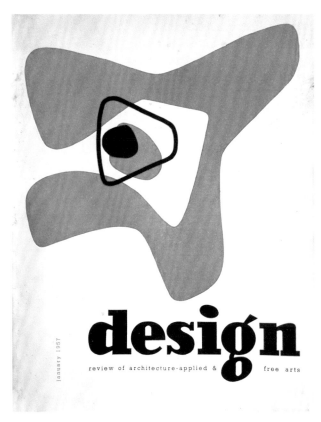

Fig. 5   Cover of the inaugural issue of *Design* (January 1957)

In addition to setting South Asian architecture within a transnational perspective, *Marg*, along with *Design*, frequently featured the work of foreign architects including Le Corbusier;[16] Frank Lloyd Wright, who in the late 1940s was working on offices and stores for Calico Mills in Ahmedabad; and Richard Neutra, who designed the US Embassy in Karachi with Robert Alexander in the 1950s (see fig. 2 on p. 162). At the same time, the work of leading South Asian architects, many of whom had been trained abroad, was, if less extensively, published and discussed in European and North American architecture magazines, especially when it involved international collaborations. This occurred, for instance, with Muzharul Islam and Stanley Tigerman's master-plan research for Five Polytechnic Institutes in East Pakistan (see fig. 21 on p. 55 and fig. 22 on p. 58).[17] Such examples attest to the intensity of architectural mobility in post-Independence contexts—through both the physical movement of architects and firms and the dissemination in the media of texts, photographs, blueprints, and master plans—as well as its embedded hierarchies.[18]

Entrenched inequities indeed still structured architectural discourse and the attribution of projects after Independence. As Dipesh Chakrabarty explains regarding India, the period from the late 1940s to the 1960s corresponded to a so-called developmental phase that was still turned toward the West in an attempt to catch up with it.[19] This may explain why the state often privileged Western cultural interlocutors even as it expressed the desire to move away from Western-centric approaches. In addition to the aforementioned magazines, architectural print media encompassed the official reports of European and North American architecture firms, foundations, and organizations collaborating with South Asian states on development-aid programs and urban master plans. Among the most ambitious projects was Constantinos A. Doxiadis's plan for Islamabad (see pp. 186–89), for which Doxiadis Associates (DA) was selected in the late 1950s. DA's in-house bulletin extensively documented different aspects of the project and thereby showcased the firm's construction capacity and design potential (fig. 6). Moreover, starting in 1957, Doxiadis, through his Center of Ekistics in Athens, published the scholarly magazine *Ekistics* (named after his neologism for "the science of human settlements"), which featured contributions by Pakistani and, from 1971, Bangladeshi geographers, educationalists, and planners.[20] Also in the 1950s, the United Nations enlisted Michel Écochard, director of town planning in the French protectorate of Morocco, as a consultant on the issue of refugees in Karachi, which led to a report detailing an unrealized plan for the satellite city of Landhi (1953) and the master plan and campus buildings for the University of Karachi (1958).[21] In addition, the Ford Foundation opened its first foreign office in New Delhi in 1952. It was involved in the city's 1962 master plan, as well as in Pakistan's city planning through the Harvard Development Advisory Group.[22] These kinds of reports, embedded in local discussions on economic development and social stratification, moreover helped mobilize architecture in the promotion of state-led modernization.

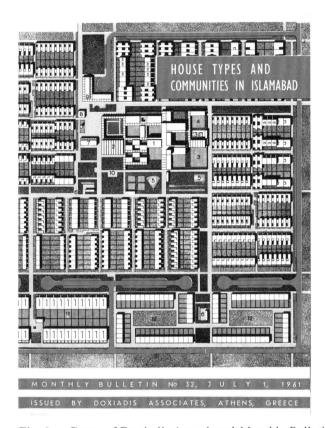 

Fig. 6   Cover of Doxiadis Associates' *Monthly Bulletin*, no. 32 (July 1961). Special issue, "House Types and Communities in Islamabad."
         Constantinos A. Doxiadis Archives
Fig. 7   Cover of *Designs for Low Cost Housing*. New Delhi: Ministry of Works, Housing and Supply, 1954

In this regard, the capacity to communicate the thinking behind vastly transformative projects to different audiences by enlisting diverse platforms, including films and exhibitions, was key. Attesting to the strategic relationship between state and the media, officially organized exhibitions and conferences came with their own printed matter, brochures, and posters, and contributed to the popular dissemination of government policies. In 1954, *Marg* published a supplement dedicated to the International Exhibition on Low-Cost Housing organized in New Delhi by India's Ministry of Works, Housing and Supply, which also published its own brochure (fig. 7), while the *Journal of the Ceylon Institute of Architects* covered the Ceylon Industrial Exhibition of 1965 in Colombo and its numerous prefabrication projects.[23] When Charles Correa, Pravina Mehta, and Shirish Patel sought to present their design for New Bombay (now Navi Mumbai)—a planned city located on the mainland coast of Maharashtra, opposite the Bombay Peninsula, and intended to decongest the historic metropolis—the scheme was the focus of a special issue of *Marg*. It was also promoted with the film *City on the Water* (1975; fig. 8), directed by Correa and produced by the Films Division of India. This state-run organization also made other shorts with an architectural focus, such as Ravi Prakash's *Search for Shelter* (1950), Pratap Parmar's *Housing for the People* (1972), and B. D. Garga's *Roof Above* (1976), revealing the civic mission with which architecture was invested.[24] In contrast, the alternative-minded but influential British-born South India–based architect Laurie Baker produced self-published pamphlets that reflect his commitment to the reduction of building costs, the use of vernacular materials, and sustainable ways of living (fig. 9).[25]

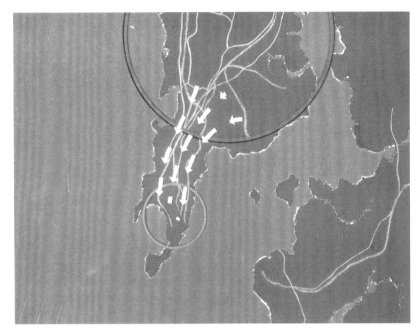

Fig. 8   Charles Correa (1930–2015). *City on the Water*. 1975. Film: 8mm, color, 16 minutes 35 seconds. Films Division, Government of India

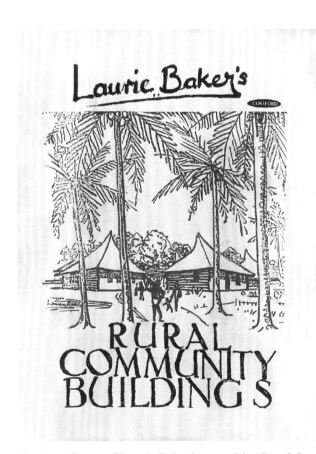

Fig. 9   Cover of Laurie Baker's pamphlet *Rural Community Buildings*. Thrissur, India: COSTFORD, 1986

Returning to *Marg*, within this wider context of architectural media, its legacy stands out for how it not only promoted modernist architecture in India but also invested anew in the precolonial past while expressing skepticism of revivalist tendencies. It was among the first forums to historicize major contemporary projects and to renew art and architectural narratives, valorizing both past and present achievements. It was only with the Festivals of India in the mid-1980s—for which Indian government officials, critics, artists, and architects mounted exhibitions in France, the United Kingdom, the United States, the Soviet Union, and Japan—that significant book-length studies spanning the historical and the contemporary would be released, as catalogues to these exhibitions.[26]

Tellingly, whereas these state-backed festivals projected a coherent, nationally focused image of Indian architectural developments on the world stage, the contemporaneous independent media took on international perspectives with renewed strength. Foremost among them, the journal *Mimar*, launched in 1981 by the Aga Khan Trust for Culture, emerged as a platform for the profession across "developing countries," including those of South Asia. Covering new projects as well as iconic earlier ones, such as Brazilian architect Lina Bo Bardi's works and Louis I. Kahn's National Parliament House in Dhaka (1962–82), it reflected on the modernist legacy and advanced the transnational agenda of previous magazines—directing attention this time away from Europe and North America and toward postcolonial stakes.

1   Tata first supported *Marg* through office space and advertisements—and from 1951 to 1985, after its founders could no longer finance the review, by making *Marg* a division of Tata Sons.
2   Architect Minnette de Silva's sister, Marcia de Silva, known as Anil, was initially responsible for the layout. See Rachel Lee and Kathleen James-Chakraborty, "*Marg* Magazine: A Tryst with Architectural Modernity," *ABE Journal* no. 1 (2012), https://doi.org/10.4000/abe.623. From 1955 onward, the journal was designed by artist and illustrator Dolly Sahiar.
3   Mulk Raj Anand, "Planning and Dreaming," *Marg* 1, no. 1 (October 1946): 5.
4   On revivalism, see Rahul Mehrotra, *Architecture in India since 1990* (Mumbai: Pictor, 2011), 25.
5   Devika Singh, "Approaching the Mughal Past in Indian Art Criticism: The Case of *MARG* (1946–1963)," *Modern Asian Studies* 47, no. 1 (January 2013): 167–203.
6   Samina Iqbal, "*Pakistan Quarterly*: Site of Substance" (conference paper), "It Begins with a Story: Artists, Writers, and Periodicals in Asia," Asia Art Archive and Sharjah Art Foundation, Sharjah, November 2018).
7   In the case of *Marg*, South Asian connections were drawn especially between India and Ceylon. Along with de Silva, Ceylonese and Ceylon-based contributing editors would over time include the renowned painter George Keyt; architect Andrew Boyd; de Silva's sister, writer and art historian Anil de Silva, a founding member of the Indian People Theatre's Association who served as Marg's first assistant editor; and Jehangir P. J. Bilimoria, who would participate in the inaugural meeting of the Ceylon Institute of Architects in 1957.
8   Anand, "Planning and Dreaming," 3.
9   "Architecture and You," *Marg* 1, no. 1 (1946): 13.
10 Ibid., 15. Speaking at a seminar on architecture in 1959, Nehru, too, fervently advocated a move beyond the "static" last centuries and encouraged the championing of new directions, designs, and ideas. "Inaugural Address by Shri Jawaharlal Nehru, Prime Minister," in *Seminar on Architecture*, ed. Achyut Kanvinde (New Delhi: Lalit Kala Akademi, 1959), 5–9.
11 On Koenigsberger, see, for instance, Rachel Lee, "Constructing a Shared Vision: Otto Koenigsberger and Tata & Sons," *ABE Journal* no. 2 (2012), https://doi.org/10.4000/abe.356.
12 Anoma Pieris, *Architecture and Nationalism in Sri Lanka: The Trouser under the Cloth* (London, Routledge, 2012), 131. See also Minnette de Silva's autobiography, *The Life & Work of an Asian Woman Architect* (Colombo: Smart Media Productions, 1998).
13 Minnette de Silva, "A House at Kandy, Ceylon," *Marg* 6, no. 3 (June 1953), 4–11.
14 In the 1960s and 1970s, *Design* documented the Chandigarh homes of Indian architects involved in the Project. See, for instance, "When Architects Design for Themselves: Chandigarh Architects Design Their Own Houses in Le Corbusier's City," *Design* 15 no. 2 (February 1971): 15–22. Senior architect at Chandigarh Urmila Eulie Chowdhury recounted her experience on All India Radio; see M. S. Batra, "Architect: Mrs Eulie Chowdhury (interview)," in *A.I.R. Miscellany* 5 (1965): 43–44.
15 Jai Sen, "The Unintended City," *Seminar*, no. 200 (April 1976), https://www.india-seminar.com/2001/500/500%20jai%20sen.htm.
16 For a later, critical take on Le Corbusier and the replication of social inequalities in Chandigarh, see Mulk Raj Anand, "Needed: A More Experimental Architecture for India," *Design* 23, no. 11 (November 1979): 17.
17 Raymond Lifchez, "Master Plan Study Gives East Pakistan New Approaches for Tropical Architecture," *Architectural Record*, September 1968, 153–60.
18 On architectural mobility, see Łukasz Stanek, *Architecture in Global Socialism: Eastern Europe, West Africa, and the Middle East in the Cold War* (Princeton, NJ: Princeton University Press, 2020).
19 Dipesh Chakrabarty, "The Legacies of Bandung: Decolonisation and the Politics of Culture," *Economic and Political Weekly* 40, no. 46 (November 12–18, 2005): 4,814.
20 For example, Nafis Ahmad and A. K. M. Hafizur Rahman, "Development of Industry in Chittagong," *Ekistics* 15, no. 90 (May 1963): 301–4; Khalid Shibli, "Administration of Urban Development: Pakistan," *Ekistics* 23, no. 135 (February 1967): 92–97; Khalid Ashfaq, "Housing West Pakistan, 1970–2000," *Ekistics* 38, no. 224 (July 1974): 13–21; and M. A. Qadeer, "Do Cities 'Modernize' the Developing Countries? An Examination of the South Asian Experience," *Ekistics* 39, no. 233 (April 1975): 229–35.
21 See Ijlal Muzaffar, "Boundary Games: Ecochard, Doxiadis and the Refugee Housing Projects under Military Rule in Pakistan, 1953–1959," in *Governing by Design*, ed. Daniel M. Abramson, Arindam Dutta, Timothy Hyde, and Jonathan Massey (Pittsburgh, PA: University of Pittsburgh Press, 2012), 147–76.
22 Tom Avermaete and Maristella Casciato, *Casablanca Chandigarh: A Report on Modernization* (Zurich: Park Books, 2014), 66–67. In the field of design, *The India Report* (1958), by Charles and Ray Eames, was a response to an invitation from the Indian government and sponsored by the Ford Foundation. See Saloni Mathur, "Charles and Ray Eames in India," *Art Journal* 70, no. 1 (Spring 2011): 34–53; and Claire Wintle, "Diplomacy and the Design School: The Ford Foundation and India's National Institute of Design," *Design and Culture* 9, no. 2 (July 2017): 207–24.
23 Pieris, *Architecture and Nationalism in Sri Lanka*, 127.
24 Charles M. Correa, Pravina Mehta, and Shirish B. Patel, "Bombay: Planning and Dreaming," special issue, *Marg* 18, no. 3 (June 1965).
25 See Gautam Bhatia, *Laurie Baker: Life, Works & Writings* (New Delhi: Penguin, 1991).
26 See Raj Rewal, Jean-Louis Véret, and Ram Sharma, eds., *Architecture in India* (Paris: Electa Moniteur, 1985); and Carmen Kagal, ed., *Vistāra: The Architecture of India* (Bombay: Tata Press, 1986).

"SHELTERED OPENNESS": THE MODERN HOUSE

Kazi Khaleed Ashraf

Modernity appeared in South Asia in a slow, simmering process entangled with both the marauding enterprise of European colonialists and a commercial as well as intellectual resurgence among a new native elite. While the progressive groups of Bengal and India were eager to embrace European modernity in episodic changes focused on institutions, their enthusiasm stopped literally at the doorstep of the house.

Venerated as well as repudiated, "home" has always been a contested category in the subcontinent. While the traditional home in South Asia is considered an introspective place, erected both tectonically and ritually, "homelessness" as practiced by ascetics and renouncers was glorified as well. With multiple households living in each dwelling, the home is also a place in which the individual is subordinated to deep-rooted norms. If modernity signifies the celebration of the self, the traditional home appears antithetical to the modern project. All of these conditions perhaps account for the fitful development of the modern house in South Asia.

Other than sporadic examples—from Claude Batley's neotraditional residences in Bombay in the early decades of the twentieth century to Rabindranath Tagore's historically styled houses in Santiniketan (see Pieris, p. 37)—colonial-period experiments in private housing design in South Asia are few. (The bungalow, more on which below, is an exception). By contrast, the "home" in the village of Sewagram where Mohandas Gandhi lived from 1936 to 1948 was deliberately constructed as a hut in a rural ethic and now appears as a prescient rethinking of the house paradigm.[1] A manifestation of a political and spiritual discourse, and of a contrapuntal modernity, Gandhi's home, popularly known as Bapu Kuti, recalls the ideological shift from *grihya* (home/household) to *kuti* (hut) as practiced in ancient renunciatory traditions (fig. 1).

Fig. 1   Mohandas Gandhi (1869–1948) at his hut Bapu Kuti, Ahmedabad, India. 1946

In maintaining the vast machine of the colonial empire through relentless building projects, European architects and engineers presented to middle- and upper-class Indians the image of the "modern home" encapsulated in that now universalized building type, the bungalow. While the primary impulse was pragmatic, the evolution from *bangla* (or village hut) to bungalow is perhaps the biggest and most underrated architectural event triggered in the subcontinent.[2] The bungalow—adopted from the vernacular architecture of Bengal; configured out of climatic concerns, metrics of comfort, and fear of tropical "miasma"; and providing prototypes for various economic groups—created the most pervasive residential paradigm in modern South Asia, from ubiquitous villas and suburban houses to dubious "farmhouses" dotting the fringes of the contemporary metropolis. Two aspects of the bungalow paradigm would keep modern architects in thrall: climatic parameters in configuring a house, on the one hand, and in situating a building, on the other.

Although superseded by a high architectural poetics, climate was a primary driver in Le Corbusier's iconic residences in Ahmedabad: Villa Shodhan and the Sarabhai House (both 1951–56). A major influence on residential design for the upper class, both houses transcend their "utilitarian roots" and serve as examples of architectural virtuosity.[3] By replicating the spatial drama of the Swiss-French architect's Villa Savoye (1928–31), Villa Shodhan (fig. 2) introduces a radical type of architectural volume in the Indian scene, while the Sarabhai House (fig. 3), with its sprawling character and intimate relation with the site, prods a deeper spatial-psychological sensibility.

Fig. 2   Villa Shodhan, Ahmedabad, India. 1951–56. Le Corbusier (Charles-Édouard Jeanneret, 1887–1965). Interior view. Photographer unknown. c. 1956. Architecture & Design Study Center, The Museum of Modern Art, New York

Fig. 3   Sarabhai House, Ahmedabad, India. 1951–56. Le Corbusier (Charles-Édouard Jeanneret, 1887–1965). Interior view. 1955. Photograph: Lucien Hervé. Architecture & Design Study Center, The Museum of Modern Art, New York

In most South Asian dwellings, across various social strata and geographic contexts, the living space overflows to the "outside," producing a mediating realm between outer and inner domains and giving houses a perennial quality of "sheltered openness."[4] Charles Correa would conceptualize that quality as a "place in the sun," integral to "open-to-sky" interior courtyards and ambulatory spaces.[5] Such tenets for dwellings also offer a convenient alliance with the modernist intertwining of exterior and interior spaces. Moving away from the pragmatism of the bungalow, the house by the late 1950s became an architectural statement, an ensemble expressing transparency, porosity, and openness under a parasol. Achyut Kanvinde's Balkrishna Harivallabhdas Residence in Ahmedabad (1962–64; fig. 4), Correa's Parekh House in Ahmedabad (1966–68), Muzharul Islam's own house in Dhaka (1964–69; fig. 5), Balkrishna V. Doshi's Tejal House in Ahmedabad (1994), and Geoffrey Bawa's Jayewardene House in Mirissa, Sri Lanka (1996), all belong to the "parasol house" type.

Fig. 4   Balkrishna Harivallabhdas Residence, Ahmedabad, India. 1962–64. Achyut Kanvinde (1916–2002). Exterior view. c. 1964. Kanvinde Archives

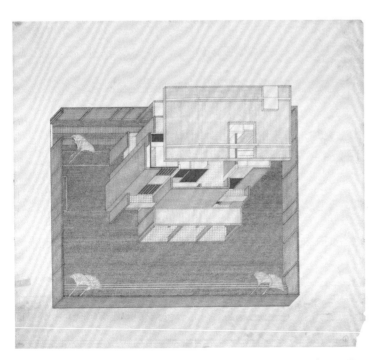

Fig. 5   Muzharul Islam's residence, Dhaka, East Pakistan (Bangladesh). 1964–69. Muzharul Islam (1923–2012)/Vastukalabid. Plan oblique. Muzharul Islam Archives

The Sri Lankan architects Minnette de Silva and Geoffrey Bawa, inspired by the documentation of vernacular architecture carried out by the designer Barbara Sansoni (fig. 6) and artist/architect Laki Senanayake, developed a distinctive regionalist mode. An early articulation of the "tropical modernist" house, and a laboratory for a regionalist expression, is de Silva's Karunaratne House in Kandy (1947–51; see pp. 178–81), considered to be among the first modern houses in the country.[6] Writing in the magazine *Marg* in 1953, de Silva described the house as an experiment in "modern regional architecture in the tropics."[7] In that building, and others that followed, de Silva assembled the ingredients that were to define architecture in Sri Lanka, by relating building and landscape, overlapping inside and outside, and rejuvenating the vernacular courtyard (*midula*) in modern form.

Fig. 6   Barbara Sansoni (b. 1928). *Yakadagala.* 1964. Hand-colored print, 8 × 10⁵⁄₁₆ in. (20.3 × 26.2 cm). Barbara Sansoni Archives

In Bawa's work, the bungalow/house received two distinct conceptual revisions: the "house in a garden" as in his magnum opus, the garden estate Lunuganga (1948–98; see Portfolio, nos. 8, 20), and the "house as a garden" represented by his Colombo home on 33rd Lane (1960–98; fig. 7), in which, as historian David Robson argues with regard to the Ena de Silva House (1960–62; see figs. 3–6 on pp. 162–63), the bungalow is refashioned to be "inward-looking," dismantled and reassembled in a tight urban setting.[8] As "meta-bungalows," Bawa's houses transcend the pragmatic parameters of the bungalow as such to be more akin to sensuous artifacts operating in tandem with landscape conditions.

Symptomatic of a rising middle class but reflecting diverse aspirations in different cities, houses were defining a new lifestyle in a Westernized milieu as a fusion of the old colonial *babu* culture (the upper-middle-class adoption of English norms), European modernism, and, from the 1960s onward, Americanization. The result, as a successor to the bungalow model, was the generic villa in an open lot, a house type that was supported by urban-planning dictums. Noteworthy works were produced under those conditions. In what was then East Pakistan (now Bangladesh), Muzharul Islam designed a few hundred houses between 1960 and 1970 as various tectonic, spatial, constructional, and expressive experiments. The socialist enterprise of the Indian government in the 1950s and 1960s also produced some remarkable housing designs. Propounding the dictum "form follows climate," Correa conducted innovative experiments with climatic parameters, most notably with the concept of the Tube House (1961–62; see figs. 4, 5 on p. 123), aspects of which were taken up in the sectionally organized Ramkrishna House in Ahmedabad (1961–64), as well as his own house with a solar parasol (unbuilt, 1968).

The interiors of many of those houses were also indicative of a new aesthetic: their furnishings ranged from ethnic and traditional accoutrements to a quasi-Gandhian sparseness. Such interiorscapes, conceived as a *raumplan*, with fluid spaces, steps going up and down, low walls, and visual overlays, are best expressed in Kanvinde's own house in New Delhi (1965–67; fig. 8).

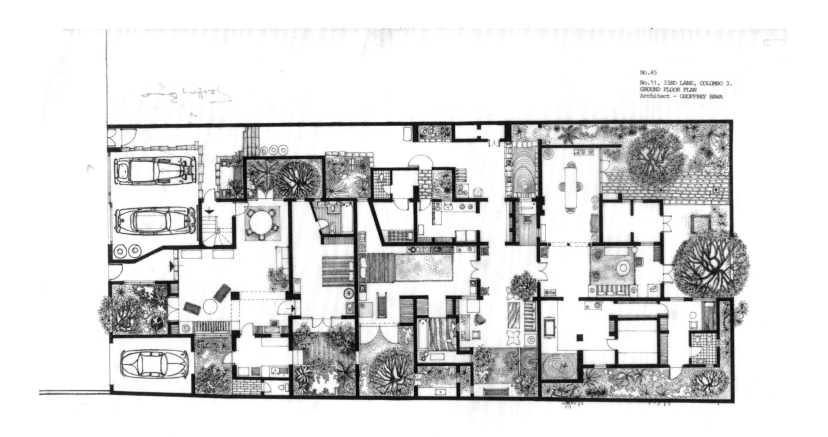

Fig. 7   No. 11, 33rd Lane House, Colombo, Ceylon (Sri Lanka). 1960–98. Geoffrey Bawa (1919–2003). Ground-floor plan. Ink and pencil on tracing paper. 11$^{15}/_{16}$ × 19$^{9}/_{16}$ in. (30.3 × 49.7 cm). The Lunuganga Trust

Fig. 8   Kanvinde Residence, New Delhi, India. 1965–67. Achyut Kanvinde (1916–2002). Interior view, with the architect seated at center. 1966. Photograph: Madan Mahatta. Kanvinde Archives

146

Configured as concrete-and-brick assemblages with cantilevered elements, many houses of the 1960s and 1970s presented a quasi-Brutalist framework, from Doshi's Chinubhai House (1959–60; fig. 9) to Hasmukh Patel's house for Indubhai Sheth of the Ahemedabad circle (1973) to the Yasmeen Lari House (1973; see figs. 12–13 on p. 22) in Karachi. By contrast, Kamil Khan Mumtaz's early projects in Lahore, the Kot Karamat farmhouse (1970) and his own residence (1977–80; fig. 10); Bashirul Haq's own house-studio in Dhaka (1979); Nayyar Ali Dada's Shakir Ali House (now museum, 1982) in Lahore; and the "eco-friendly" buildings by Laurie Baker in the Indian states of Kerala

Fig. 9   Chinubhai House, Ahmedabad, India. 1959–60. Balkrishna V. Doshi (b. 1927)/Vāstu Shilpā. Exterior view. Vāstu Shilpā Foundation Archives

Fig. 10   Mumtaz Residential Complex, Lahore, Pakistan. 1977–80. Kamil Khan Mumtaz (b. 1939). Exterior view. 1987. Photograph: Kazi Khaleed Ashraf. Aga Khan Documentation Center, MIT Libraries

and Mysore (Karnataka after 1973) introduced a new brick ethos as well as a new take on the meaning of the home. Deliberately resituating the traditional thematic of the house in a modern framework, these architects adopted brick as a redemptive material that was conducive to creating an architecture closer to the ground and to its site, and a darkened ambience that stood in contrast to the skeletal or planar aesthetics of previous decades.

In the larger global debate of the 1980s between "universalization" and "local culture," in which ideas of postmodernism and regionalism surged, a more social concern for housing dampened a glorified narrative for the house. The house, in fact, became a site for the restoration of older cultural typologies and values, and in some cases a flamboyant demonstration of the excesses of a neoliberal economy, which is especially evident in the Antilia in Mumbai (2003–10), still considered the world's most expensive private home, a twenty-seven-story tower. By shifting from the ideology of a modern dwelling to a spectacular theater, the house now espouses a contrarian prescription to modernism.

1   Gandhi's ideological hut was bypassed in most architectural narratives, though it received a cameo in Charles Correa's traveling exhibition *Vistāra: The Architecture of India* (1986). With regard to the parameters of building materials and how they can be accessed, the hut is now discussed as emblematic of a sustainable practice.
2   See Anthony D. King, *The Bungalow: The Production of a Global Culture* (Oxford, UK: Oxford University Press, 1995).
3   With the brise-soleil and parasol roof, Le Corbusier developed an architectural-typological language for climate control from his early work in North Africa, as seen in the first sketch for Villa Baizeau in Carthage, Tunisia (1928). See Stanislaus von Moos, *Le Corbusier: Elements of a Synthesis* (Cambridge, MA: MIT Press, 1979), 128.
4   Peter Serenyi, "Timeless but of Its Time: Le Corbusier's Architecture in India," *Perspecta* 20 (1983): 108.
5   Charles Correa, "A Place in the Sun," *Journal of the Royal Society of Arts* 131, no. 5,322 (May 1983): 328–40.
6   Shiromi Pinto, "Minnette de Silva: The Brilliant Female Architect Forgotten by History," *The Guardian*, December 14, 2018; and Amy Sherlock, "Born 100 Years Ago, Remembering the 'Tropical Modernist' Architect Minnette de Silva," *Frieze Masters*, no. 7 (September 2018), https://frieze.com/article/born-100-years-ago-remembering-tropical-modernist-architect-minnette-de-silva.
7   Minnette de Silva, "A House at Kandy, Ceylon," *Marg* 6, no. 3 (June 1953): 4–11. The article is discussed on pp. 178–81 of this volume.
8   David Robson, *Geoffrey Bawa: The Complete Works* (London: Thames & Hudson, 2002), 75.

ARCHITECTURE AND ENVIRONMENT

Prajna Desai

"The air flows through the house and up through the *midula* to upper floors,"[1] Sri Lankan architect Minnette de Silva wrote of Pieris House 1 (1952–56; fig. 1), her first project in Colombo, where an attenuated double-pitched Kandyan roof topped a two-story plan with *pilotis* that raised the living quarters above hyphenating ground-floor spaces (fig. 2), including the type of interior courtyard known as a *midula*, that collectively looked onto both street and garden. De Silva's hybrid approach of rewiring functionalist aesthetics into dissected recuperations of what Pierre Bourdieu called "habitus" was based on the idea that geography and place took priority over arbitrary universalist values.[2] Her emphasis on preserving rather than fusing formal and material irregularities and differences straddled the gap between the Buddhist revivalism of official Ceylonese architecture and the aesthetics of European modernism, and reinvigorated residential design in Kandy and Colombo from the 1950s onward.

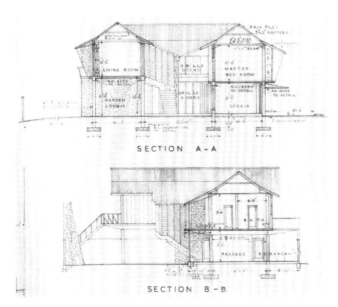

Fig. 1   Pieris House (Pieris House 1), Colombo, Ceylon (Sri Lanka). 1952–56. Minnette de Silva (1918–1998). Sections and plan. 1″ = 1'-0″. Reproduced in de Silva's autobiography, *The Life & Work of an Asian Woman Architect* (Colombo: Smart Media Productions, 1998), 181

Fig. 2   Pieris House (Pieris House 1), Colombo, Ceylon (Sri Lanka). 1952–56. Minnette de Silva (1918–1998). Interior view of the ground floor. Photograph: David Robson

149

De Silva's unapologetic regionalism was axiomatic rather than alternative, whether vis-à-vis European modernism or something else. The confidence with which it spoke from a cultural position that challenged the assumed centrality of Europe in architectural discourse also rendered it largely illegible within the milieu of the Congrès Internationaux d'Architecture Moderne (CIAM) and subsequent scholarly appraisals of regionalism.[3] Barring some recent academic redressals by architectural historians, her work has historically been interpreted as an offshoot of the Architectural Association School of Architecture in London and so as part of the "tropical modernism" that Jane Drew, Maxwell Fry, and Otto Koenigsberger promoted for postcolonial contexts.[4] Although often misread as a less sophisticated counterpart to Latin American modernist architecture, her all-encompassing environmental approach delineated crucial relationships among geography, place, social life, and contemporary history. Its singularity is, however, perhaps most acutely grasped through the stimulus it gave to Geoffrey Bawa, Sri Lanka's most prolific and influential architect, and his heterotopic project of modern architecture.[5]

From the 1960s onward, Bawa adapted Palladian scenographic principles to Ceylon's topography, sensuously transfiguring material locale through a cornucopia of forms from the island and beyond: linked courtyards, clustered pavilions, and atrium-like verandas that were combined with tiled roofs, economically distributed walls, and lofty piers. If the various buildings, terraces, and artworks dotted around the garden on his Lunuganga Estate, which he worked on from 1948 to 1998 (figs. 3, 4; see Portfolio, nos. 8, 20), crystallized an improvisational sensibility, the breach and recuperation of geophysical valences was later showcased in buildings that functioned as allegories of origin and place. Prominent among them is the Parliament Building in Colombo (1979–82), which was built with largely imported materials on an artificial island in a manmade lake, a technocratic reification of statecraft that encapsulated political centralization in its layout. A decade later, Kandalama Hotel (1991–94; fig. 5) reprised Bawa's phenomenological vernacular through its geomantic relationship with the topographic monolith of the ancient rock fortress of Sigiriya and its links with Sri Lanka's majoritarian mythos of Sinhala Buddhist origins.

The intimate relationship between architecture and the natural world that played a key role in the work of many of South Asia's leading architects in the years following Independence was, especially in India, often a focus of concerns about equality and privilege, privacy and leisure, which sometimes played out in the context of housing policy. Yet the intertwined relationship of environment, society, and cultural sensibilities constituted a decisive principle in the very different work of two Indian architects: Charles Correa and Laurie Baker.

At the core of Correa's motifs of increment and flow was the notion of *vistāra* (expansion) and a corresponding spatial language of volumetric voids.[6] Increment produced a polycentric traditional Indian "settlement" of post-and-beam boxes interspersed with open courts in the Gandhi Memorial Museum (1958–63; fig. 6) in Ahmedabad; an interlocking garden aesthetic for Bombay's Jeevan Bima Nagar mid-rise housing (1969–72); and low-rise

Fig. 3   Lunuganga Estate, Bentota, Ceylon (Sri Lanka). 1948–98. Geoffrey Bawa (1919–2003). Perspective drawing by Sumangala Jayatillaka. 1988. Ink and colored pencil on tracing paper. The Lunuganga Trust

Fig. 4   Lunuganga Estate, Bentota, Ceylon (Sri Lanka). 1948–98. Geoffrey Bawa (1919–2003). Site plan. 1984. Ink and pencil on tracing paper. The Lunuganga Trust

Fig. 5   Kandalama Hotel, Dambulla, Sri Lanka. 1991–94. Geoffrey Bawa (1919 2003). Site section. Ink and pencil on tracing paper, 23 1/4 × 33 1/16 in. (59 × 84 cm). The Lunuganga Trust

Fig. 6   Gandhi Memorial Museum, Ahmedabad, India. 1958–63. Charles Correa (1930–2015). Exterior view. c. 1963.
Photograph: Pranlal Patel. Charles Correa Foundation

housing in Belapur (1983–86; see fig. 10 on p. 127), part of the New Bombay project, the master plan for which Correa codesigned with Pravina Mehta and Shirish Patel, where open courtyards and free margins predigested the Indian proclivity for piecemeal growth. In all these projects, flow—as a kind of flexible formalism—forged connections between optically misaligned sequenced courts, linked terraces, and stretched embankments in tensile formations. Perhaps the most exceptional project in this vein, which also reads as a constructive spatial critique of government-sanctioned corporate control over landscape and environment, is Goa's Kala Academy (1973–1983), an arts center that offers unbroken continuity with the street on one side and the Mandovi River on the other (fig. 7), built at

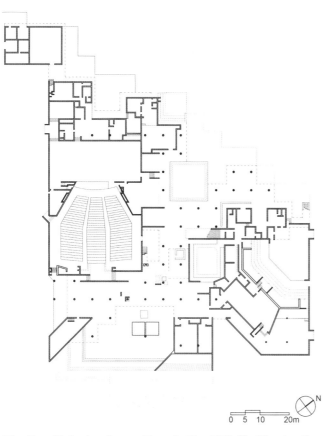

0 5 10   20m

Fig. 7   Kala Academy, Goa, India. 1973–83. Charles Correa (1930–2015). Plan. Charles Correa Foundation a time when an oligopolistic mining industry was stripping verdant Goa for iron ore to pay for oil imports after the 1970s energy crisis. From boulevard through pergola, terraces transition across reception, gallery, theater, and lawn, lapping an amphitheater to a walkway spilling onto the river, poeticizing the kind of free passage Prime Minister Indira Gandhi's securitization rendered elusive with the Emergency of 1975 to 1977.

Laurie Baker's economical housing, by contrast, advanced the architectural viability of a Gandhian socio-ecological impulse.[7] Attuned to the landscape of the Indian state of Kerala, the center of his activity, Baker paired empirical method with local, time-tested organic materials and introduced the use of certain industrial elements in ways that were neither fashionable in Western contexts nor widely known in Kerala, thus disturbing the customary capital flows between institutional budgets and the construction industry. Making use of filler slabs, for instance, to reduce the need for both concrete and steel, and building with thermally effective and material-conserving rat-trap bond masonry, he transformed the utilitarian into a desirable sensorium. Deploying the curve's beauty and thermal properties, latticed brick masonry vaults and funicular shell roofing complemented the natural surroundings of his buildings, typically small farms on home plots and lush backyard forests. His largest project was the Centre for Development Studies in Trivandrum (1967–71; see pp. 214–17), which negotiated formal and conceptual complexity across buildings with diverse functions. Predating the 1973 oil crisis, the project preemptively absorbed inflation's effects on imports of construction materials, making what would later be recognizable as a low-carbon counterproposal to oil money's transformation of paddy-field Kerala with the "Gulf houses" built by a returning workforce flush with income from employment in the construction and oil industries in Dubai and its neighbors from the 1980s onward. The establishment of the Centre of Science and Technology for Rural Development (COSTFORD) in Trivandrum in 1985 captured the lasting ethos of Baker's architectural model.

In East and West Pakistan, multiple environmental flashpoints that differed in inflection and chronology were spurred by instrumental religion and contestations of identity. Each such event necessitated reassessing architectural choices. Among them were Partition and its inevitable outcome in Bangladeshi Independence in 1971, General Zia Ul Haq seizing power in Pakistan in 1977 with a military coup followed by the institution of sharia law, and the Aga Khan First Chairman's Award to Egyptian architect Hassan Fathy in 1980, which was an encouragement and inspiration for many architects in South Asia to think through the environment.

In 1950s East Pakistan, Muzharul Islam had posited a kind of environmental modernism based on a secular Bengali foundation in the image of Dhaka as a "complex in a garden, and the garden and the complex in the center of the city."[8] Islam's site-sensitive architecture was a modulation of functionalist abstraction. His designs for the Public Library (1953–54; see Portfolio, nos. 21, 22) and the College of Arts and Crafts (later the Institute of Fine Arts) (1953–56; fig. 8; see Portfolio, no. 11) at the University of Dhaka rejected both colonial hybrids and Islamic historical forms that could be construed as aligned with the political ruling class in West Pakistan. The Institute of Fine Arts—in the totality of its fluid entrance, curved staircase, galleries on *pilotis*, full-length wooden louvers, and exposed brick—has a methodological kinship with de Silva's Pieris House 1. It was informed by Rabindranath Tagore's ideas about an openness to external influence that is a result of a fluid interrelationship between "the home and the world,"[9] and borrowed aspects from the plein-air blueprint of the school at Santiniketan that Tagore had founded outside Calcutta in 1901.

A comparable attachment, albeit to overtly modern expression, appeared in West Pakistan in the work of Mehdi Ali Mirza and Kamil Khan Mumtaz. However, the rapprochement Pakistani architect Yasmeen Lari proposed between modernism and the Islamic philosophy of moderation offered a more persuasive ecological argument, too. Like de Silva's middle way between the International Style and contemporary architectural vocabularies drawn from Sri Lanka, Lari's environmentalism opposed both theocratic politics and what she called the "instant Islamic" brand of architecture in Pakistan.[10] Combining cheap brick and domestically rolled imported steel in Lahore's low-income Anguri Bagh Housing (1972–75; see pp. 222–25) and pushing for unostentatious self-assisted construction using mud at Bahawalpur's Army Barracks (1981; figs. 9, 10)—

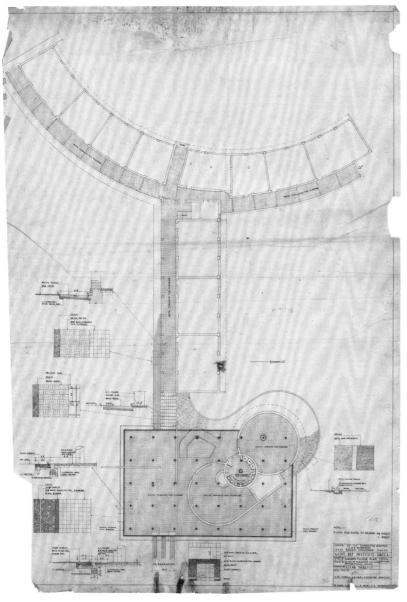

Fig. 8 College of Arts and Crafts (Institute of Fine Arts), University of Dhaka, East Pakistan (Bangladesh). 1953–56. Muzharul Islam (1923–2012). Plan drawing. 1955. Ink and pencil on paper. Muzharul Islam Archives

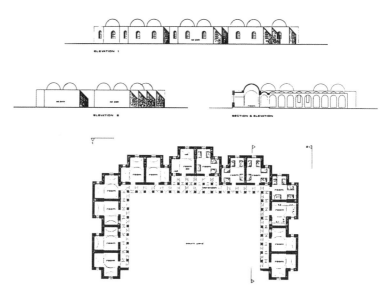

Fig. 9 Army Barracks, Bahawalpur, Pakistan. 1981. Yasmeen Lari (b. 1941). Exterior view during construction. 1983. Photograph: M. Hasan. Aga Khan Trust for Culture

Fig. 10 Army Barracks, Bahawalpur, Pakistan. 1981. Yasmeen Lari (b. 1941). Site plan, section, and elevations. 1983. Aga Khan Trust for Culture a project characterized by surprise gardens in enclosed spaces—she asserted the contemporary value of certain landscape sensibilities left over from the city's Mughal history by integrating them with living vernaculars.

In conclusion, I would like to briefly discuss Urmila Eulie Chowdhury (1923–1995), an architect little known outside India despite being an indispensable collaborator, pivotal from its genesis, on the design and construction of Chandigarh. The city's distinctive combination of tree-lined avenues and concrete-heavy government and residential architecture is no doubt a notable chapter in any history of landscape and modern architecture in post-1947 India. However, Chowdhury's multidimensional role enacts an equally important, if different, story about architecture's relationship to environment in South Asia.

Chowdhury, a culturally embedded translator of social and professional infrastructure, went beyond design, organization, and execution in ways that complicate the modernist image of architect-auteur. Through her, architecture reads as a kind of ecology, a system where landscape and climate both encompass and transcend region, physical nature, and the atmospheric to include cultural temperature, social practices, and site-specific professional know-how. A letter she sent to Le Corbusier in 1962 explaining the need for a public restroom near the dam of Chandigarh's Sukhna Lake notes that its placement should "preserve the view of the Himalaya range" and ends with a confident note of assurance: "A sketch will be sufficient for me to prepare the design."[11] Implicit in her language, and in Chowdhury's architectural legacy more generally, is the idea that design is but one part of architecture's relationship to landscape, a notion that returns us to the emphasis on cultural texture and grain that de Silva in Ceylon equally sought to frame as the necessary model for an architecture of the environment.

1   Minnette de Silva, *The Life & Work of an Asian Woman Architect* (Colombo: Smart Media Productions, 1998), 180. The *midula* takes up ritual and social referents from indigenous Sri Lankan domestic architecture.

2   Minnette de Silva, "A House at Kandy, Ceylon" *Marg* 6, no. 3 (June 1953): 4–11(see pp. 178–81 in this volume); and de Silva, "Experiments in Modern Regional Architecture in Ceylon," *Journal of the Ceylon Institute of Architects* (1965–66): 13–17.

3   CIAM stalwart Sigfried Giedion's writings on contemporary architecture, which sought to resolve "a specific regional problem," in South America, California, Africa, and "India," which he used as a blanket term for India and its immediate neighbors, omitted de Silva entirely. See, for instance, Giedion, "The Regional Approach," *Architectural Record* 115, no. 1 (January 1954): 132–37.

4   On tropical modernism, see Jiat-Hwee Chang, *A Genealogy of Tropical Architecture: Colonial Networks, Nature and Technoscience* (London: Routledge, 2016).

5   See David Robson, *Geoffrey Bawa: The Complete Works* (London: Thames & Hudson, 2002); Tariq Jazeel, *Beyond Bawa: Modern Masterworks of Monsoon Asia* (London: Thames & Hudson, 2007); and Shanti Jayewardene, *Geoffrey Manning Bawa: Decolonising Architecture* (Colombo: National Trust Sri Lanka, 2017).

6   See Charles Correa, "Open to Sky Space: Architecture in a Warm Climate," *Mimar*, no. 5 (1982): 30–35. Correa's expansion motif was prominent in his 1986 exhibition *Vistāra*, the catalogue to which was published as *Vistāra: The Architecture of India*, ed. Carmen Kagal (Bombay: Tata Press, 1986); see also Charles Correa, *The Blessings of the Sky* (Tokyo: Gallery MA, 1995).

7   See Gautam Bhatia, *Laurie Baker: Life, Works & Writings* (New Delhi: Penguin, 1991); and Atul Deulgaonkar, *Laurie Baker: Truth in Architecture* (Pune, India: Jyotsna Prakashan, 2015).

8   Kazi Khaleed Ashraf and Saif Ul Haque, eds., *Vastukatha: Selected Sayings of Architect Muzharul Islam* (Dhaka: Bengal Institute, 2019), 50.

9   Adnan Morshed, "Modernism as Postnationalist Politics: Muzharul Islam's Faculty of Fine Arts (1953–56)," *Journal of the Society of Architectural Historians* 76, no. 4 (December 2017): 532–49.

10 Yasmeen Lari quoted in Hasan-Uddin Khan, "Profile: Yasmeen Lari," *Mimar*, no. 2 (1981): 45.

11 Urmila Eulie Chowdhury to Le Corbusier, October 24, 1962, Fondation Le Corbusier, Paris.

TRYST WITH DESIGN

Saloni Mathur

Design and architecture in South Asia, as elsewhere, are deeply entangled disciplines, with a high degree of overlap between institutions, practices, individuals, and ideas. At the core of discourses of design in the subcontinent are the centuries-old traditions of "craft." The term refers to the small-scale, rural or village practices of artisanal production connected to vernacular forms and ways of life. British art reformers in the nineteenth century—influenced by the British Arts and Crafts Movement and design reformers such as William Morris, John Ruskin, Owen Jones, George Birdwood, and Henry Cole—famously viewed these aesthetic traditions as ancient and timeless, when they were in fact a dynamic locus of active reinvention in response to the forces of industrialization and modernity. Their colonial frameworks would be radically upturned in the subcontinent by the beginning of the twentieth century, with the rise of pioneering nationalist art historians and intellectuals such as Ananda K. Coomaraswamy (1877–1947), E. B. Havell (1861–1934), and Rabindranath Tagore (1861–1941), alongside the *swadeshi* (or "self-sufficiency") movement, which emerged in opposition to the partition of Bengal in 1905, and which advocated the making of local products and a boycott of all foreign goods (fig. 1).[1]

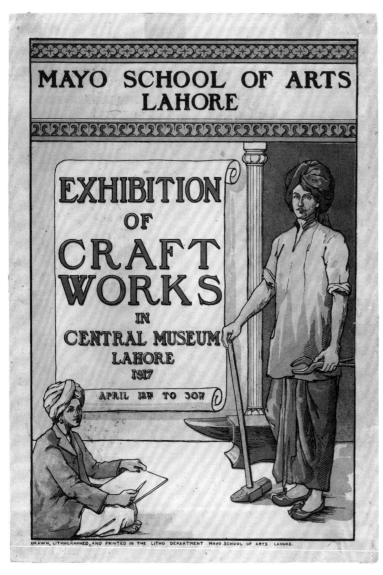

Fig. 1   Poster for the Mayo School of Arts Exhibition of Craft Works at the Central Museum, Lahore, Pakistan, April 12–30, 1917. Lithograph, 18³/₁₆ × 12⁵/₈ in. (46.2 × 32 cm). NCA Archives

The embattled arena of craft thus emerged at the center of a powerful nationalist discourse and the fight for independence in the first half of the twentieth century, with the figure of Gandhi and his spinning wheel as perhaps the most iconic symbol of the nationalist struggle (fig. 2).[2] The tensions between tradition and modernity, indigenism and internationalism, and rural and urban that have shaped the enduring legacies and colonial hierarchies of craft thus crucially inform the story of design that emerges across the new nation-states of South Asia in the second half of the twentieth century (fig. 3).The experience of Partition between India and Pakistan in 1947, the further breakup of East and West Pakistan leading to the creation of Bangladesh in 1971, the subsequent wars within (i.e., the 1983–2009 Sri Lankan Civil War) and between these nations, and the ongoing hostility between India and Pakistan further complicate a comprehensive history of modern design in the region. Nonetheless, a unique relationship between decolonization and design, characterized by broad humanistic principles, assertions of self-determination, and the utopian aspirations of nation-building led to a renewed self-awareness about the very meaning of design across South Asia from the 1950s on.

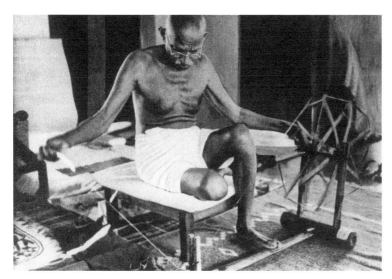

Fig. 2   Mohandas Gandhi at his spinning wheel. c. 1940.

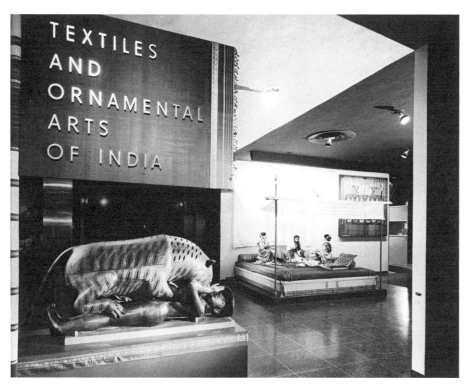

Fig. 3   View of the exhibition *Textiles and Ornamental Arts of India*, The Museum of Modern Art, New York, April 11–September 25, 1955. Photograph: Alexandre Georges. The Museum of Modern Art, New York

157

In the new geopolitical landscape following the end of British rule, the intertwined activities of designers, architects, visual artists, critics, and intellectuals, supported by funding bodies including UNESCO, the Ford Foundation, and the United States Information Agency (USIA), resulted in experimental practices, pedagogies, and several important new institutions of design (see Karim, pp. 129–34). These initiatives were often conversant with long-standing traditions of craft and produced unique conceptions of self and nation while implicating artists and artisans, markets, governments, and modern definitions of heritage. In Nehru's India, for example, the American architects and designers Charles and Ray Eames were the catalysts for the establishment of the National Institute of Design (NID) in Ahmedabad in 1961, India's premier institution for design education (figs. 4, 5). For two years prior to its opening, a large-scale exhibition mounted by The Museum of Modern Art, New York, titled *Design Today in America and Europe*, had traveled to nine major Indian cities to draw attention to the place of design within modernization, attracting over a million visitors.[3] The four hundred household objects displayed in the show, including chairs, lamps, kitchen utensils, and glassware, were eventually gifted to the NID and became the basis for a permanent study collection to teach students to create similar objects suited to their own society. With an emphasis on industrial design, the NID's philosophy and curriculum was modeled on the principles of the Bauhaus in Germany before World War II and the Ulm Design School in the postwar period, especially the latter's investment in cultural regeneration in the wake of German fascism (fig. 6).[4]

Fig. 4   Graphics seminar at the National Institute of Design, Ahmedabad, India. c. 1969. Faculty members, from left: unidentified, Helena Perheentupa, H. Kumar Vyas, Mahendra Patel, Mohand Bhandar, and Rajen Choudhary. NID Archives
Fig. 5   Charles Eames (1907–1978) teaching students at the National Institute of Design, Ahmedabad, India. 1964. NID Archives

In Pakistan, the colonial-era Mayo School of Arts in Lahore was upgraded to the National College of Art in 1958, where experiments in modern painting and design embraced the cosmopolitan heritage of the Muslim and Persianate world.[5] In Dhaka, the East Pakistan (later Bangladesh) Small and Cottage Industries Corporation, which was established in 1957, prioritized the traditional artisanship and handicraft industries of the rural inhabitants of the region. Later, in Colombo, the National Design Centre, established in 1983, similarly oriented itself toward handloom weaving and other handicrafts indigenous to the island nation (fig. 7).[6] The role of women in design initiatives during these decades is especially noteworthy: not merely their prominent place in specific craft industries (in Bangladesh, for example, women currently comprise some 50 percent of the

Fig. 6   Student Naveen Patel at the printing table in the textile design studio at the National Institute of Design, Ahmedabad, India. c. 1960. NID Archives

country's approximately one million weavers),[7] but also the role of prominent women, including architects, in the revival of these handicraft traditions. Exemplary figures, such as Laila Tyabji (b. 1947), Gira Sarabhai (1923–2021), and Pupul Jayakar (1915–1997) in India, and Barbara Sansoni (b. 1928), Ena de Silva (1922–2015), and Chandramani Thenuwara (b. 1934) in Sri Lanka, laid the foundations for new sensibilities toward design, and textiles in particular, in their respective countries.[8]

Similarly, national languages such as Urdu, Hindi, Bengali, Tamil, and Sinhala, and the curves of their different scripts, inspired major experiments within modernist painting and textile design, along with innovations in typography and graphic design. At times, these aesthetic endeavors led to regional cooperation and national visibility in ways that sustained and empowered the grassroots artisan; at other times, the visual medium of design became co-opted by commercial interests or appropriated by the needs of politicians and the state.

The developmentalist paradigm that dominated the 1960s and 1970s gave birth to a problem-solving ethos within the arena of design, and a preoccupation with the intellectual challenges of "design in a developing society" or "design in the non-Western world." In contrast to the privileged role of design in industrial development, participants in this

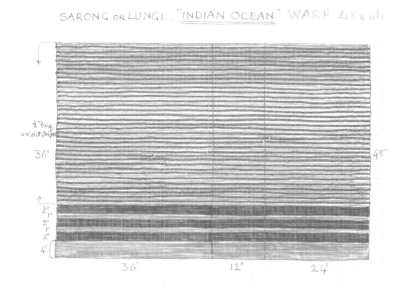

Fig. 7   Barbara Sansoni (b. 1928). "Indian Ocean" design for a sarong or lungi. Notebook page. 69/16 × 9 in. (16.7 × 22.8 cm). 1988. Barbara Sansoni Archives

milieu often advocated a socially responsible practice of design that prioritized poor communities, local traditions, inexpensive materials, and indigenous skills.[9] During these decades, governments implemented protectionist policies aimed, if unevenly, at supporting traditional practices such as textile handicrafts and the handloom industries, and the building of new spaces to support work in these fields. State and national efforts repeatedly focused on bridging the gap between the craftsperson and the consumer through the marketing of cottage industries to urban patrons in conjunction with grassroots collectives and NGOs, and through a range of exhibitory formats such as shopping emporia, art fairs, melas, museums, and gift shops. Today, across South Asia, the term "cottage industries"—referring to the practice of making out of one's cottage or home, a notion which has its roots in the Industrial Revolution in Britain in the late eighteenth and early nineteenth centuries—is a general signifier of state support for the economic and cultural ecosystems of craft.

A shift in this paradigm during the 1980s, marked by the emergence of an increasingly interconnected global economy, has led to renewed debates on and discourses of design.[10] These discussions provoke broader questions surrounding the historiography of design in postcolonial societies, and epitomize the ongoing process of reinvention that characterizes its trajectories in postcolonial South Asia. They also illuminate the ways in which the era of decolonization has challenged normative design history, and point to the historically contingent nature of design itself as a heterogenous, contested, and polyvocal field.

1   See Sumit Sarkar, *The Swadeshi Movement in Bengal, 1903–1908* (New Delhi: People's Publishing House, 1973).
2   See Susan S. Bean, "Gandhi and *Khadi*, the Fabric of Indian Independence," in *Cloth and Human Experience*, ed. Annette B. Weiner and Jane Schneider (Washington, DC: Smithsonian Institution Press, 1989), 355–76; Rebecca M. Brown, *Gandhi's Spinning Wheel and the Making of India* (London: Routledge, 2013); Arindam Dutta, *The Bureaucracy of Beauty: Design in the Age of Its Global Reproducibility* (New York: Routledge, 2006); and Saloni Mathur, *India by Design: Colonial History and Cultural Display* (Berkeley: University of California Press, 2007).
3   See Farhan Sirajul Karim, "MoMA, the Ulm and the Development of Design Pedagogy in India," in *Western Artists and India: Creative Inspirations in Art and Design*, ed. Shanay Jhaveri (London: Shoestring, 2013), 122–39.
4   See ibid., 122–39; and Saloni Mathur, "Charles and Ray Eames in India," *Art Journal* 70, no. 1 (Spring 2011): 34–53. See also "Indian Design and Design Education," special issue, *Design Issues* 21, no. 4 (Autumn 2005).
5   See Iftikhar Dadi, *Modernism and the Art of Muslim South Asia* (Chapel Hill: University of North Carolina Press, 2010); and Saima Zaidi, ed., *Mazaar, Bazaar: Design and Visual Culture in Pakistan* (Oxford, UK: Oxford University Press, 2010).
6   See Annemari de Silva, *Craft Artisans and State Institutions in Sri Lanka* (Colombo: International Centre for Ethnic Studies, 2019).
7   Muhammad Rabiul Islam Liton, Tahmidul Islam, and Subrata Saha, "Present Scenario and Future Challenges in Handloom Industry in Bangladesh," *Social Sciences* 5, no. 5 (October 2016): 70. See also Muhammad Abdul Latif, *Handloom Industry of Bangladesh, 1947–90* (Dhaka: University Press, 1997).
8   Notably, Gira Sarabhai, who trained with Frank Lloyd Wright in Arizona from 1947 to 1951 (and designed the NID building in Ahmedabad in 1961 with her brother Gautam) rejected the label "architect" and preferred to be called "designer." See Madhavi Desai, *Women Architects and Modernism in India: Narratives and Contemporary Practices* (London: Routledge, 2017). See also David G. Robson, "Introduction: Ena de Silva and the Aluwihare Workshops," *Journal of Modern Craft* 1, no. 3 (March 2008): 405–14; and Mary N. Woods, *Women Architects in India: Histories of Practice in Mumbai and Delhi* (London: Routledge, 2017). For more on Chandramani Thenuwara, see Nethra Samarawickrema, "The Fabric of Her Life and Work," *Sunday Times* (Colombo), June 6, 2010, http://www.sundaytimes.lk/100606/Plus/plus_18.html.
9   See Rajeshwari Ghose, "Design, Development, Culture, and Cultural Legacies in Asia," *Design Issues* 6, no. 1 (Fall 1989): 31–48.
10   See Gui Bonsiepe, "Design and Democracy," *Design Issues* 22, no. 2 (Spring 2006): 27–34; Victor Margolin, "Design for Development: Towards a History," *Design Studies* 28, no. 2 (2007): 111–15; and Margolin, *The Politics of the Artificial: Essays on Design and Design Studies* (Chicago: University of Chicago Press, 2002); Victor Papanek, *Design for the Real World: Human Ecology and Social Change* (New York: Pantheon, 1973); Sulfikar Amir, "Rethinking Design Policy in the Third World," *Design Issues* 20, no. 4 (2004): 68–75.

MAROONED MODERNS: PRESERVATION AND THE LONG SHADOW OF COLONIALISM

Mrinalini Rajagopalan

In 1812, Lady Maria Nugent, wife of the East India Company Commander-in-Chief Sir George Nugent, toured the Taj Mahal. She spent several hours at the monument, wrote her name on one of its minarets, and compared its exquisite *pietra dura* to the most beautiful Sèvres china. Enraptured, she exclaimed that the Taj Mahal ought "to have a glass case made for it. What a pity that it should be exposed to decay!"[1] A nineteenth-century Englishwoman's reaction to a seventeenth-century Indian monument might seem an odd segue to modern architecture in South Asia. Yet the histories of preservation in Bangladesh, India, Pakistan, and Sri Lanka are hopelessly entangled with their colonial pasts.

Due to its colonial origins and contemporary pressures of nationalism, the apparatus of preservation in South Asia has largely proved an incapable steward for modern architecture. Despite renewed interest in and recognition of South Asia's contribution to modern architecture, many modern buildings in the region are threatened by demolition or benign neglect. Colonial preservationists cast South Asia's cultural heritage as static and unchanged from antiquity; they privileged individual structures as objects of display, often at the expense of their larger social and environmental contexts. Most importantly, colonial preservation was guided by an impulse to "save" monuments from the vagaries of weather and from South Asians themselves, who were seen as historically unaware and prone to vandalizing their own heritage.[2] The international charters of preservation that followed in the wake of the World Wars also perpetuated this rationale of salvage and privileged Western concepts of monumentality, aesthetic value, and cultural import.[3] Contemporary attempts to rethink heritage policies through a framework of democratic participation have persisted with top-down approaches and little regard for local perspectives on heritage.[4] In addition, nationalist impulses in the region have targeted modern architecture and its idealization of secular principles and rationality over ethnic and religious identities (figs. 1, 2).

Fig. 1   World Health Organization South-East Asia Regional Headquarters, New Delhi, India. 1962–64. Demolished 2019. Habib Rahman (1915–1995). Exterior view. c. 1964. Habib Rahman Archives

Fig. 2   US Embassy, Karachi, Pakistan. 1955–61. Listed as a protected heritage site in 2012 to avert potential demolition. Richard Neutra (1892–1970) and Robert Alexander (1907–1992). Exterior view. 1961. Photograph: Rondal Partridge

Lost in the bureaucratic shuffle of preservation are the granular histories of the many millions of South Asians who both encountered and shaped modernity via modern architecture. Architectural experimentation was integral to the process of South Asia's decolonization. More than simply ornaments of newly independent nation-states, modern buildings were central to the experience of modernity for innumerable citizens of Bangladesh, India, Pakistan, and Sri Lanka. A decolonial reckoning with preservation thus necessitates a rethinking of architectural authorship in more capacious ways and a recognition of works of modern architecture as sites of public history rather than the creations of single "genius" authors.[5] With this mission in mind, I offer three mini-polemics about modern buildings that have been at the center of recent preservation debates.

1. The Ena de Silva House: In 1948, a young woman wearing Kandyan headgear and a bejeweled costume appeared as the "Spirit of Sri Lanka" in a pageant to celebrate the nation-state's independence. Ena de Silva would go on to become a well-known artist, advocate of the island's craft traditions, and patron to architect Geoffrey Bawa. In South Asia, as elsewhere, women played key roles in championing modern art and architecture, a history that has only recently begun to be uncovered.[6] Between 1960 and 1962, Bawa, working at the time with Ulrik Plesner, designed a house for and in collaboration with de Silva, bringing together colonial bungalow and Sri Lankan courtyard typologies for an urban plot in

Fig. 3   House for Osmund and Ena de Silva (Ena de Silva House), Colombo, Ceylon (Sri Lanka). 1960–62. Disassembled and reconstructed at the Lunuganga Estate, Bentota, Sri Lanka, 2016. Geoffrey Bawa (1919–2003) and Ulrik Plesner (1930–2016)/ Edwards Reid & Begg. View onto the courtyard at its original site

162

Colombo (fig. 3). The creative symbiosis between architect and artist would continue through both their careers, with de Silva's batik and textile arts often occupying pride of place in the architect's most prestigious projects, such as Sri Lanka's Parliament Building (1979–82).

In 2016 the Ena de Silva House was dismantled and rebuilt on Bawa's estate in Lunuganga, sixty miles south of Colombo (figs. 4–6).[7] In the process of dismantling the structure, architects and archaeologists discovered many of de Silva's creative contributions to the house. Her proclivity for colors and textures was apparent in design decisions such as the embedding of antique china plates in countertops.[8] De Silva was more than simply a bourgeois consumer of modern architecture; rather, she was a maker of her modern environment.

The relocation of the Ena de Silva House from its original urban setting to a bucolic sprawling estate contravenes Article 7 of the 1964 Venice Charter, which states that a "monument is inseparable . . . from the setting in which it occurs," albeit allowing exceptions where "the safeguarding of [the] monument demands it."[9] Such universalisms ignore the long histories of reconstruction and relocation as a form of preservation in Asia, from the twenty-year cyclical rebuilding of the Ise shrine in Japan to the reuse of the third-century BCE Ashokan pillars in medieval mosques in India.[10] De Silva herself sourced the satinwood columns for her house from a property elsewhere. A critical treatment of the relocated house may therefore recognize de Silva's creative agency and place it within

Fig. 4   Aerial view of the House for Osmund and Ena de Silva (Ena de Silva House) during its reconstruction at the Lunuganga Estate, Bentota, Sri Lanka. July 2016. Photograph: Sebastian Posingis

Fig. 5   Doors, windows, shutters, and other materials from the House for Osmund and Ena de Silva (Ena de Silva House), Colombo, prior to its reconstruction at the Lunuganga Estate, Bentota, Sri Lanka. 2016

Fig. 6   H. U. Rohan Gunasiri and R. M. Sumedha Bhadrakalpanie Rajapaksha tracing the placement of individual cobblestones in the front courtyard of the House for Osmund and Ena de Silva (Ena de Silva House), Colombo, prior to its reconstruction at the Lunuganga Estate, Bentota, Sri Lanka. 2016 longer regional histories of reuse, translocation, and translation. While the relocation of the house certainly alters the original dialogue between its context and formal layout, the value of such a radical intervention should also be considered in light of the demolition of several modern buildings by other Sri Lankan architects, such as Minnette de Silva and Valentine Gunasekara.

2. Kamalapur Railway Station: Designed by Daniel C. Dunham and Robert G. Boughey and completed in 1968, this railway station in Dhaka, with its cast-in-place concrete parabolic roof, was a harbinger of Bangladesh's modernisms to come (fig. 7; see Portfolio, no. 30; see pp. 202–5). When the station opened, Dhaka was the regional capital of East Pakistan; three years later it would become the national capital of a sovereign Bangladesh. The station also marks a critical moment in Bangladesh's modernist history, between 1962, when Louis I. Kahn was commissioned to design East Pakistan's parliament building, and its inauguration in 1982 as the National Parliament House of Bangladesh. Far from

Fig. 7 Kamalapur Railway Station, Dhaka, East Pakistan (Bangladesh). 1968. Daniel C. Dunham (1929–2000) and Robert G. Boughey (b. 1940)/Louis Berger and Consulting Engineers. Building under construction. c. 1968. Photograph: Daniel C. Dunham

the hallowed halls of the seat of government, which were accessible only to the nation's elite, Kamalapur Railway Station represented the infrastructure of quotidian modernisms. It was in large part a building that welcomed rural migrants into the bustling metropolis. For so many the white sails of thin concrete were the first glimpse of an urban skyline. Seen through the windows of a train as pennants dancing on the horizon, arriving new-comers would later experience those sails as a shade-giving canopy when they passed between the slender concrete columns to make their way, and indeed their lives, in Dhaka.

The demolition of Kamalapur Railway Station was approved in late 2020, the structure a casualty of a new metro rail line for Dhaka.[11] In response to the outcry against demoli-tion, once again led largely by the international architectural community, proposals were mooted of either dismantling and rebuilding the original station at another site or erecting a "similar" structure to house the new metro.[12] If realized, as may well be the case by the time this volume goes to press, the demolition would not only deprive Bangladesh of a modernist building, but also evict the laborers who built the station from the history of modern architecture. Could Kamalapur Railway Station be reimagined from the perspec-tive of the rural migrant arriving at the bustling metropolis of Dhaka for the first time? Is it possible to write an architectural history of modernism from the viewpoint of the many Bangladeshis who passed by the station as they left for Malaysia, Dubai, or Abu Dhabi to build the Petronas Towers, the Burj Khalifa, or the Louvre Abu Dhabi? Kamalapur Station also has a place in the global history of architecture as a modernist structure that served as a waypoint for the migrant builders of avant-garde architectures in Dhaka and elsewhere.

3. The Hall of Nations: Jawaharlal Nehru, the first prime minister of India, had famously prophesied that factories would be the temples of the newly independent nation-state. Commissioned to commemorate the twenty-fifth anniversary of Indian independence by

Fig. 8   Visitors to the Asia '72 international trade fair in front of Raj Rewal and Mahendra Raj's then recently completed and since demolished Hall of Nations, Pragati Maidan, New Delhi, India. 1972. Photograph: Virendra Prabhakar

A reinforcement detail for space frame member connection in the Hall of Nations

3rd Asian International Trade Fair Exhibition Grounds New Delhi.

Under Construction by

PURI CONSTRUCTION PRIVATE LTD.

27, BARAKHAMBA ROAD, NEW DELHI-1

Phones : 44333, 279617, 621670

Architects : RAJ REWAL & KULDIP SINGH

Consulting Engineers : ECI.

Supervising Engineers : CPWD.

Design June 1972   53

Fig. 9   Page from *Design* (June 1972), with a photograph illustrating rebar used for the space-frame construction of Raj Rewal and Mahendra Raj's Hall of Nations, Pragati Maidan, New Delhi, India

Nehru's daughter, Indira Gandhi, when she was herself prime minister, the Hall of Nations Complex was completed in 1972 by architect Raj Rewal and engineer Mahendra Raj (see pp. 218–21). Nehru's vision of socialism and self-sufficiency was designed into the robust musculature of the building. A monumental concrete space frame floated over a vast exhibition hall that showcased all manner of Indian industry, from books to tractors and textiles to military vehicles. Rewal and Raj had initially conceived of the Hall of Nations as a steel structure, but the lack of resources and available technology led to a redesign in concrete (see Stierli, p. 19). Five hundred families lived and worked on-site; their tasks included hand-pouring the concrete for the impressive space frame that became an iconic feature of Delhi's modern landscape (figs. 8, 9).[13]

In 2017, the Hall of Nations Complex was demolished, falling prey to the same "great man" celebrity that had been its original raison d'être. A combination of neoliberal development that called for its replacement with a new "state of the art" convention center, and a political leadership unsympathetic to the Nehru legacy (and that also happens to be rivals to the Nehru-Gandhi political dynasty), brooked no consideration of the monument's architectural value. Might its fate have been different had it been thought of as an example of concrete craftsmanship rather than a built paean to one man or one moment?

South Asia, like many other parts of the Global South, pioneered new breakthroughs in concrete design in the decades following decolonization. Enforced frugality, a dearth of mechanized production, and a surplus of manual labor often led to innovative designs born out of necessity. The Global South has not been accorded its due in the mainstream narrative of modernist ingenuity.[14] While political capriciousness and capitalist development are rarely derailed by nuanced historical commentary, cases such as the Hall of Nations may prompt new narratives of modernism to include not only an architect and a structural engineer but also several hundred laborers and their families innovating modernism beside them (fig. 10).

Fig. 10   A young girl and a child at the World Agriculture Fair, Pragati Maidan, New Delhi, India. Background: The State Trading Corporation Pavilion, designed by Luc Durand (1929–2018), under construction. 1959. Photograph: Harji Malik

Lady Nugent's breathless plea in 1812 for preserving the Taj Mahal like a fossil encased in glass stands in sharp contrast to the fate of many a modern building in South Asia today. Concrete leviathans built in the heady days of decolonization, many of these modern structures are now considered obstacles to new dreams of development, have become targets of political ideologies, or have fallen into terminal disrepair. Modern architecture finds itself marooned in South Asia's historical timeline.[15] It neither belongs to the region's glorious past of temples, mosques, and imperial capitals nor does it have a place in the subcontinent's spectacular future of smart cities and other grand projects of neoliberalism. Decolonizing preservation would require a radical departure from the consumptive tourist's gaze that Lady Nugent so guilelessly championed and which unfortunately continues to be the basis of preservation policy in South Asia. In contrast, a reclamation of structures such as the Ena de Silva House, Kamalapur Railway Station, or the Hall of Nations Complex as sites of public history could anchor the intellectual and creative labor of women, laborers, and global migrant workers as makers of modern architecture in their own right. In this decolonial vein, preservation might also prompt a more inclusive history of South Asian modernity writ large.

1   Maria Nugent, *Lady Nugent's East India Journal: A Critical Edition*, ed. Ashley L. Cohen (New Delhi: Oxford University Press, 2014), 167.
2   For details, see Mrinalini Rajagopalan, introduction to *Building Histories: The Archival and Affective Lives of Five Monuments in Modern Delhi* (Chicago: University of Chicago Press, 2016).
3   For a critique of universal values and the Eurocentricisms that undergird international charters of preservation, see Howayda al-Harithy, "[Reframing] World Heritage," *Traditional Dwellings and Settlements Review* 17, no. 1 (Fall 2005): 717; and Tim Winter, "Heritage Studies and the Privileging of Theory," *International Journal of Heritage Studies* 20, no. 5 (June 2014): 556–72. The Conserving Modern Architecture Initiative, launched by the Getty Conservation Institute in 2012, is a worthy effort to rethink prevailing preservation norms for modern architecture. The geographical focus of the initiative at the moment, however, remains largely European and American.
4   In an essay focused on the General Assembly of the International Council on Monuments and Sites, held in Delhi in 2017, anthropologist Sudeshna Guha remarks that despite its theme of "History and Democracy," the conference evaded questions of public participation and the potential to increase the orbit of stakeholders beyond experts, politicians, and developers. Sudeshna Guha, "Decolonizing South Asia through Heritage- and Nation-Building," *Future Anterior* 16, no. 2 (Winter 2019): 30–45.
5   Architectural historian Dolores Hayden has pioneered new modes of preservation in Los Angeles with a non-monumental approach that privileges the landscapes of labor, migration, and community as public histories. See Hayden, *The Power of Place: Urban Landscapes as Public History* (Cambridge, MA: MIT Press, 1997).

6   For a history of Indian women architects see Mary N. Woods, *Women Architects in India: Histories of Practice in Mumbai and Delhi* (London: Routledge, 2017); and Madhavi Desai, *Women Architects and Modernism in India: Narratives and Contemporary Practices* (London: Routledge, 2017). In India, the sisters-in-law Gira and Manorama Sarabhai were committed patrons of modern art and architecture. For a history of women promoters of modern architecture in the United States, see Alice Friedman, *Women and the Making of the Modern House: A Social and Architectural History* (New Haven, CT: Yale University Press, 2007).

7   Ena de Silva had not lived in the house for several decades when she decided to sell it for financial reasons. Calls for preservation came from the architectural community and the government. The decision to rebuild the house at Lunuganga was a compromise whereby the house could be preserved and de Silva could receive fair compensation for her property. De Silva died in 2015, before the reconstruction was completed. There are some parallels between the afterlives of the Ena de Silva House and the Villa Savoye. Madame Savoye abandoned the house built by Le Corbusier because she found it unlivable and later wished to sell the land on which the house stood. Once again, calls for preservation came not from the client herself but rather from the architectural community and institutions such as the French Ministry of Culture and The Museum of Modern Art, New York, which wished to monumentalize the structure as an icon of modern architecture. See Kevin D. Murphy, "The Villa Savoye and the Modernist Historic Monument," *Journal of the Society of Architectural Historians* 61, no. 1 (March 2002): 68–89.

8   This information comes from a wall text at the relocated Ena de Silva House, shared with author by architects Channa Daswatte and Amila de Mel.

9   International Council on Monuments and Sites, "International Charter for the Conservation and Restoration of Monuments and Sites," 1964 (adopted 1965), https://www.icomos.org/charters/venice_e.pdf.

10 See Jordan Sand, "Japan's Monument Problem: Ise Shrine as Metaphor," *Past and Present* 226, suppl. 10 (February 2015): 126–52; and chapter 5 of Rajagopalan, *Building Histories*.

11 As of this writing, the demolition has been approved by the prime minister's office. For more on the threats to modernist architecture in South Asia, see Adnan Z. Morshed, "Cities Without Stories: South Asia Needs to Preserve Its Disappearing Modernist History," *Architect's Newspaper*, January 11, 2021: https://www.archpaper.com/2021/01op-ed-south-asia-needs-to-preserve-its-disappearing-modernist-history/.

12 There is little information on what the terms "replica" or "similar" mean and how such a program of rebuilding will be executed. For current (as of early 2021) information on Kamalapur Station, see Aaron Smithson, "Bangladesh Authorities Consider Demolishing Iconic Kamalapur Railway Station for an Elevated Metro Line," *Architect's Newspaper*, January 4, 2021, https://www.archpaper.com/2021/01/dhaka-demolishing-iconic-kamalapur-railway-station-for-elevated-metro-line/; and Tuhin Shubhra Adhikary, "Demolition of Iconic Kamalapur Station Plaza: PMO Gives Go-Ahead," *Daily Star* (Dhaka), January 30, 2021, https://www.thedailystar.net/frontpage/news/demolition-iconic-kamalapur-station-plaza-pmo-gives-go-ahead-2036121.

13 Raj Rewal in Anupriya Saraswat, "Reclaiming from the Ruins: Discussing the Hall of Nations with Raj Rawal," ArchitectureLive!, June 9, 2017, https://architecturelive.in/reclaiming-from-the-ruins-discussing-the-hall-of-nations-with-raj-rewal/.

14 Some key contributions to an expanded history of modernism include Martino Stierli and Vladimir Kulić, eds., *Toward a Concrete Utopia: Architecture in Yugoslavia, 1948–1980* (New York: The Museum of Modern Art, 2018); Oliver Elser, Philip Kurz, and Peter Cachola Schmal, eds., *SOS Brutalism: A Global Survey* (Zurich: Park Books, 2017); Fernando Luiz Lara, *The Rise of Popular Modernist Architecture in Brazil* (Gainesville: University Press of Florida, 2008); and Adrian Forty, *Concrete and Culture: A Material History* (Chicago: University of Chicago Press, 2012).

15 In India, for example, an arbitrary ceiling of sixty to a hundred years determines whether a building can be considered historic.

TRANSFORMATIVE PROJECTS

GOLCONDE GUESTHOUSE

Architects   Antonin Raymond (1888–1976) with George Nakashima (1905–1990),
              François (František) Sammer (1907–1973), and Chandulal Shah (d. 1945)
Built   1937–42
Location   Pondicherry (Puducherry), French India (India)

With its unequivocal embrace of architectural modernism and its exposed concrete construction, the Golconde guesthouse (see Portfolio, no. 14) was without precedent on the subcontinent when it was built between 1937 and 1942 in the then French colony of Pondicherry. The building was commissioned by the Sri Aurobindo Ashram, which was founded in 1926 by the Calcutta-born anticolonial activist and spiritual reformer Sri Aurobindo and the French artist Mirra Alfassa (known as The Mother), in order to accommodate the rapidly growing community. It was financed through a large donation from the Muslim Nizam, or prince, of Hyderabad, and that city's Golconda diamond mines gave the building its French name. The absence of skilled contractors or labor and the dearth of available construction materials (in particular steel) made Golconde a major logistical operation and a pioneering achievement.[1]

The building features an austere palette and a simple layout of two longitudinal wings held together by a central service core. The environmentally sensitive design responds to the local climate via its north-south orientation, individually operable asbestos cement louvers that allow for efficient cross-ventilation, and communal spaces on the open-air ground floor. While the building's exterior is manifested as an exquisite concrete frame poured on-site, the monastic interiors of the individual rooms are defined by the custom-designed hardwood joinery and furniture, which augment a powerful statement of architectural rationalism with a Japanese sensibility. Indeed, the two architects in charge of the project, the Czech-born American Antonin Raymond and the Japanese American George Nakashima, came to India by way of Japan, where they had been key agents in establishing architectural modernism from the early 1920s onward.

The remarkably simple separation of communal spaces on the ground floor and in the private quarters on the three upper floors relates to the ashram's ethos of communal living and renders the building a "manifest union of technology, aesthetics, and social reform."[2] The emphasis on community is also evident in the process of construction, which was executed exclusively by members of the ashram under the supervision of Nakashima, François (František) Sammer, Chandulal Shah, and, after Nakashima's return to the United States in 1939, Udar Pinto. The building not only was pioneering for its use of ferroconcrete construction for aesthetic ends, but also laid the foundations for the climate-responsive design that would be explored and expanded by a whole generation of South Asian architects in the decades to come. Golconde remains in use as a guesthouse and serves as a striking example of the successful preservation of concrete construction in challenging climatic conditions.

Martino Stierli

---

1   For more details on the logistics behind the building's construction, see Stierli in this volume, p. 12.
2   Pankaj Vir Gupta, Christine Mueller, and Cyrus Samii, *Golconde: The Introduction of Modernism in India* (New Delhi: Urban Crayon, 2010), 30.

Golconde guesthouse, Pondicherry (Puducherry), French India (India). 1937–42. Antonin Raymond (1888–1976), George Nakashima (1905–1990), François (František) Sammer (1907–1973), and Chandulal Shah (d. 1945). Drawing: François (František) Sammer. Pencil and watercolor on paper, mounted, 18 × 22¾ in. (45.7 × 57.7 cm). Antonin Raymond and Noémi Pernessin Raymond Collection, The Architectural Archives, University of Pennsylvania

Site plan. Ink and pencil on paper, 6 × 14 in. (15.2 × 35.6 cm). David L. Leavitt Collection, The Architectural Archives, University of Pennsylvania

Indira Gandhi (right) at Golconde guesthouse during the second visit of her father, Prime Minister Jawaharlal Nehru, to the Sri Aurobindo Ashram, September 29, 1955

Interior view. c. 1940s–1950s

Workers preparing wooden formwork for laying concrete. c. 1940

173

NEW SECRETARIAT BUILDING

Architect   Habib Rahman (1915–1995)
Built   1949–54
Location   Calcutta (Kolkata), India

Architect Habib Rahman's fourteen-story New Secretariat Building, one of some fifty projects built during the post-Independence decades by the West Bengal Public Works Department (PWD), is an iconic experiment in steel-frame and concrete-slab construction and a testament to Rahman's overseas training, Indian engineering, and local labor.
It was also the first steel-frame skyscraper in India. With a degree in architecture from the Massachusetts Institute of Technology and time spent at Walter Gropius's office from 1945 to 1946,[1] Rahman tested the Harvard design approach in an aesthetic comparable to those of Achyut Kanvinde and Muzharul Islam, who were also educated in North America. Unlike for them, however, the PWD was a pragmatic choice for a practitioner with Muslim heritage such as Rahman, in a Hindu-dominant, post-Partition Calcutta, which his subsequent rise to senior architect of this institution substantiated.[2] His career exemplifies many of the formal strategies through which state and national government architecture was being modernized following the end of British rule.

Whereas Rahman's first public project, the Gandhi Ghat memorial of 1947–49 (see Portfolio, no. 33), just north of Calcutta, explored abstracted cultural motifs, the New Secretariat Building (see Portfolio, no. 34) displayed his greater affinity for the structural rationalism and aesthetic restraint of the International Style. The building's function was to house the administrative offices of the government of the Indian state of West Bengal, which came into existence when the future Bangladesh—then East Bengal—became part of Pakistan through Partition. The design comprised a tripartite complex made up of the fourteen-story tower and two low-rise buildings—one rectangular and the other forming a partial crescent around a small internal plaza. The building's formal properties were likely inspired by international examples such as Oscar Niemeyer's Ministry of Education and Health in Rio de Janeiro (1937–43).[3] The tower was raised at street level on *pilotis*; its narrow depth and louvered facade explored pragmatic climatic responses in an era when mechanical systems were rarely used. The vertical servicing of a multistory structure, never previously attempted in India, proved to be the greatest challenge.[4] After its completion in 1954, the New Secretariat Building was a model for several comparable administrative structures that Rahman designed as chief architect of New Delhi's Central PWD, most notably the World Health Organization South-East Asia Regional Headquarters (1962–64; see fig. 1 on p. 161), which was demolished in 2019.

Anoma Pieris

---

1   Hiralba Jadeja, "Architecture of Habib Rahman: A Critical Inquiry into the Reinterpretation of His Early Influences into the Context of India"(undergraduate thesis, CEPT University, Ahmedabad, 2013), section 2.1.3.
2   Peter Scriver and Amit Srivastava, *India*, Modern Architectures in History (London: Reaktion, 2015), 130.
3   Jadeja, "Architecture of Habib Rahman," section 2.1.4.
4   Malay Chatterjee, "Habib Rahman and his Times," *Architecture + Design* 13, no. 2 (1996): 22.

THE NEW SECRETARIAT

New Secretariat Building, Calcutta (Kolkata), India. 1949–54. Habib Rahman (1915–1995). Cover of brochure, 8^1/$_2$ × 5^1/$_2$ in. (21.6 × 14 cm). 1954. Habib Rahman Archives

Habib Rahman in his Calcutta office with a drawing of the New Secretariat Building and models of Gandhi Ghat, the New Secretariat Building, and the Komagata Maru Memorial. c. 1950. Habib Rahman Archives

Steel frame structure of the New Secretariat Building during construction. c. 1951. Habib Rahman Archives

176

Habib Rahman at the New Secretariat Building in Calcutta during its construction. c. 1951. Habib Rahman Archives

Steel frame during construction. 1951. Habib Rahman Archives

"A HOUSE AT KANDY, CEYLON"

Author   Minnette de Silva (1918–1998)
Publication *Marg* 6, no. 3 (June 1953)

Minnette de Silva's "A House at Kandy, Ceylon" occupies a central place in the history of South Asian modernism. Published in the Bombay-based magazine *Marg*, where de Silva was a contributing editor, it is ostensibly a commentary on the Sri Lankan architect's own Karunaratne House (1947–51), but reveals itself to be a critique of modernism's universalist claims and a call to be mindful of regional specificities. Because industrialization had already destroyed European craft traditions, she argues, architects in the West were "too late" in staging their modernist revolution. "For us it is much easier," she writes, "We have our crafts with us, still valid in our modern society. We must bring them back into an architecture which must be designed to suit our contemporary living."

Trained at the Architectural Association School of Architecture in London, de Silva stood at the forefront of a cadre of South Asian modernists endeavoring to give architectural expression to the region's emergent post-Independence identities. When she returned to independent Ceylon in 1948, her memory of the previous year's CIAM conference in Bridgwater, UK, must have been still fresh. There, she had befriended Le Corbusier, Siegfried Giedion, Jaqueline Tyrwhitt, and Maxwell Fry and Jane Drew, and engaged with new, challenging ideas, among them "regional modernism."[1] Decades before Kenneth Frampton's discussion of "critical regionalism," the critic J. M. Richards took a similar line at the conference, and aspects of "A House at Kandy" reveal a keen interest in Richards's ideas. Richards insisted on the existence of specific "conditions of climate and social custom . . . in particular localities" and recommended the use of "local materials" and the incorporation of "traditional forms."[2] De Silva sought ways to bring these principles to bear on the creation of a specifically South Asian built environment, endowing her Karunaratne House with, for instance, an enclosed veranda and a large living area suitable for family gatherings and Buddhist ceremonies. Her use of local timbers such as jak and halmilla was in keeping with her advocacy of independent Ceylon's economic self-reliance—"I used local timbers to show that we didn't have to import teak from Burma and I used them in a natural state exposing the knots and faults," de Silva would write in her autobiography, *The Life & Work of an Asian Woman Architect*.[3] The seamless integration of these features with a reinforced concrete framework indicated both respect for tradition and a desire for economy. The veranda and the large living room proved cost-effective, and in the *Marg* article de Silva emphasizes that they gesture toward tradition without compromising the demands of modern life.

In July 1953, de Silva left for France to attend the ninth CIAM meeting, in Aix-en-Provence. A letter that she sent to Tyrwhitt shortly afterward suggests a desire to "reform *Marg* on a wider . . . basis."[4] De Silva problematized what she perceived to be the magazine's narrow focus on India and sought to foreground the dynamic research on regional modernism undertaken in Ceylon; "A House at Kandy" is an important reflection of this effort. Remarkably, the letter identifies her practice as a "Studio of Modern Architecture, Arts, Crafts," corroborating how much the essay is a self-assured manifesto for overcoming the disciplinary divisions between these three aspects of cultural production.

Da Hyung Jeong

1   "Architectural Expression," paper delivered by J. M. Richards at CIAM 6, seq. 17, Box 004, Papers of the Congrès Internationaux d'Architecture Moderne (CIAM), 1928–70, Frances Loeb Library, Harvard Graduate School of Design, Cambridge, MA.
2   Ibid.
3   Minnette de Silva, *The Life and Work of an Asian Woman Architect* (Colombo: Smart Media Productions, 1998), 125.
4   Minnette de Silva to Jaqueline Tyrwhitt, November 1953, 42-JT-18-2/3, gta Archiv, ETH Zürich, Switzerland.

Minnette de Silva with a draftsman. 1956. Photograph: Brian Brake

Left: Karunaratne House, Kandy, Ceylon (Sri Lanka). 1947–51. Minnette de Silva (1918–1998). Interior view of the dining room. c. 1951. Photograph published in Minnette de Silva, "A House at Kandy, Ceylon," *Marg* 6, no. 3 (June 1953): 9; and in de Silva's autobiography, *The Life & Work of an Asian Woman Architect* (Colombo: Smart Media Productions, 1998), 124. Right: View of the front facade. c. 1951

Exterior view of the garden front

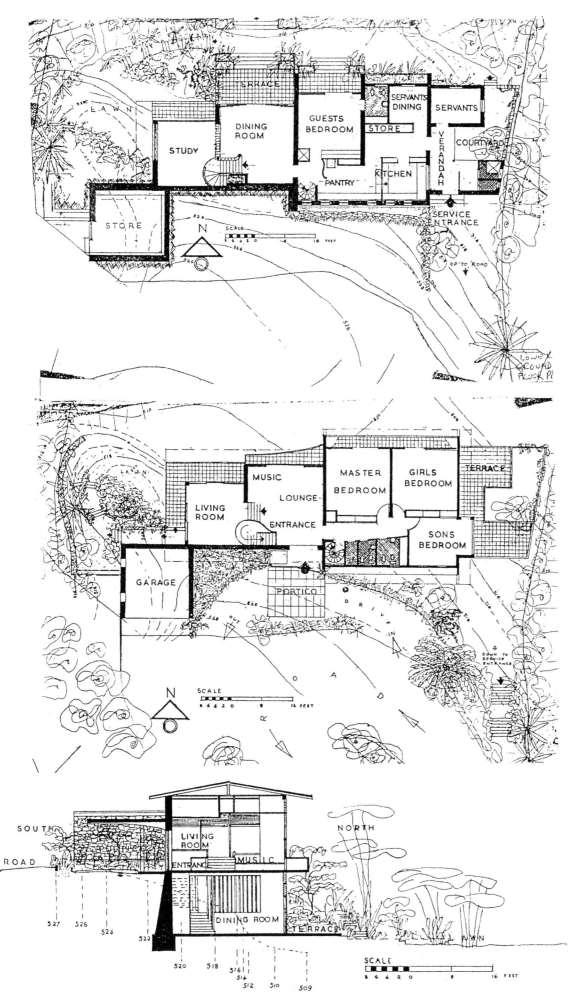

Plans and cross section

INDIA INTERNATIONAL CENTRE

Architect   Joseph Allen Stein (1912–2001)
Built   1958–62
Location   New Delhi, India

Plans for a new scholarly establishment in Delhi envisioned by John D. Rockefeller in 1958 motivated an emergent elite in India to capitalize on its intersections with foreign philanthropy. The country's first vice president, Sarvepalli Radhakrishnan, and others, proposed The Rockefeller Foundation fund an "International House for India." The American expatriate architect Joseph Allen Stein, who was known as an advocate of equitable approaches to community-centered design, was ultimately commissioned to design the campus for this nongovernmental cultural institution. The interconnected buildings of the India International Centre (IIC) express the continuities of Stein's holistic understanding of modernism and reflect the aim formulated in the institution's founding charter: "to promote understanding and amity between the different communities of the world."[1]

Crown Prince Akihito of Japan laid the foundation stone for the principal building in 1960. Upon its completion in 1962, the Centre became a locus for policy debates, aesthetic research, and social interactions to ensure the continuities of a new multinational India. Stein also designed the nearby arts and cultural center Triveni Kala Sangam (1957–63), as well as the Ford Foundation Headquarters (1952) and other buildings similarly deploying environmentally sensitive and socially resonant aesthetics.

Stein's IIC campus offers uninterrupted collective spaces at ground level. Multiple galleries and performance areas, a library, dining and lounge areas, and temporary residential rooms are distributed among glass-enclosed spaces in the upper stories. Fired clay screens (*jali*)—some with blue tiles, contained within precast concrete frames—sheath the administrative wing, while concrete panels with exposed aggregate punctuate the ends of the buildings. Shallow curved arches perching atop both an entry structure and the principal building evince a restrained visual dynamism. Delhi's monumental past is accessed in the adjacent Lodi Garden, where fourteenth- to sixteenth-century tombs and mosques are visible from the Centre's outdoor areas. Its own designed landscapes and bodies of water, by contrast—along with the heterogeneous materials used, which include stone, brick, and concrete—foreground ideas of breaking down monolithic historic forms. The materials used in the buildings' interiors were sourced from throughout the world, illustrating not only Nehru's forging of an industrialized economy but also how the IIC embodied a hopeful transnationalism.

The opening of one corner of the IIC's garden attracted much attention in 1970. Initially designed as part of the overall landscape plan envisioned by Stein and placed within a square parterre near the edge of the road, the busts of Mohandas Gandhi and Martin Luther King Jr. serve as beacons for passersby as well as members and guests of the Centre. Inaugurated by Prime Minister Indira Gandhi, whose Emergency of 1975 to 1977 would dismantle civil protections, political equity, and economic viability across the country, the Gandhi-King Plaza today extends Stein's and the IIC's signaling of individual and collective humanism.

Sean Anderson

1   "Aims and Objectives," India International Centre website, accessed September 5, 2021, https://iicdelhi.in/sites/default/files/2020-03/ IIC_Aims%20and%20Objectives.pdf. For more information on the project, see Joseph Allen Stein, N. H. Ramachandran, and Geeti Sen, "The India International Centre: Concept and Design; Joseph Allen Stein in Conversation with N. H. Ramachandran and Geeti Sen," *India International Centre Quarterly* 22, no. 4 (Winter 1995): 118–28; and Jeffrey M. Chusid, "Joseph Allen Stein's Experiments in Concrete in the US and India," *APT Bulletin: The Journal of Preservation Technology* 48, no.1 (2017): 23–31.

India International Centre (IIC), New Delhi, India. 1958–62. Joseph Allen Stein (1912–2001). Exterior view. 1962.
Photograph: Rondal Partridge

Interior view. 1962. Photograph: Rondal Partridge

Interior view of corridor. 1962. Photograph: Rondal Partridge

184

Exterior view. 1962. Photograph: Madan Mahatta

View of the auditorium, with the architect seated in the foreground. 1962. Photograph: Rondal Partridge

ISLAMABAD

Architects   Constantinos A. Doxiadis (1913–1975), Vedat Dalokay (1927–1991),
              Hassan Fathy (1900–1989), Anwar Said (b. 1940), Louis I. Kahn (1901–1974),
              Edward Durell Stone (1902–1978), and others
Built   1958–67, with later additions
Location   Islamabad, Pakistan

Greek architect Constantinos A. Doxiadis and his firm Doxiadis Associates (DA) established new large-scale planning projects throughout the world that centered a dynamic framework he termed *ekistics*, "the science of human settlements." Using this systematic research-based approach, he and his collaborators sought to comprehend "urban landscapes as complex matrices of mutable and evolving networks of information."[1]

When Islamabad ("City of Islam") was officially established at the foothills of the Himalayas as the new capital of Pakistan in 1967, the government hoped it would promote a unified sense of nationhood spanning East and West Pakistan. DA's master plan organized urban space into eight zones made up of sectors within which class and other social determinants determined the size and arrangement of residential, commercial, and religious buildings. Researchers investigated and photographically documented everything from "the way local residents colonized the roadside or back-lanes" to "the traces of an unauthorized path trodden across designated green spaces, the color of washing hung out to dry."[2] The charts and drawings decoding such information became part of a schematized ordering of urban spatial forms allowing for dynamic growth along extensive axial road systems, furthering Doxiadis's vision of Islamabad as a "Dynapolis." As Markus Daechsel writes, DA's master plan "exemplified both a new way of making sense of the world and new possibilities of governance. . . . Far more emphasis was placed on everyday urban functions than on the usual requirement to symbolize national aspirations."[3]

Somewhat removed, at least geographically, from the political theater playing out in the country and region, which would ultimately affect the design of the capital's central parliamentary and embassy zones, Doxiadis and other architects and planners working for the Capital Development Authority (CDA) remained resolute in their faith in a transformative human-centered urbanity. In 1968 Doxiadis described Islamabad as a "city [in which] we can hope that man, relieved of all stresses that arise from his conflict with the machine, will allow his body to dance, his senses to express themselves through the arts, his mind to dedicate itself to philosophy or mathematics, and his soul to love and to dream."[4]

Ultimately, however, although much of the overall organization of the city proposed in the master plan continued to inform urban development, few of the buildings that DA envisaged were implemented. Louis I. Kahn's schematic plan for the Presidential Complex and Edward Durell Stone's subsequent proposal for the same project remained unbuilt. As Islamabad's expansion progressed, dramatic revisions to DA-designed housing schemes as well as principal government buildings were made, in part to give the city a more explicitly "Islamic" character. Localized, sector-based mosques, markets, and public spaces devised by CDA architect Anwar Said remain, while prominent additions, including Turkish architect Vedat Dalokay's iconic and monumental Faisal Mosque (1969–86), fall outside the scope of the original plan.

Sean Anderson

1   Ahmed Zaib Khan Mahsud, "Rethinking Doxiadis' Ekistical Urbanism," *Positions*, no. 1 (Spring 2010): 17.
2   Markus Daechsel, "Sovereignty, Governmentality and Development in Ayub's Pakistan: The Case of Korangi Township,"
     Modern Asian Studies 45, no. 1 (January 2011): 157.
3   Markus Daechsel, *Islamabad and the Politics of International Development in Pakistan* (Cambridge, UK: Cambridge University Press,
     2015), 5.
4   Constantinos A. Doxiadis, *Ekistics: An Introduction to the Science of Human Settlements* (London: Hutchinson, 1968), 317.

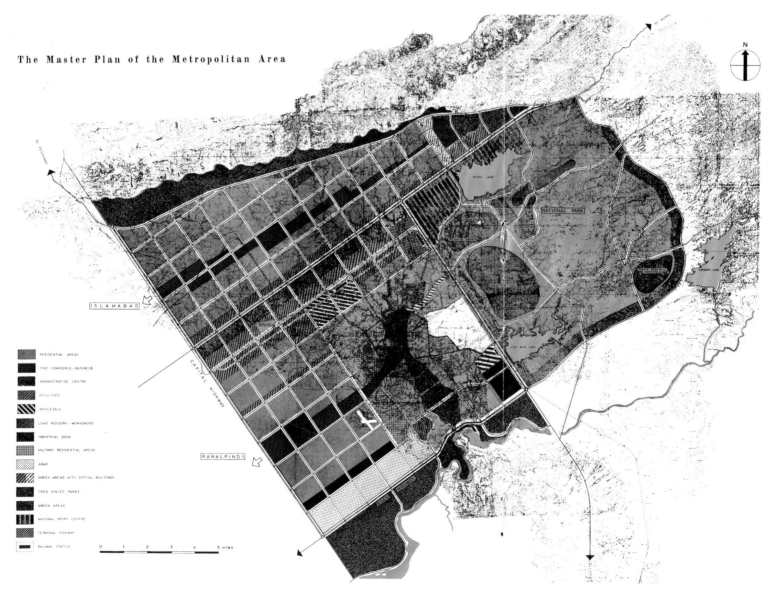

The Master Plan of the Metropolitan Area

RESIDENTIAL AREAS
CIVIC - COMMERCE - BUSINESS
ADMINISTRATIVE CENTRE
EMBASSIES
WHOLESALE
LIGHT INDUSTRY - WORKSHOPS
INDUSTRIAL ZONE
MILITARY RESIDENTIAL AREAS
ARMY
GREEN AREAS WITH SPECIAL BUILDINGS
OPEN SPACES - PARKS
GREEN AREAS
NATIONAL SPORT CENTRE
TERMINAL HIGHWAY
RAILWAY STATION

0 1 2 3 4 5 miles

ISLAMABAD

RAWALPINDI

CAPITAL HIGHWAY

NATIONAL PARK

Master plan of the metropolitan area of Islamabad. Doxiadis Associates, *Monthly Bulletin*, no. 64 (March 1964). Constantinos A. Doxiadis Archives

Photograph of a model of the central part of Islamabad. 1960. Constantinos A. Doxiadis Archives

VIEW FROM THE COURT THROUGH THE GROUND FLOOR OF THE MAIN BLOCK

D-PA 2830

DOXIADIS   ASSOCIATES — CONSULTING   ENGINEERS

Perspective of the Court Complex (unbuilt). Page 235 of Doxiadis Associates' "On Architecture in Islamabad" (report no. 56, April 22, 1961). Constantinos A. Doxiadis Archives

A VILLAGE WITHIN THE AREA OF
THE NEW CAPITAL

THE STRUCTURE OF A COMMUNITY

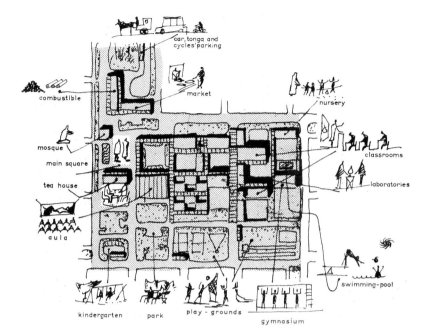

A VERANDAH

Stone is the main building material.
Flat roofs, stone walls and timber
columns are the main architectural
characteristics.

A SHELTER

Shelters and verandahs are
indespensible - they provide protection
against sun and rain.

A SHOP

Protection against sun is provided by
a thatched roof.
The two-level floor arrangement is
done for functional reasons.

D-PA 2701

Left: Illustration from p. 177 of Doxiadis Associates' "On Architecture in Islamabad" (report no. 56, April 22, 1961). Constantinos A. Doxiadis Archives
Right: Page 123 of Doxiadis Associates' "On Architecture in Islamabad" (report no. 56, April 22, 1961). Constantinos A. Doxiadis Archives

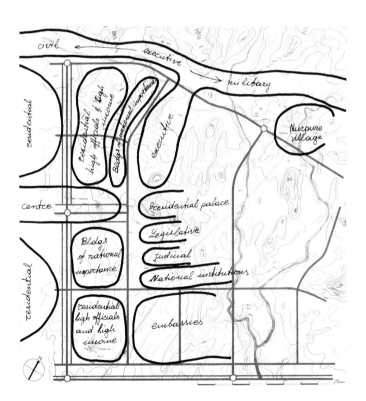

INTERRELATION OF FUNCTIONS IN THE ADMINISTRATIVE CENTER

The main reason for which the new Capital of Pakistan is being created is that the proper environment should be
provided for the administrative functions of the Country. The hills lying Northwest of Rawal Lake form an ideal setting
for the administrative sector, at the core of the city of ISLAMABAD and at the end of the main axis. Thus, and on the
basis of the theory and principles of the City of the Future—DYNAPOLIS— the administrative sector as well as the central
sector of the city both begin at the core of ISLAMABAD. The Capitol complex will be at the heart of the synthesis.
It is from here that the administrative sector will have to be developed towards and following the direction of the
Margala Hills, in order to spread along them in the future. The sketch on this page is a Zoning Map of the
Administrative Center of ISLAMABAD.

Back cover of Doxiadis Associates' *Monthly Bulletin*, no. 18 (October 1960). Constantinos A. Doxiadis Archives

SARDAR VALLABHBHAI PATEL MUNICIPAL STADIUM

Architect   Charles Correa (1930–2015)
Engineer   Mahendra Raj (b. 1924)
Built   1959–66
Location   Ahmedabad, India

Commissioned by the Ahmedabad Municipal Corporation, the Sardar Vallabhbhai Patel Municipal Stadium was originally envisaged as a multipurpose sports complex with a number of separate facilities. Only the cricket stadium (see Portfolio, no. 4) was ultimately realized, and in its early years it functioned as a venue for international cricket matches.[1] As such, it served as a theater for cultivating and projecting national ambitions, which were embodied in its architectural expression. The building was one structure among several making up an entire landscape of new cultural and educational facilities built in Ahmedabad in the post-Independence period with the support of a group of wealthy textile millowners, such as Kasturbhai Lalbhai, Surottam Hutheesing, Gautam Sarabhai, and Chinubhai Chimanlal. The last served as the city's mayor between 1950 and 1962 and was, along with the architect Gira Sarabhai, instrumental in hiring Le Corbusier for various projects in the city, including several private residences for the families of this circle of wealthy industrialists as well as the celebrated Ahmedabad Textile Mill Owners' Association (ATMA) Building (1951–56; see fig. 13 on p. 48).[2] In spite of some key differences, for example that the Ahmedabad elites were also keen to promote local textile craft traditions, the millowners advocated a progressive municipal politics broadly in line with the aims of Prime Minister Jawaharlal Nehru's national project of industrialization and urbanization. Their patronage of modern architecture was instrumental for its promotion within the political project of decolonization on both a local and a national level.

As a recreational facility, the stadium met the objective of providing for a broad spectrum of "social services."[3] Charles Correa and engineer Mahendra Raj's circular design is a proud expression of this collective ethos. Built for thirty-five thousand spectators, the stadium introduced a modular folded-plate concrete frame structure, a technology Raj had familiarized himself with during his time in the New York–based office of Ammann & Whitney.[4] It is this feature that lends the building its highly recognizable formal and spatial quality, best perceived in the exterior interstitial space between the inclined "legs" of the folded plates and the underside of the seating. The roof cantilevers some sixty-five feet and is likewise based on folded-plate technology, which allows it to seemingly float freely above the stands without any additional supports. It provides shelter for a section of the stadium in an otherwise open, airy configuration. The use of exposed concrete, while standard for the expression of self-reliance in newly independent nations across the world, was more of an anomaly in the oeuvre of Correa, who would be an early critic of the modernist project and gravitate toward a regionalist register in later years.

Martino Stierli

1   Hasan-Uddin Khan, ed., *Charles Correa* (Singapore: Concept Media, 1987), 147.
2   See Peter Serenyi, "Timeless but of Its Time: Le Corbusier's Architecture in India," *Perspecta* 20 (1983): 94.
3   K. M. Kantawala, "Growth of the City of Ahmedabad," *Social Welfare* 10 (1964): 43.
4   "1960s: Municipal Stadium," in *The Structure: Works of Mahendra Raj*, ed. Vandini Mehta, Rohit Raj Mehndiratta, and Ariel Huber (Zurich: Park Books, 2016), 64.

Sardar Vallabhbhai Patel Municipal Stadium, Ahmedabad, India. 1959–66. Architect: Charles Correa (1930–2015). Engineer: Mahendra Raj (b. 1924). Exterior view. 2010. Photograph: Ariel Huber

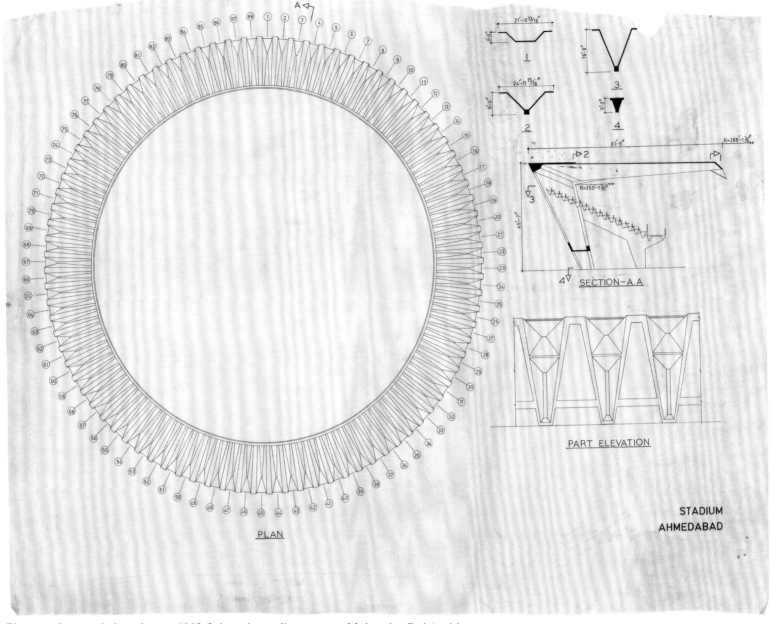

Plan, section, and elevation. c. 1965. Ink and pencil on paper. Mahendra Raj Archives

Photograph of model. Mahendra Raj Archives

View of the stands from below. 2010. Photograph: Ariel Huber

193

POLONTALAWA HOUSE

Architects   Geoffrey Bawa (1919–2003) and Ulrik Plesner (1930–2016)
Built   1963–65
Location   Polontalawa, Ceylon (Sri Lanka)

Less well known than Geoffrey Bawa's institutional architecture but more explicitly evocative of the moral economy that was the tour de force of his aesthetic, the Polontalawa House is an excellent example of symbiosis between Bawa and the Danish architect Ulrik Plesner leading to a culturally sensitized approach. This project was among the first in which the duo used the humility of vernacular architecture as a means to decolonize programs that had previously enhanced European prestige. The client, the Swiss Bauer Company, a fertilizer producer that had amassed a small plantation empire, introduced the first electrified factory to the island and in 1941 built a modernist multistory office and apartment complex in Colombo. The residence Bawa and Plesner envisioned for the plantation's director was undoubtedly cast in a mold similar to company-owned bungalows, which were evolving from an indolent colonial model to a modernist version of it.

The thousand acres of scrub jungle by the Deduru Oya (one of Sri Lanka's longest rivers) was dotted with large, rounded, rose-colored boulders and proved impossible to survey. The house had to be designed in situ according to the architects' instructions, using a method for which Bawa later became renowned. Plesner describes standing on the tallest, ten-foot-high boulder and directing village laborers to lay out the house in full scale, using string elevated on bamboo poles to indicate corners, gables, and ridges.[1] At the end of the third day, the house was mapped out in the air in string. Once a month, Plesner would drive up to issue directives to laborers as the house incrementally took shape. A six-foot-high stone boundary wall prevented wild animals from entering the site.

The Polontalawa House captures the poetics of shelter with an overhanging roof form balanced on boulders and columns defining a space with minimal containment: a timber post-and-beam structure holds up the eaves of the tile-bearing corrugated roof, which is placed on a latticed frame, the living spaces flowing freely beneath it.[2] There are no walls, with the exception of those in two small bedrooms accessed by crossing a bridge from the principal living areas. The floor levels are elevated off the ground. Although overlooked in the first Bawa monograph,[3] this design best encapsulates the architects' conviction about the primacy of the roof. Ultimately more significant, however, is its abandonment of modernist rationalization in the complete embrace of a situated and humanistic design practice.

Anoma Pieris

1   Ulrik Plesner, *In Situ: An Architectural Memoir from Sri Lanka* (Copenhagen: Aristo 2012), 248.
2   See Ulrik Plesner, "Polontolawa House, Sri Lanka," *Living Architecture*, no. 5 (1986): 98–103.
3   Brian Brace Taylor, *Geoffrey Bawa* (Singapore: Concept Media, 1986).

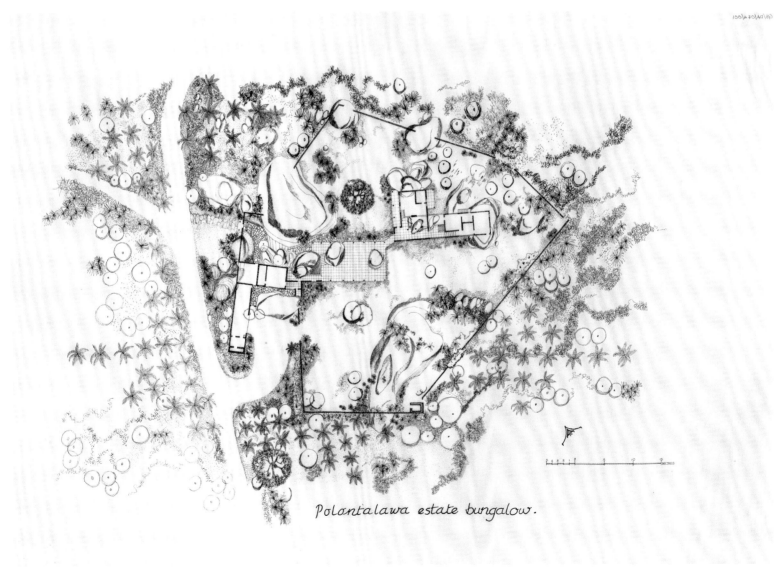

Polontalawa estate bungalow.

Polontalawa House, Polontalawa, Ceylon (Sri Lanka). 1963–65. Geoffrey Bawa (1919–2003) and Ulrik Plesner (1930–2016)/Edwards Reid & Begg. Plan drawing. Ink and pencil on tracing paper, 18⁷/₁₆ × 26 in. (46.9 × 66 cm). The Lunuganga Trust

Interior view

Interior view looking onto the courtyard. Plesner Archives

Interior view. Plesner Archives

SCHOOL OF ARCHITECTURE, CENTRE FOR ENVIRONMENTAL PLANNING AND TECHNOLOGY

Architect	Balkrishna V. Doshi (b. 1927)
Built	1962–68; with later additions
Location	Ahmedabad, India

The Ahmedabad Education Society established the School of Architecture in 1962 with funding from the state of Gujarat. The buildings for the institution, which became part of the Centre for Environmental Planning and Technology (CEPT) after the addition of a School of Planning in 1972, were designed by Balkrishna V. Doshi, its founding director, and completed in 1968 (see Portfolio, no. 24). With an ethos that was grounded in social and intellectual pluralism and acknowledged India's complexities, Doshi designed the campus architecture to promote spaces of collaborative learning about all aspects of the built environment, while relaying the Centre's Sanskrit motto *gnanam vignanamsahitam*, or "knowledge with science and spirituality." Eschewing rigid dualisms of past and future, Doshi and the founding director of the School of Planning, American-born architect Christopher Benninger (b. 1942), pursued unique design pedagogies that could revitalize tradition while also activating ideas around democratic ideals through the configuration of the campus and its studios as well as an autonomous curriculum. It was important for both Doshi and Benninger that the study of architectural design and planning depart from colonial-era technocratic disciplinary boundaries and for it instead to allow an exploration of artistic and conceptual ideas rooted on the Indian subcontinent but not beholden to it. Since its founding, many of CEPT's graduates, from each of the five faculties it expanded to encompass, have become significant architects, artists, planners, and thinkers in South Asia and throughout the world.

CEPT's campus buildings are emblematic of the institution's holistic philosophy. Approaching the center of the campus and the primary studio building of the School of Architecture from the road, one crosses small grass-covered hillocks to emerge in an open area framed by trees and open-tiered brick-and-concrete structures. The central entrance to the school features two symmetrical funnel-shaped staircases conceived by Doshi as means of catalyzing self-reflection. The sense of the school's expansiveness is immediate: on a floor floating above a plaza level, the generously sized studios and offices are designed without doors to enable cross breezes and productive adjacencies under dispersed light from clerestory windows. The dimensioning of the design studio spaces has been imagined as itself an instructional aid. "Everything goes inside," Doshi said in 2018, "So why not really continue it? Why create doors? Or why create restrictions? So I always wrote, in the [CEPT] campus, my whole idea was that an educational campus should be without doors. No boundaries. And that philosophy I continue."[1]

Among Doshi's other buildings on the CEPT campus is the Lalbhai Dalpatbhai Institute of Indology (1957–62; see fig. 17 on p. 52; Portfolio, no. 1), adjacent to which is the Amdavad ni Gufa art gallery (1992–95), a subterranean "spatial sculpture" designed in collaboration with the renowned Indian artist M. F. Husain (1915–2011).[2] Built to emulate a cavern of shadows, light, and color, the space has a seemingly boundless darkened interior, with reflections hidden beneath a network of light-filled domes. With its stalagmite pillars and large paintings, the structure is an exploration of CEPT's and Doshi's centering of spaces that amplify the self, imagination, and nature.

Sean Anderson

1   Balkrishna V. Doshi quoted in Ashish Malhotra, "'A Bolt From the Blue': Doshi on Winning the Pritzker," Bloomberg CityLab, March 20, 2018, https://www.bloomberg.com/news/articles/2018-03-20/indian-architect-doshi-talks-about-winning-the-pritzker.
2   Doshi characterizes the gallery as a "spatial sculpture" in Anthony Paletta, "A Modernism for India," *Washington Examiner*, October 14, 2018, https://www.washingtonexaminer.com/weekly-standard/pritzker-prize-winning-architect-b-v-doshi-a-modernism-for-india.

School of Architecture, Centre for Environmental Planning and Technology (CEPT), Ahmedabad, India. 1962–68. Balkrishna V. Doshi (b. 1927)/
Vāstu Shilpā. Interior view. Vāstu Shilpā Foundation Archives

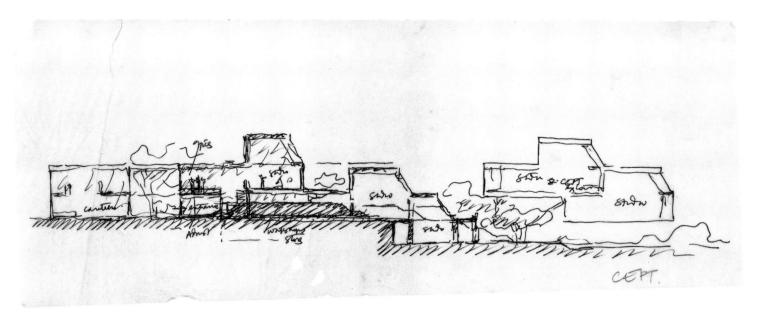

Sketch of section. c. 1962. Ink and pencil on tracing paper, 7⅝ × 19¾ in. (19.4 × 50.1 cm). Vāstu Shilpā Foundation Archives

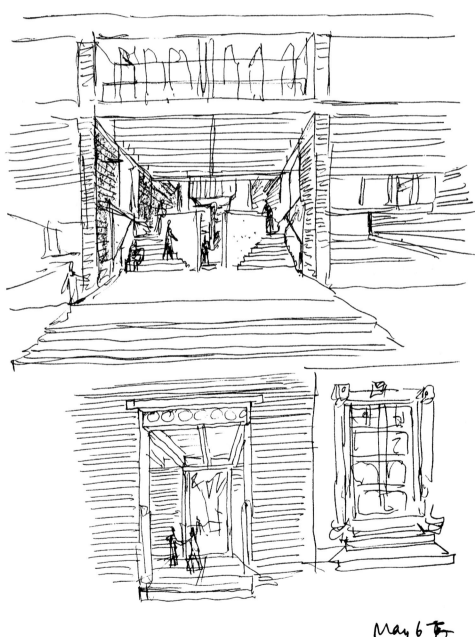

Perspective sketches. c. 1962. Ink and pencil on paper. Vāstu Shilpā Foundation Archives

Balkrishna V. Doshi (right of center) with students at CEPT. c. 1970s. Vāstu Shilpā Foundation Archives

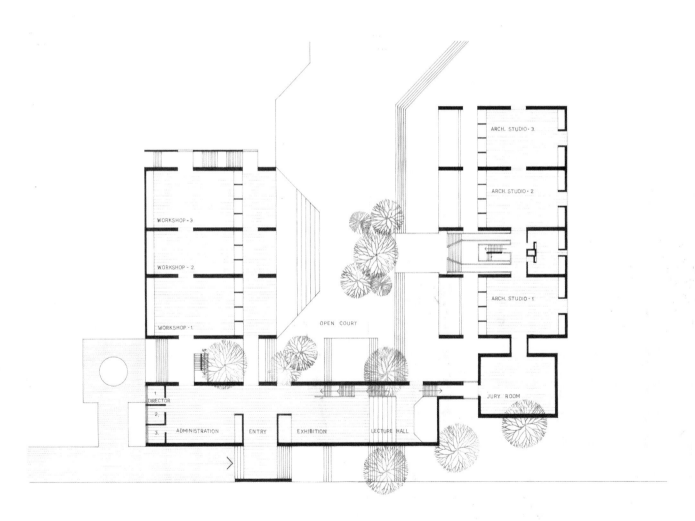

CENTRE FOR ENVIRONMENTAL PLANNING AND TECHNOLOGY

VASTU SHILPA AHMEDABAD				
ARCHITECT	B. V. DOSHI			
DELT	K. B. JAIN	PLAN AT ⊕⊕		
SCALE	1 INCH = 16 FEET			
DATE	JULY 1967			

Site plan. 1″ = 16′-0″. 1967. Ink and pencil on paper. Vāstu Shilpā Foundation Archives

KAMALAPUR RAILWAY STATION

Architects   Daniel C. Dunham (1929–2000) and Robert G. Boughey (b. 1940)
Built   1968
Location   Dhaka, East Pakistan (Bangladesh)

The Dacca Realignment Scheme, part of East Pakistan's Second Five-Year Plan (1960–65), was an acknowledgment of the growing significance of the eastern capital (now transliterated as Dhaka) as a transportation hub and of the attendant need for an expansion of its facilities. Along with the modernization and fundamental rearrangement of railway tracks, it called for the relocation of Dhaka Station. A site in Kamalapur, located just over a mile southeast of the city center, was chosen, and the Pakistani branch of Louis Berger's United States–based civil-engineering firm was commissioned to design the new station building.

In a 1960 letter confirming the Harvard-trained architect Daniel C. Dunham's employment, Berger underscored the importance of the young architect's familiarity with the principles of "tropical architecture."[1] At Harvard, Dunham had investigated the problems and advantages of thin-shell concrete roofing, particularly of the "umbrella" type that would become the basis of the design for Kamalapur Railway Station he executed with Robert G. Boughey (see Portfolio, no. 30). Such roofs, popularized by Jørn Utzon's 1957 design for the Sydney Opera House, offered the possibility of a powerfully expressive architecture Dunham and Boughey meaningfully exploited by giving the arches of the vaults a profile reminiscent of local Islamic architecture. The cool, shaded public space afforded by the canopy became a focal point of urban life, while the offices and ticketing facilities were accommodated in two-story enclosed spaces, with the upper level accessible via a modernist spiral staircase, a device serving in this context as a metaphor for the hopes and aspirations associated with Independence.

Speaking at the 1963 conference of the Institute of Engineers, Pakistan, Dunham underscored that nothing, not even the provision of modern conditions, should compromise the *venustas* (beauty) of a building. He lamented that Pakistan had trained many engineers but very few architects—the Bengali architect Muzharul Islam, also present at the conference, agreed, remarking that "architecture, as a profession, virtually does not exist in East Pakistan today."[2] Convinced that a sound architectural education was of paramount importance to the nation's future, Dunham left Berger's firm to teach at the East Pakistan (later Bangladesh) University of Engineering and Technology, where he played an important role in training the subsequent generation of architects.

In November 2020, Bangladesh railway authorities announced a plan to demolish the station, citing the need to make way for a new rapid-transit line. The decision provoked international criticism, and at press time the building's fate remains uncertain.[3]

Da Hyung Jeong

1   Louis Berger to Daniel C. Dunham, October 3, 1960, courtesy of Kate Dunham, New York.
2   Muzharul Islam, "The Problems Faced by an Architect in East Pakistan," *Pakistan Engineer* 3, no. 4 (October 1963): 181
3   Aaron Smithson, "Dhaka Demolition: Bangladesh Authorities Consider Demolishing Iconic Kamalapur Railway Station for an Elevated Metro Line," *Architect's Newspaper*, January 4, 2021, https://www.archpaper.com/2021/01/dhaka-demolishing-iconic-kamalapur-railway-station-for-elevated-metro-line/.

Kamalapur Railway Station, Dhaka, East Pakistan (Bangladesh). 1968. Daniel C. Dunham (1929–2000) and Robert G. Boughey (b. 1940)/Louis Berger and Consulting Engineers. Exterior view showing the corner staircase. c. 1980

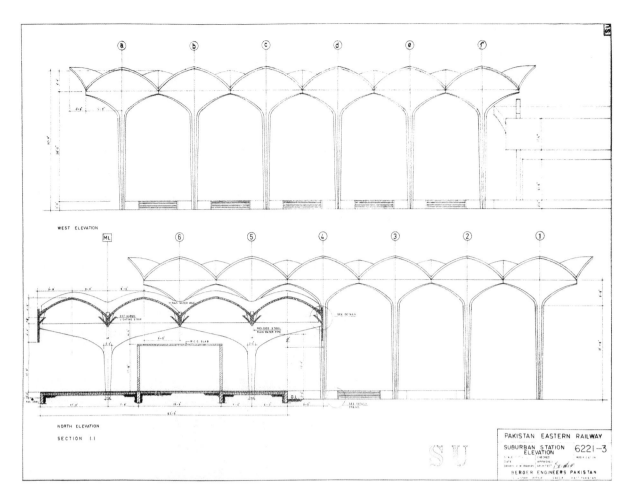

Elevations. ¼" = 1'-0". c. 1962. Ink on paper, 10⅝ × 14³⁄₁₆ in. (27 × 36 cm). Robert G. Boughey

Exterior view. c. 1967

Interior view. c. 1980

CHITTAGONG UNIVERSITY

Architect   Muzharul Islam (1923–2012)
Built   1965–71
Location   Chittagong, East Pakistan (Bangladesh)

In his decades-long critical practice of architecture in East Pakistan and its successor state, Bangladesh, Muzharul Islam sought an affirmation of the kind of learned decency he associated with particular elements of Bengali society. While he rarely spoke of "architecture," preferring the Bengali word *sthapatyashilpa*, a term encompassing all aspects of architecture from its imagining to construction and occupation, Islam expressed in his writings and projects a desire to reconfigure the modes by which society adapted to transformations within modern village and city life. His was a practice built through an ethics of political and community engagement, including activism around the Bangladesh Liberation War of 1971. Aligning his knowledge of Western notions of abstraction—expanded through studies in the United States and long affiliations with European and American architects—with close attention to the narratives of Bengali culture, Islam has been credited with single-handedly bringing modernist sensibilities to the architecture of Bangladesh.

Witnessing the decline of Bengali village systems, Islam asserted that individual buildings embodied the contradictions of politics and the urban environment. This also informed his approach to the design and building of institutions. Inseparable from his concurrent university projects—including the Jahangirnagar University (1967–70) outside Dhaka, as well the Five Polytechnic Institutes (1965–71) he designed collaboratively with Chicago-based architect Stanley Tigerman—the planning of Chittagong University (see Portfolio, no. 25), a residential institution in the country's southeast riverine delta, involved not only an astute observation of context but a responsiveness to the ways in which projections about the university's future should shape its composition.

In planning the Chittagong campus, Islam spent approximately one year observing the 1,600 acres of forested hilly terrain of which some six hundred would be reserved as the principal site for the university. He approached the scheme with great sensitivity to the natural surroundings: the angular geometries of the design's plan and elevation served to organize how structures and individuals would congregate across the campus, since, for the architect, building on steeper terrain was impossible because "the hills are something you cannot create."[1] In the first plans, dynamic brick and concrete housing blocks, classrooms, and administrative buildings are clustered along the edges of the hills Reflecting a desire to leave the site's ecosystems undisturbed, the arrangement of several structures took monsoon flooding in the area into account. Grouping terraced and reticulated buildings along axial "streets" allowed for walks of around fifteen minutes between them, while also providing unimpeded views. With its complex geometries emulating those of the surrounding landscape, the university's campus extends Islam's interest in a convergence of materiality, form, and nature.

Sean Anderson

1   Kazi Khaleed Ashraf, ed., *An Architect in Bangladesh: Conversations with Muzharul Islam* (Dhaka: Loka, 2014), 173.

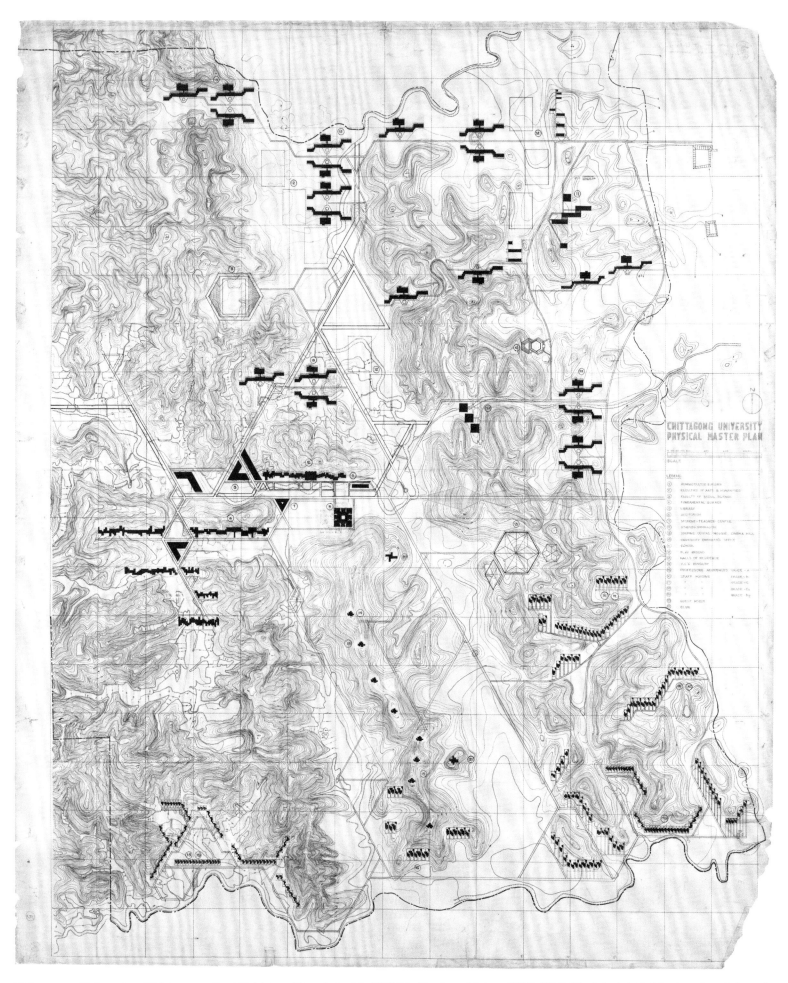

Chittagong University, Chittagong, East Pakistan (Bangladesh). 1965–71. Muzharul Islam (1923–2012)/Vastukalabid. Master plan. Ink and pencil on paper, 36¹/₂ × 33¹/₂ in. (92.7 × 85.1 cm). Muzharul Islam Archives

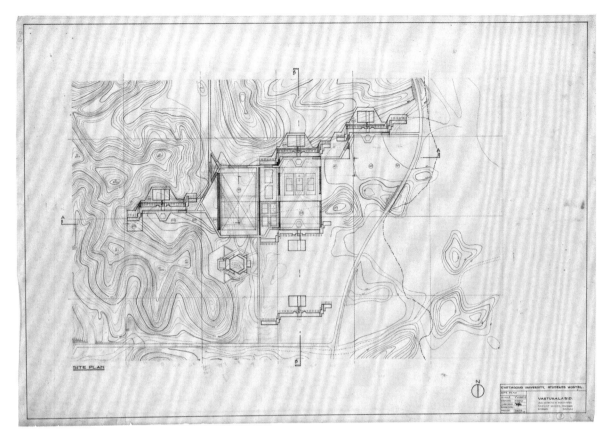

Site plan. 1″ = 100′-0″. 1968. Ink and pencil on paper. Muzharul Islam Archives

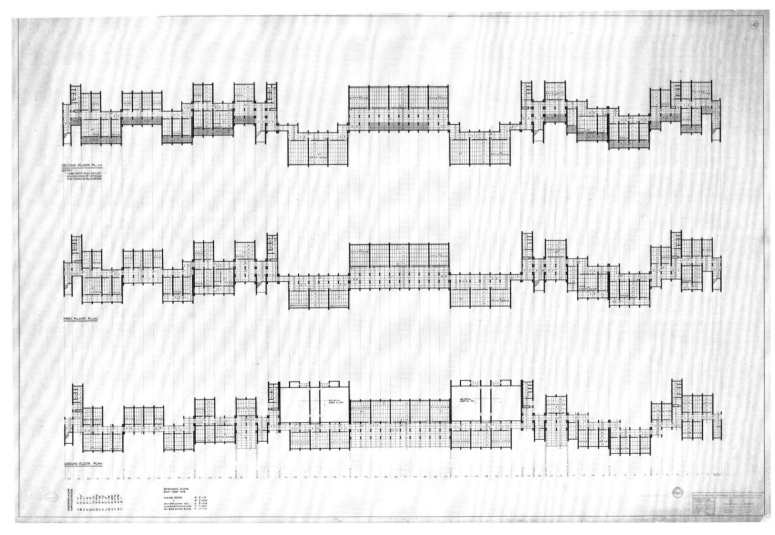

Plan of the humanities building. 1/16″ = 1′-0″. 1968. Ink and pencil on paper. Muzharul Islam Archives

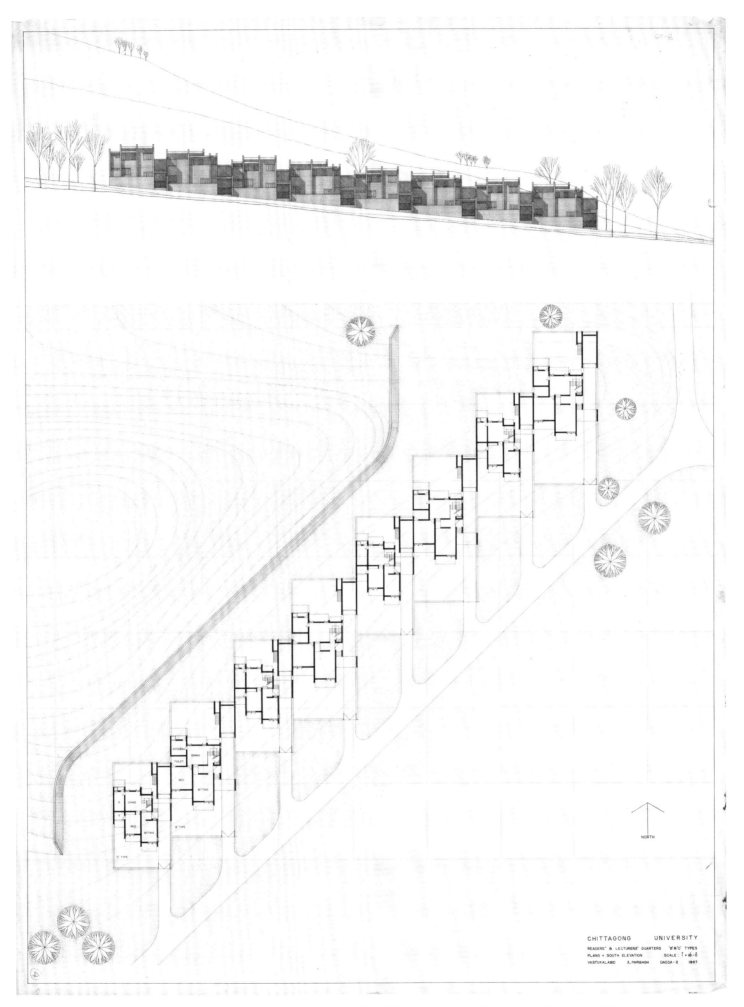

Plan and elevation of readers' and lecturers' quarters. $\frac{1}{16}$" = 1'-0". 1967. Ink and pencil on paper. Muzharul Islam Archives

TANGALLE BAY HOTEL

Architects   Valentine Gunasekara (1931–2017) and Christopher de Saram (1939–2018)
Engineer   Jayati Weerakoon (1928–2021)
Built   1969–72
Location   Tangalle, Ceylon (Sri Lanka)

Perched on the edge of a rocky promontory outside the southern coastal town of Tangalle, Valentine Gunasekara and Christopher de Saram's seventy-room Tangalle Bay Hotel is distinctly modernist, and thereby strikingly different from the many regionalist designs that later made Sri Lanka a popular destination for global tourism. It alludes neither to the local vernacular nor to the colonial past.[1] Its linear form, of a berthed ocean liner with plug-in terraced accommodation wings, can thus come as a surprise in a locality unused to the formalist rigor of the California modernism the design is inspired by. The curvilinear, double-height interior—with its elevated undulating sky bridge, reached by cylindrical stairways—and the terraced rooms cascading down to the ocean transport visitors experientially to the long voyages across the sea most familiar to the postwar generation, setting them in exhilarating proximity to the surf. The hotel rejects the sentimental appeal of the indigenized colonial citadel that has displaced colonial rest houses as the new paradigm for modern hospitality.

A distinguishing feature of the Tangalle Bay Hotel is its accessibility. Unlike contemporaneous projects that insulate their clientele behind boundary walls, the hotel is open to its surroundings and was used by locals for festivals and family gatherings—an important expression of Gunasekara's social orientation. The design speaks explicitly of two modernist lineages. Its passive environmental systems originate in the Tropical Architecture program at the Architectural Association School of Architecture in London, where both architects studied, while the sweeping horizontal views of the landscape from a building placed within it are a legacy of Gunasekara's exposure to the architecture of America's West Coast. He learned to appreciate the plasticity of concrete during a tour of the United States in 1966, spending six months at Eero Saarinen's office under Kevin Roche. Conversations with Louis I. Kahn, Richard Neutra, and Charles and Ray Eames on their work in the subcontinent followed, emboldening Gunasekara to experiment with expressive modernist forms.

Gunasekara abhorred socially divisive cultural expressions, and the Tangalle Bay Hotel was the apotheosis of his quest for a distinctive vocabulary unfettered by the weight of the feudal and colonial past. He was determined to introduce rationalized modular building systems and innovative technologies, and to upskill his local labor contractor, Sirisoma. Working closely with engineer Jayati Weerakoon, he introduced prefabrication and phased construction, both of which were in the labor-intensive domestic building industry. Today, Gunasekara is received in two ways—as an uncompromising modernist or as someone ahead of his time. The sinuous lines of the Tangalle Bay Hotel, wrapped around the rocky cliff face, were equally capable of causing consternation and delight.

Anoma Pieris

---

1   See Anoma Pieris, "Modernity at the Margins: Reconsidering Valentine Gunasekara," *Grey Room*, no. 28 (Summer 2007): 56–85; and Pieris, *Imagining Modernity: The Architecture of Valentine Gunasekara* (Colombo: Stamford Lake, 2007).

Tangalle Bay Hotel, Tangalle, Ceylon (Sri Lanka). 1969–72. Architects: Valentine Gunasekara (1931–2017) and Christopher de Saram (1939–2018). Engineer: Jayati Weerakoon (1928–2021). Exterior view from the water. Photograph: Nihal Fernando

Perspective drawing. 1970. Ink and pencil on paper, 20 × 30 in. (50.8 × 76.2 cm). Valentine Gunasekara Archives

Exterior view. Valentine Gunasekara Archives

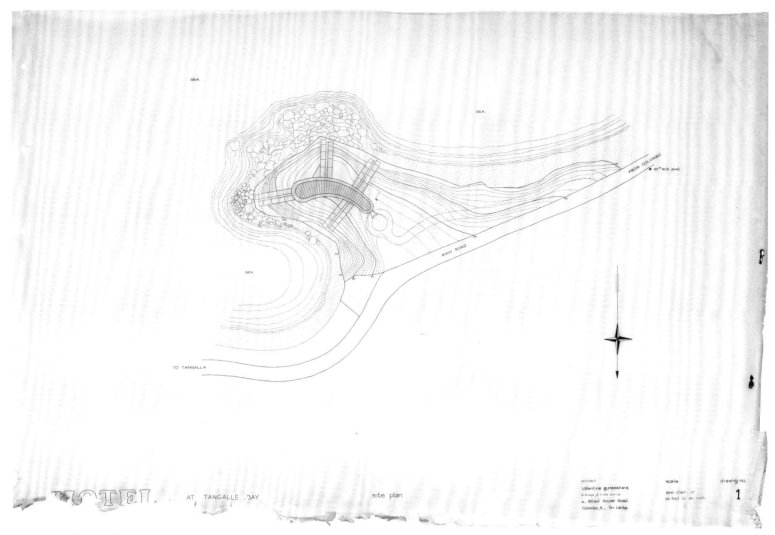

Site plan. 1″ = 66′-0″. Ink and pencil on paper, 19¾ × 30 in. (50.2 × 76.2 cm). Valentine Gunasekara Archives

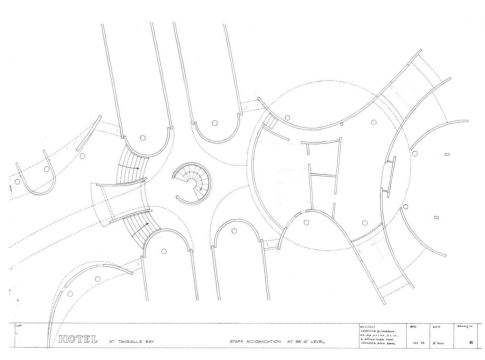

Left: Interior view. Valentine Gunasekara Archives
Right: Plan of staff accommodation. ¼″ = 1′-0″. 1973. Ink and pencil on paper, 20 × 30 in. (50.8 × 76.2 cm). Valentine Gunasekara Archives

CENTRE FOR DEVELOPMENT STUDIES

Architect   Laurie Baker (1917–2007)
Built   1967–71
Location   Trivandrum (Thiruvananthapuram), India

Laurie Baker was a builder and a citizen's advocate as well as an architect. His design philosophy was not only committed to environmentally sustainable methods of low-cost construction throughout southern India, but also a means to articulate the sociocultural mores of a community and nation. Baker was born in Britain, and his ethos was rooted in Quaker ideals, which resonated with Gandhian principles of self-reliance and communal agency. He carried out his first work in India alongside his wife, Elizabeth Jacob, establishing and managing hospitals for leprosy patients in the remote Himalayas. Rigorously following a set of twenty self-fashioned ethical principles, from "Discourage EXTRAVAGANCE & SNOBBERY" to "BE HONEST IN DESIGN, Materials, Construction, Costs & MISTAKES" to "Get your CONSCIENCE out of DEEP FREEZE & USE it,"[1] Baker developed projects that were informed by his belief that "vernacular architecture almost always has good answers to all our problems."[2]

Founded in 1970 by noted economist K. N. Raj (1924–2010), the Centre for Development Studies is a ten-acre postgraduate educational institution that promotes a decentralized approach to research and training focused on policy-making, planning, and development economics, from a global perspective. Established with funding from the government of Kerala in a residential area of the state capital, Trivandrum, the principal administrative building of the campus is both metaphoric "front door" and physical center for a number of interconnected classroom buildings, a library, an auditorium, guesthouses, and student dormitories. Baker's interest in imbuing infrastructure with ideas of self-reliance is evident in the articulation of the campus's materiality, function, and spaces, through which he corroborated the pedagogical mission of the Centre.

Baker's predominantly brick structures are based on studies of vernacular architecture and exchanges with builders and craftspeople throughout India. For many of the Centre's buildings, non-orthogonal geometries establish a rigorous system of interdependent public and private spaces, many of which are covered by porticoes and reached by elevated walkways and bridges. The dominant circular library features multiple levels of reading rooms and book stacks, with an internal staircase perforated by small openings that allow air to flow through all areas of the building. Most of the external load-bearing brick walls throughout the campus are perforated by *jali* (latticed screens with geometric organization), which are found throughout Baker's oeuvre. In the chapel, corbeled lacelike patterns provide light in addition to airflow, while also creating a regiment of shadows inside the structure. Such elements are found among Baker's other local buildings, including the equally dynamic Indian Coffee House (c. 1980; see Portfolio, no. 38) adjacent to Trivandrum's main train station.

If, for Baker, "building becomes much more fun with the circle,"[3] one recognizes that in its capaciousness, the circle provides a metaphor for the architect's attention to interdependence and community-based understanding. At the Centre for Development Studies, Baker's profound insights confirm that communities and the individuals that compose them can respond to and build with equitable approaches to material and experience.

Sean Anderson

1   An undated handwritten list of these principles is published in Laurie Baker, "Teachings and Travel Writings," *a+u: Architecture and Urbanism*, no. 363 (December 2000): 4.
2   Laurie Baker, "Cementlessness," *Hindustan Times* (New Delhi), November 4, 1974, as quoted in Gautam Bhatia, *Laurie Baker: Life, Works & Writings* (New Delhi: Penguin, 1991), 48.
3   "Baker on 'Laurie Baker' Architecture," undated, in ibid., 233.

Centre for Development Studies, Trivandrum (Thiruvananthapuram), India. 1967–71. Laurie Baker (1917–2007). Exterior view. 2021.
Photograph: Randhir Singh

The JALI is one of India's oldest ways of giving light & ventilation & security to a room. Formerly pierced stone was carved to give patterned holes in stone slabs, but we can carry on this decorative & efficient alternative to the window. The patterns possible by using Bricks are endless. & far less costly than a window.

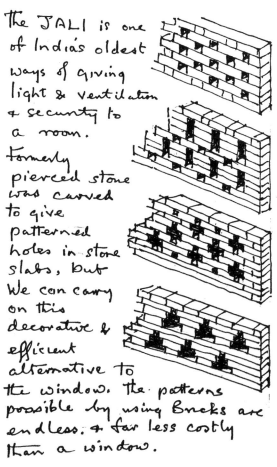

Annotated drawing published in Laurie Baker's *Houses: How to Reduce Building Costs* (Thrissur, India: COSTFORD, 1986)

Interior view. 2021. Photograph: Randhir Singh

216

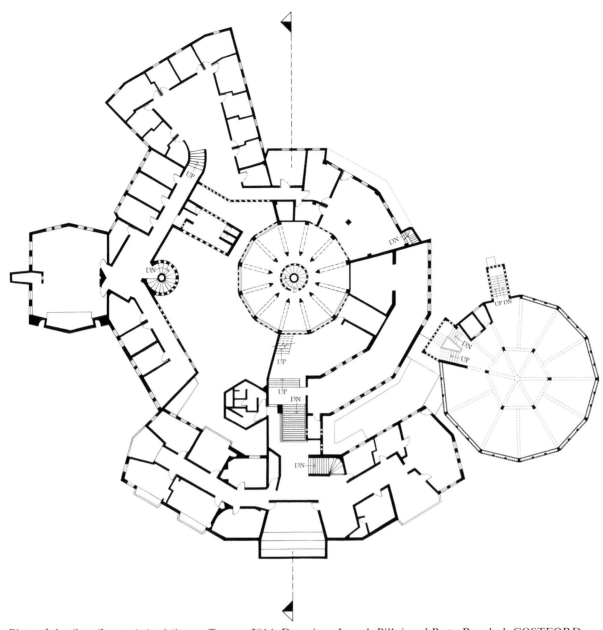

Plan of the first floor of the Library Tower. 2014. Drawing: Jayesh Pillai and Rutu Panchal. COSTFORD

Laurie Baker sketching on-site with construction workers. c. 1976. Photograph: Jack Skeel

HALL OF NATIONS AND HALLS OF INDUSTRIES

Architect   Raj Rewal (b. 1934)
Engineer   Mahendra Raj (b. 1924)
Built   1970–72; demolished 2017
Location   New Delhi, India

As the centerpiece of Pragati Maidan (progress grounds), a large-scale venue for exhibitions and conventions in central New Delhi, the Hall of Nations and Halls of Industries Complex holds a prominent place in the Indian collective imaginary as an architectural symbol of the optimism that characterized the immediate post-Independence decades. The Hall of Nations and the smaller Halls of Industries adjacent to it (see Portfolio, no. 29) were together intended to serve as the main exhibition pavilions for the international trade fair Asia '72, which marked the twenty-fifth anniversary of Indian independence. After Indian architect Raj Rewal and his then collaborator, architect Kuldip Singh, won the competition for the project, Rewal and structural engineer Mahendra Raj were chiefly responsible for the final design. Their scheme called for a series of five truncated pyramids connected by a syncopated circuit of oversize ramps. This arrangement also defined a central open area that could be used as an outdoor space for events and gatherings.[1]

The exhibition complex exemplifies an integrated design approach in which architectural and structural elements are virtually indistinguishable. Rather than impeding the realization of the ambitious design, material and economic limitations served as an opportunity to produce a unique architectural expression. The large-scale free-span structures were originally designed in steel, yet the lack of sufficient quantities of it at an affordable price meant that the intricate, triangular space frames of the enclosures were executed in ferroconcrete. Such a material translation was made possible through the work of the on-site project engineer, Durai Raj, and more generally the abundance of both mental and manual labor in India. It included the calculation of the intricate structural system by engineers at the Indian Institute of Technology Kanpur as well as the fabrication of the extremely complex formwork and casting of concrete by countless workers on-site.[2] It is precisely such idiosyncrasies that render the project emblematic of the ways in which the "universal" principles of modernism were actively undermined and decisively reshaped by the specificity of place, and the inventiveness of South Asian architects and engineers.[3]

The Hall of Nations and Halls of Industries were materialized in a short period, transitioning from the drawing board to a reality on the ground in less than two years. The complex was inaugurated by Prime Minister Indira Gandhi in November 1972, and its forward-looking image circulated around the world. As seen in a set of photographs by Indian photographer Madan Mahatta, the selectively clad concrete latticework of the pavilions allowed light to penetrate deeply into the wide-open, flexible interiors, while preventing excessive solar gain. Despite the outcry of architects and preservationists, the Hall of Nations Complex was hurriedly demolished without prior warning on the night of April 23–24, 2017, as part of a larger "redevelopment plan" for Pragati Maidan, violently depriving India and South Asia of one of the most dynamically expressed, technologically innovative, and symbolically charged examples of twentieth-century architecture.[4]

Evangelos Kotsioris

1   Brian Brace Taylor, *Raj Rewal* (London: Concept Media, 1992), 74–80.
2   Mahendra Raj, "Hall of Nations & Halls of Industries: Large Exhibition Hall Complex; A Case Study," in *The Structure: Works of Mahendra Raj*, ed. Vandini Mehta, Rohit Raj Mehndiratta, and Ariel Huber (Zurich: Park Books, 2016), 142–51.
3   Giordano Tironi, *Humanisme et architecture: Raj Rewal, construire pour la ville indienne* (Lausanne, Switzerland: L'Âge d'Homme, 2013), 131–35.
4   Raj Rewal, "Demolishing Nehru," *Indian Express* (Mumbai), November 15, 2018.

Hall of Nations, Pragati Maidan, New Delhi, India. 1970–72. Demolished 2017. Architect: Raj Rewal (b. 1934). Engineer: Mahendra Raj (b. 1924). Exterior view during construction. 1972. Photograph: Madan Mahatta

Interior view. 1985. Photograph: Madan Mahatta

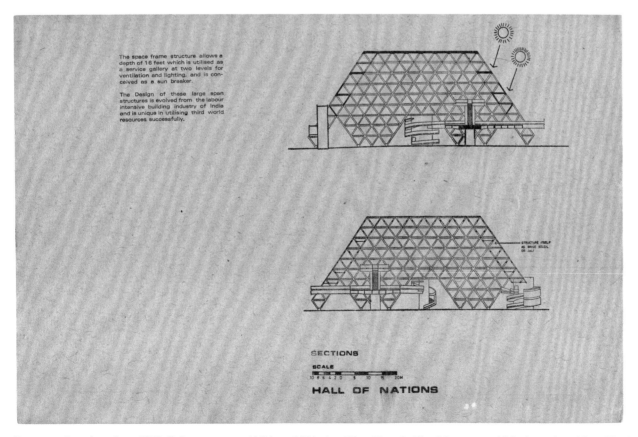

The space frame structure allows a depth of 16 feet which is utilised as a service gallery at two levels for ventilation and lighting, and is conceived as a sun breaker.

The Design of these large span structures is evolved from the labour intensive building industry of India and is unique in utilising third world resources successfully.

STRUCTURE ITSELF AS BRISE SOLEIL OR JALI

SECTIONS

SCALE
10 8 6 4 2 0   5   10   15   20M

HALL OF NATIONS

Presentation drawing. 1970. Ink on paper, 11 13/16 × 16 9/16 in. (30 × 42 cm). The Museum of Modern Art, New York

Perspective. c. 1970. Charcoal and colored pastels on tracing paper, 35 13/16 × 98 7/16 in. (91 × 250 cm). Musée National d'Art Moderne, Centre Georges Pompidou

Perspective. c. 1970. Pencil on tracing paper, 37 3/8 × 76 3/4 in. (95 × 195 cm). Musée National d'Art Moderne, Centre Georges Pompidou

ANGURI BAGH HOUSING

Architect   Yasmeen Lari (b. 1941)
Built   1972–75
Location   Lahore, Pakistan

Prime Minister Zulfikar Ali Bhutto's socialist Pakistan, which existed from 1971 to 1977, declared its three priorities to be *roti* (bread), *kapra* (clothing), and *makan* (housing). The government sought to impose strict control of the provision of these necessities. When a flood displaced several slum communities in Lahore in 1972, the state directly intervened in their resettlement, soliciting the help of the architect Yasmeen Lari to rehouse them on a 470,000-square-foot plot that had once been the site of a Mughal garden called Anguri, whence the project's name.

Trained in England at Oxford Polytechnic (now Oxford Brookes University), Lari established her practice in the mid-1960s. Its focus had initially been on private commissions, but in the 1970s she began to work in the public sector; her lifelong interest in the improvement of slum communities emerged during this time. For the 787 apartments making up the Anguri Bagh Housing, she employed mainly local unskilled labor. The walls were built using community-produced fair-faced bricks that ensured harmony with the surrounding built environment, while the floor and roof slabs were made of concrete poured in situ. The spaces of the three-story blocks interlocked and overlapped in complex ways and provided each unit with ventilation, light, and access to a rooftop as well as a courtyard, while brick *jali* screens marked the threshold between these semipublic areas and the private interiors.

The project garnered notable international acclaim. Shortlisted for the inaugural Aga Khan Award for Architecture in 1980, it was also featured at the 1982 Venice Architecture Biennale. At this exhibition, which was dedicated to architecture in Islamic countries, the project was shown alongside works by Charles Correa, Michel Écochard, Hassan Fathy, Muzharul Islam, and others; the presentation underscored Lari's key contributions to the conceptualization of Islamic modernism. In a 1981 interview, she memorably problematized what she called "instant Islamic" building styles.[1] In the Anguri Bagh Housing, she sought to build in a way that was both suitable for the social needs of its residents and in continuity with local architectural heritage. She said, "In designing this scheme I consciously tried to forget most of the lessons I had learned in the West—both design principles and planning standards."[2]

In 1975, Lari began work on the implementation of the UN-sponsored Metroville scheme in Karachi, Pakistan's first capital before Islamabad was established in the 1960s. Like the Anguri Bagh Housing, the project targeted slums, but rather than resettlement it aimed at improving living conditions in existing communities, primarily through the installation of modern amenities such as water purification systems. In a 1976 letter to one of Lari's collaborators, Canadian architect John Schreiber, S. Gulzar Haider, a professor of architecture at Carleton University, Ottawa, indicates that "a copy of the Metroville booklet" had been given to Nadine Isaacs, the architect responsible for "a 500-unit self-help housing project in Kingston, Jamaica . . . funded by the World Bank," revealing an international network of knowledge exchange centered on humanitarian efforts.[3]

Da Hyung Jeong

1   Yasmeen Lari quoted in Hasan-Uddin Khan, "Profile: Yasmeen Lari," *Mimar*, no. 2 (1981): 45.
2   Yasmeen Lari, "Angoori Bagh Housing, Lahore," *Mimar*, no. 2 (1981): 50.
3   S. Gulzar Haider to John Schreiber, January 12, 1976, Fonds 28, File 7526, McGill University Archives, Montreal.

Anguri Bagh Housing, Lahore, Pakistan, 1972–75. Yasmeen Lari (b. 1941). Exterior view. c. 1980. Photograph: Jacques Bétant.
Aga Khan Trust for Culture

An open lot with the Anguri Bagh Housing in the background. c. 1980. Photograph: Jacques Bétant. Aga Khan Trust for Culture

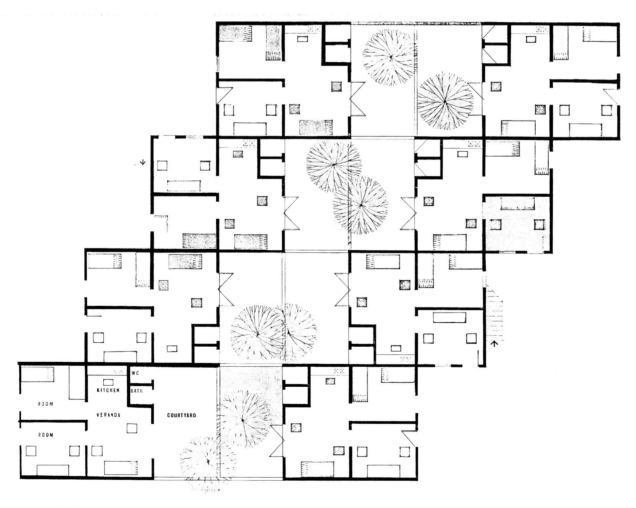

GROUND FLOOR PLAN

PEOPLES HOUSING PROGRAMME

Architect
YASMEEN LARI
Scale ... Date ...

S1/1

Ground-floor plan. c. 1980. Aga Khan Trust for Culture

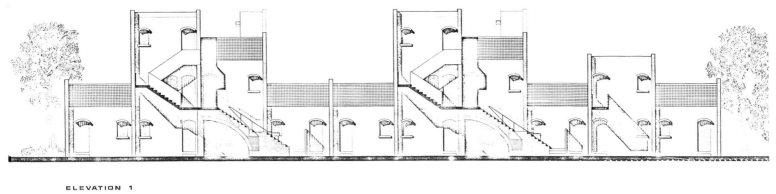

ELEVATION 1

Elevations. c. 1980. Aga Khan Trust for Culture

ELEVATION 3

Exterior view. c. 1980. Photograph: Jacques Bétant. Aga Khan Trust for Culture

LINEAR CITY

Architect   Aditya Prakash (1924–2008)
Designed   c. 1975–87; unbuilt

After completing his studies in Delhi and London, twenty-eight-year-old architect Aditya Prakash returned to his home country in 1952 to join a small team of Indian architects who would work closely with Le Corbusier, Pierre Jeanneret, Maxwell Fry, and Jane Drew on the design and realization of Chandigarh. During the first decade of his involvement in the Capital Project, Prakash designed and realized the three main cinemas of the city (Jagat, Neelam, and KC), as well as one of his most recognized projects, the Tagore Theatre (1960–62). But despite this prolific period of apprenticeship alongside the Swiss-French architect working in India, Prakash grew critical of the modern zoning principles embedded in the planning of the city, and especially of its clear-cut division between the city and the countryside and the diminishing relationship between the urban center and its surrounding farmlands and spaces of food production as it expanded outward from its core.[1]

Deeply troubled by the oil crisis and highly attuned to the environmental discourse of the early 1970s, Prakash started investigating the potential of a hypothetical settlement that would be "as self-sufficient as possible, through agriculture, horticulture, vegetable farming, animal husbandry, fishery, poultry, bee-farming, and cottage industry, and cycling the waste from one activity for utilization by the other."[2] Building upon Doxiadis Associates' linear plan for the expansion of Islamabad, R. Buckminster Fuller's ideas for the maximum use of world resources, and the emancipatory impulses of countercultural movements of the 1960s and 1970s, Prakash started formulating a theory of "self-sustaining settlements" specifically tailored to the Indian way of life. His early, abstract studies soon developed into a fully fledged visionary urbanist project, which he would later refer to as the Linear City. As in the case of Chandigarh, the Linear City would consist of repeatable sectors, but the city in Prakash's scheme would follow a straight outward path as it expanded, so as to allow a continued and intimate contact with the nonurban environment.

The sectors of the Linear City would measure one thousand by one thousand meters (meaning the area of each was approximately 250 acres). At the core of each sector, one would find a central square area (Zone A) dedicated to informal retail with *rehri* (wheel-cart) markets, food vendors, and craftsmen. The square would be surrounded by a ring of two-story residential units (Zone B), intermixed with large areas dedicated to vegetable farming and fish ponds, as well as play areas and small farms for pigs, goats, and other animals. In turn, this area would be encircled by a narrow zone of commercial activity (Zone C) in the form of single-story shopping streets, where pedestrians would mingle with the occasional animal-powered carriage or hand-pulled rickshaw; motorized traffic would be restricted to the elevated network above.[3] While Prakash's utopian mix of urban and countryside living was never realized, it constitutes a visionary proposal for a new urbanism on the subcontinent: one that did not indiscriminately adopt an imported, consumerist model of development and modernization but rather sought to imagine a symbiotic relationship between humans, plants, and animals in close proximity to one another.

Evangelos Kotsioris

1   On Le Corbusier's "reading" of the future site of Chandigarh, and the planning principles deduced from it, see Maristella Casciato, "Chandigarh: Landscaping a New Capital," in *Le Corbusier: An Atlas of Modern Landscapes*, ed. Jean-Louis Cohen (New York: The Museum of Modern Art, 2013), 370–76.
2   Aditya Prakash, "Human Settlements: A Self-Sustaining Approach," *Ekistics* 46, no. 278 (September–October 1979): 305.
3   Vikramaditya Prakash, *One Continuous Line: Art, Architecture and Urbanism of Aditya Prakash* (Ahmedabad, India: Mapin 2019), 164–181.

Linear City. c. 1975–87. Aditya Prakash (1924–2008). Perspective sketch of the informal sector. Drawing: Sandeep Virmani. Felt-tipped pen on paper, 29 1/2× 39 3/8 in. (75 × 100 cm). Aditya Prakash fonds, Canadian Centre for Architecture

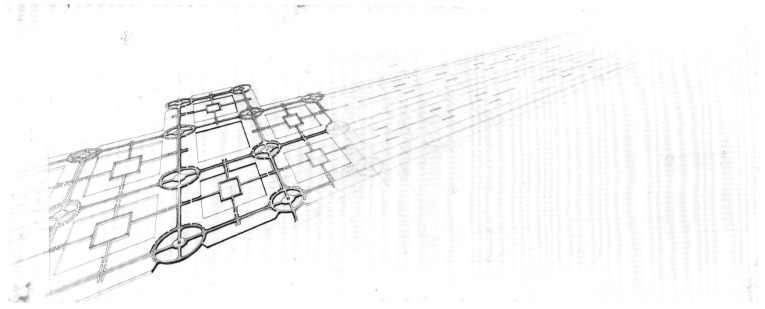

Aerial perspective of city grid. c. 1975–87. Ink and pencil on tracing paper, 14¹⁵⁄₁₆ × 39¾ in. (38 × 101 cm). Aditya Prakash fonds, Canadian Centre for Architecture

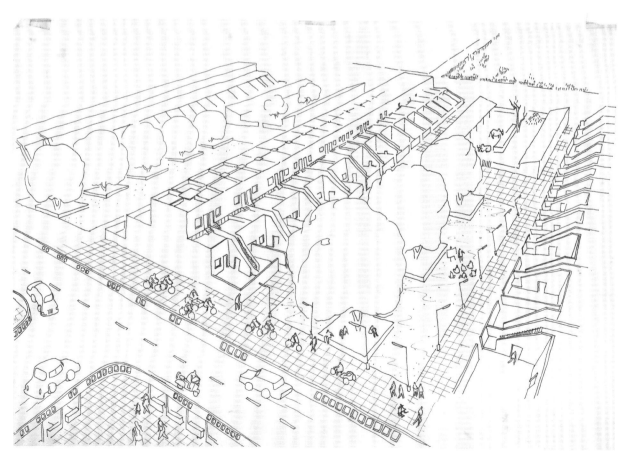

Perspective sketch of housing. c. 1975–87. Drawing: Sandeep Virmani (b. 1963). Felt-tipped pen on paper, 19¹¹⁄₁₆ × 29½ in. (50 × 75 cm). Aditya Prakash fonds, Canadian Centre for Architecture

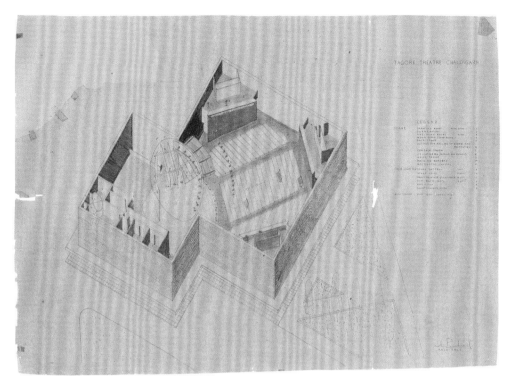

Tagore Theatre, Chandigarh, India. 1960–62. Aditya Prakash (1924–2008). Axonometric drawing. c. 1960. Felt-tipped pen and colored pencil on paper, 27⁹⁄₁₆ × 39 in. (70 × 99 cm). Aditya Prakash fonds, Canadian Centre for Architecture

Tagore Theatre, Chandigarh, India. 1960–62. Aditya Prakash (1924–2008). Photograph of model. c. 1960. Aditya Prakash fonds, Canadian Centre for Architecture

"C" TYPE MOSQUE (AHLE-HADITH MOSQUE)

Architect   Anwar Said (b. 1940)
Built   1969–73/1975–77
Location   Islamabad, Pakistan

While working as the principal architect of the Capital Development Authority (CDA) of Islamabad, Anwar Said—an architect born in Peshawar, some hundred miles away—designed a series of prototypical mosques that could be implemented throughout the residential districts of the new capital of Pakistan. The concept envisaged small, medium, and large ("A," "B," and "C" type) mosques that could be implemented at various scales of urban design. Said's approach was a direct response to the master plan for Islamabad, designed by Doxiadis Associates, which imagined the city as a hierarchical mosaic of nested "sectors," each of which would function as a self-contained entity complete with its own housing, civic facilities, schools, shops, and spaces of prayer, all accessible on foot.[1] Invoking a similar, almost structuralist ethos, Said's designs relied on the repetition and variation of basic geometric forms to produce complex spatial relationships.

One of the realized examples of Said's "C" type design is the Ahle-Hadith Mosque, the largest mosque of Islamabad's sector G-6/1 (see Portfolio, no. 31). The unusual, diamond-shaped plan of the building revolves around a central courtyard whose open porticoes accommodate an ablution area. Large enough to cater to a community of six thousand, the complex also incorporates a small library and the imam's quarters. The geometric form of the building is created through the tessellation of the structural module of a groin vault with pointed arches on a square grid. Four of those modules are doubled in scale and aggregated without internal partitions to formulate a double-height central prayer hall for 440 people (1,500 when combined with the courtyard). All exterior arches of the complex are glazed and covered with precast concrete screens, allowing ample light in while preventing spaces from getting overheated. Said's interpretation of the mosque is characterized not only by its abstracted forms, but also by a remarkable economy of construction means. The thin shells of the concrete vaults, for instance, were cast in place by reusing the same formwork multiple times.

Having studied architecture at the University of Liverpool in the early 1960s, Said later explicitly pointed to the influence of foreign modern architects—including Le Corbusier, Mies van der Rohe, and Louis I. Kahn—on his work. For projects like the "C" type mosque, he has further cited such heterogeneous design references as the work of the sixteenth-century Ottoman architect Sinan and the sense of movement embedded in Baroque architecture.[2] It is precisely through the negotiation of such external and internal vectors that Said's mosque types for the CDA sought to propose a pan-Islamic architecture of worship—and in doing so, to make a locally inflected version of modernism an integral part of Islamabad's daily life.[3]

Evangelos Kotsioris

---

1   Zahir-ud-Deen Khawaja, "The Importance of Mosque Design in the Urban Environment of Pakistan's New Capital—Islamabad," *Proceedings of Symposium on Mosque Architecture* vol. 3B, *The Urban Design of Mosques* (Riyadh, Saudi Arabia: College of Architecture & Planning, King Saud University, 1999), 59–70.
2   Anwar Said, "Ahle-Hadith Mosque G-6/1, Islamabad, 1975–1977," in *Anwar Said Architect: Complete Works* (self-pub., 2017), 102–9.
3   See Renata Holod and Hasan-Uddin Khan, *The Contemporary Mosque: Architects, Clients and Designs since the 1950s* (New York: Rizzoli, 1997), 121–4.

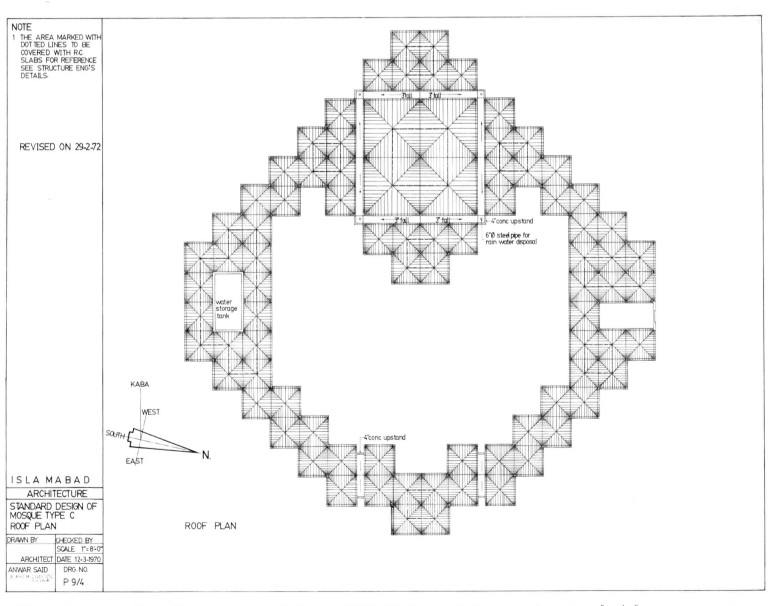

"C" Type Mosque (Ahle-Hadith Mosque), Islamabad, Pakistan. 1969–73/1975–77. Anwar Said (b. 1940). Roof plan. 1″ = 8′-0″. 1970–72. Ink and pencil on paper, 25 3/4 × 33 9/16 in. (65.4 × 84.4 cm). Courtesy Anwar Said

231

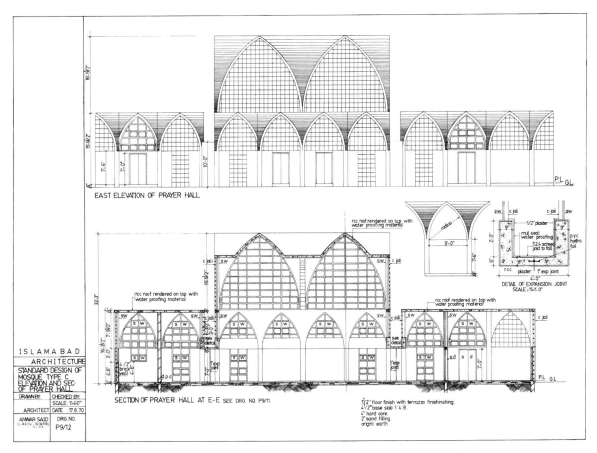

Elevation and section of the prayer hall. 1″ = 4′-0″. 1970. Ink and pencil on paper, 25 3/4 × 33 9/16 in. (65.4 × 84.4 cm). Courtesy Anwar Said

Exterior view. 1985. Photograph: Jacques Bétant. Aga Khan Trust for Culture

View to courtyard. 1985. Photograph: Jacques Bétant. Aga Khan Trust for Culture

Aerial view. 1985. Photograph: Jacques Bétant. Aga Khan Trust for Culture

NATIONAL COOPERATIVE DEVELOPMENT CORPORATION OFFICE BUILDING

Architect   Kuldip Singh (1934–2020)
Engineer   Mahendra Raj (b. 1924)
Built   1978–80
Location   New Delhi, India

In addition to his designs for a number of innovative multiunit housing projects, the New Delhi–based architect Kuldip Singh contributed to the modern transformation of his hometown with two iconic high-rise office towers: the headquarters of the National Cooperative Development Corporation (NCDC) and, completed a few years later, the formally related New Delhi Municipal Corporation (NDMC) Headquarters (Palika Kendra) (1973–83). Materialized in exposed concrete, like many of the institutional buildings of the post-Independence period in India, the two complexes were designed in conjunction with the structural engineer Mahendra Raj and are characterized by their expressive display of constructive principles. Boldly asserting their presence in New Delhi's rapidly expanding urban fabric—the NCDC tower being prominently located at the city's (colonial) core at Connaught Place and adjacent to the eighteenth-century Jantar Mantar observatory—the two high-rises embody the progressive spirit of government institutions and the techno-utopian belief in the state's power to transform and modernize society.

The NCDC Office Building (see Portfolio, no. 36) consists of two identical wings leaning against each other and conjoined toward the top, with a terraced arrangement of vertically staggered floors. This device not only makes the structure instantly recognizable through its highly idiosyncratic stepped profile but also alludes to the typology of the *gopuram*, a monumental entrance tower in traditional Dravidian temple architecture in southern India.[1] The design also brings to mind Kenzō Tange's buildings for the Tokyo Bay plan of 1967. While the building was not intentionally designed to be a symbolic representation of the client's mission, the NCDC's chairman considered its distinctive configuration of mutually supporting, upward-rising office floors to be a metaphor for the cooperative approach to development propagated by the agency.[2] All the floors have similar dimensions that allow for daylight exposure throughout, while a series of connecting walkways creates a continuous sense of space and ensures interior circulation within and between the two wings of the building. The building is predominantly glazed across its facades, and its side elevations are made up of monumental shear walls in exposed concrete, where the traces of the formwork provide an allover ornamental pattern and simultaneously expose the building's structural logic.

Singh's expressionist conceit is further articulated in the ostentatious display of the post-tensioned cable ends on the main facades, which function as latter-day triglyphs transposed to ferroconcrete construction. The structural tour de force underlying the building is evinced in Raj's many illuminating sketches and meticulous technical drawings. Besides the strong architectural expression of constructive logic, one of the building's main merits resides in the formation of a large, open, and publicly accessible space at its center, punctuated by a vertical core and a cylindrical staircase. In that regard, the NCDC building not only brings the institution in conversation with the public on a symbolic level but also literally provides shelter for it.

Martino Stierli

1   See Peter Scriver and Amit Srivastava, "National Cooperative Development Corporation (NCDC), New Delhi, India," in *SOS Brutalism: A Global Survey*, ed. Oliver Elser, Philip Kurz, and Peter Cachola Schmal (Zurich: Park Books, 2017), 329.
2   Ibid., 331.

National Cooperative Development Corporation (NCDC) Office Building, New Delhi, India. 1978–80. Architect: Kuldip Singh (1934–2020). Engineer: Mahendra Raj (b. 1924). Exterior view. 1981. Photograph: Madan Mahatta

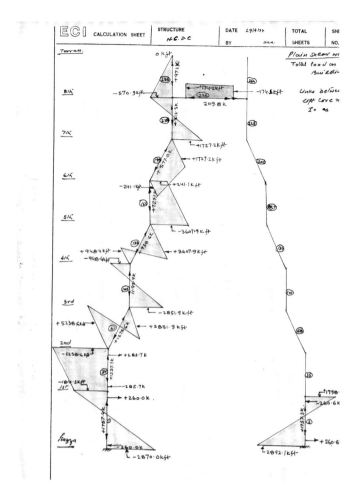

Calculation sheet. 1977. Mahendra Raj Archives

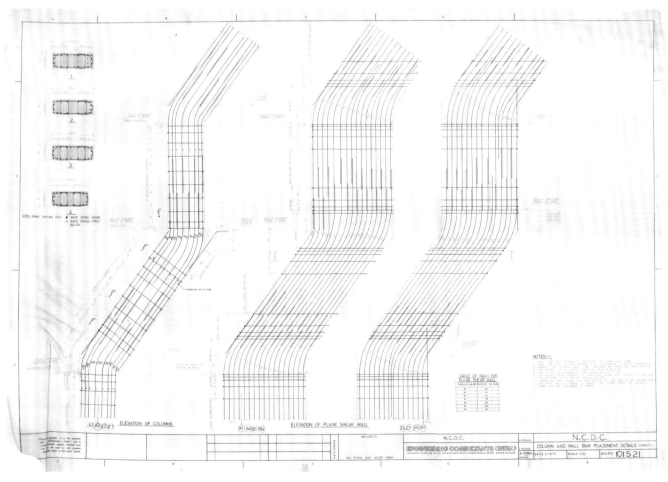

Elevation of plane shear walls and column details. 1:20. 1977. Ink and pencil on paper. Mahendra Raj Archives

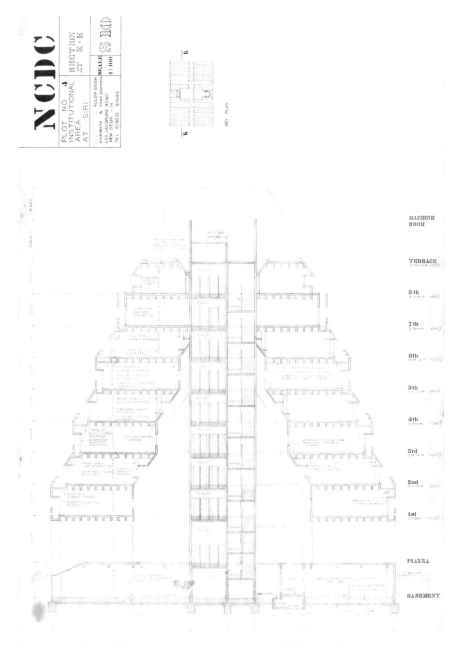

Section. 1:100. c. 1979. Ink and pencil on paper, 29 11/16 × 19 7/8 in. (74.5 × 50.5 cm). Musée National d'Art Moderne, Centre Georges Pompidou

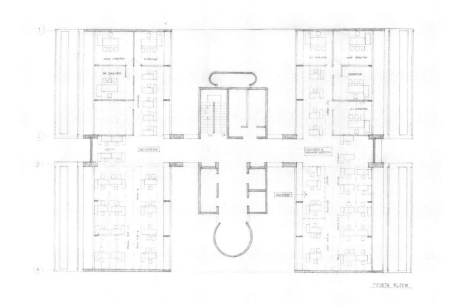

Fourth-floor plan. 1:100. 1979. Pencil on paper, 19 11/16 × 29 15/16 in. (50 x 76 cm). Musée National d'Art Moderne, Centre Georges Pompidou

CURATORIAL ADVISORY BOARD

Kazi Khaleed Ashraf
Anand Bhatt
Madhavi Desai
Ayesha Jalal
Farhan Karim
Ateya Khorakiwala
Rahul Mehrotra
Kaiwan Mehta
Adnan Z. Morshed
Ijlal Muzaffar
Vikramaditya Prakash
Peter Scriver
Devika Singh
Anooradha Iyer Siddiqi
Amit Srivastava
Riyaz Tayyibji
Mary N. Woods

LENDERS TO THE EXHIBITION

BANGLADESH
Muzharul Islam Archive

CANADA
Canadian Centre for Architecture

EGYPT
The American University in Cairo, Rare Books and Special
    Collections Library

FRANCE
Fondation Le Corbusier
Musée National d'Art Moderne, Centre Georges Pompidou

GREECE
Constantinos A. Doxiadis Archives

INDIA
Sri Aurobindo Ashram Trust
Auroville Foundation
Centre for Environmental Planning and Technology
Charles Correa Foundation
Films Division
Kiran Nadar Museum of Art
Kanvinde Rai & Chowdhury
National Institute of Design
PHOTOINK
Ram Rahman
Mahendra Raj Archives
David and Ethan Stein
Swaraj Art Archive
Vāstu Shilpā Foundation Archives

ISRAEL
Ulrik Plesner Archives

PAKISTAN
Anwar Said

SRI LANKA
The Lunuganga Trust (Geoffrey Bawa Trust)

SWITZERLAND
Aga Khan Foundation

UNITED KINGDOM
The Royal Institute of British Architects

UNITED STATES
The Architectural Archives, University of Pennsylvania
Jeffrey M. Chusid
Surane Gunasekara
Anuradha Mathur

SELECTED BIBLIOGRAPHY

PRIMARY SOURCES

Anand, Mulk Raj. "Planning and Dreaming." *Marg* 1, no. 1 (October 1946): 3–6.

"Architecture and You." *Marg* 1, no. 1 (October 1946): 7–16.

Ashraf, Kazi Khaleed, ed. *An Architect in Bangladesh: Conversations with Muzharul Islam*. Dhaka: Loka, 2014.

Ashraf, Kazi Khaleed, and Saif Ul Haque, eds. *Vastukatha: Selected Sayings of Architect Muzharul Islam*. Dhaka: Bengal Institute, 2019.

Baker, Laurie. "Cementlessness." *Hindustan Times* (New Delhi), November 4, 1974.

———. "Teachings and Travel Writings." *a+u: Architecture and Urbanism*, no. 363 (December 2000): 4–8.

Bawa, Geoffrey. "Ceylon: A Philosophy of Building." *Architects' Journal* 150, no. 42 (October 15, 1969): 939–41.

Bhatia, Gautam. *Laurie Baker: Life, Works & Writings*. New Delhi: Penguin, 1991.

Correa, Charles. "A Place in the Sun." *Journal of the Royal Society of Arts* 131, no. 5,322 (May 1983): 328–40.

———. "The Assembly, Chandigarh." *Architectural Review*, June 1964, 404–12.

———. *Housing and Urbanization*. Mumbai: Urban Design Research Institute, 1999.

———. "Programmes and Priorities." *Architectural Review*, December 1971, 329–31.

Correa, Charles, Pravina Mehta, and Shirish B. Patel, eds. "Bombay: Planning and Dreaming." Special issue, *Marg* 18, no. 3 (June 1965).

Doshi, Balkrishna V. *Paths Uncharted*. Ahmedabad, India: Mapin, 2019.

———. *Writings on Architecture & Identity*. Edited by Simone Vera Bader. Berlin: ArchiTangle, 2020.

Doxiadis Associates. "Islamabad: Programme and Plan." 2 vols. Report no. 32, DOX-PA 88 (September 30, 1961).

———. "On Architecture in Islamabad." Report no. 56, DOX-PA 115 (April 22, 1961).

Doxiadis, Constantinos A. *Ekistics: An Introduction to the Science of Human Settlements*. London: Hutchinson, 1968.

Eames, Charles and Ray. *The India Report* (1958). Ahmedabad, India: National Institute of Design, 1997.

Fry, Maxwell, and Jane Drew. *Tropical Architecture in the Dry and Humid Zones*. New York: R. E. Krieger, 1974.

Giedion, Sigfried. "The Regional Approach." *Architectural Record* 115, no. 1 (January 1954): 132–37.

Kanvinde, Achyut, ed. *Seminar on Architecture*. New Delhi: Lalit Kala Akademi, 1959.

Kanvinde, Achyut, and H. James Miller. *Campus Design in India: Experience of a Developing Nation*. Topeka, KS: Jostens, 1969.

Kanvinde, Tanuja, and Sanjay Kanvinde, eds. *Achyut Kanvinde: Ākār*. New Delhi: Niyogi, 2017.

Khan, Hasan-Uddin. "Profile: Yasmeen Lari." *Mimar*, no. 2 (1981): 45–54.

Khan, Nurur Rahman. *Muzharul Islam: Selected Drawings*. [Dhaka:] Sthapattya O Nirman, 2010.

Koenigsberger, Otto, T. G. Ingersoll, and Alan Mayhew. *Manual of Tropical Housing and Building: Climatic Design*. London, Longman, 1974.

Lari, Yasmeen. "The Lines Area Resettlement Project, Karachi." In *Urban Housing*, 56–64. Edited by Margaret Bentley Ševčenko. Designing in Islamic Cultures 2. Cambridge, MA: Aga Khan Program for Islamic Architecture, 1982.

Nehru, Jawaharlal. *Jawaharlal Nehru's Speeches*, 5 vols. New Delhi: Ministry of Information and Broadcasting, 1958–68.

Plesner, Ulrik. *In Situ: An Architectural Memoir from Sri Lanka*. Copenhagen: Aristo, 2012.

———. "On His Work as an Architect on Sri Lanka." *Living Architecture*, no. 5 (1986): 84–87.

Powell, Robert, ed. *Regionalism in Architecture*. Geneva: Aga Khan Award for Architecture, 1985.

Prakash, Aditya. "Human Settlements: A Self-Sustaining Approach." *Ekistics* 46, no. 278 (September–October 1979): 305–13.

———. "Working with the Master." *Inside Outside*, no. 40 (April–May 1985): 46–50.

Rahman, Ram. *Sunil Janah: Photographs 1940–1960; Vintage Prints from the Swaraj Art Archive*. Noida, India: Swaraj Art Archive, 2014.

de Silva, Minnette. "A House at Kandy, Ceylon." *Marg* 6, no. 3 (June 1953): 4–11.

———. *The Life & Work of an Asian Woman Architect*. Colombo: Smart Media Productions, 1998.

Stein, Joseph Allen, N. H. Ramachandran, and Geeti Sen. "The India International Centre: Concept and Design: Joseph Allen Stein in Conversation with N. H. Ramachandran and Geeti Sen." *India International Centre Quarterly* 22, no. 4 (Winter 1995): 118–28.

GENERAL REFERENCES

Anderson, Perry. *The Indian Ideology*. London: Verso, 2013.

Appadurai, Arjun. *Modernity at Large: Cultural Dimensions of Globalization*. Minneapolis: Minnesota University Press, 1996.

Bhabha, Homi K. *The Location of Culture*. New York: Routledge, 1994.

Breckenridge, Carol A., Sheldon Pollock, Homi K. Bhabha, and Dipesh Chakrabarty, eds. *Cosmopolitanism*. Durham, NC: Duke University Press, 2002.

Brown, Rebecca M. *Art for a Modern India, 1947–1980*. Durham, NC: Duke University Press, 2009.

Chakrabarty, Dipesh. *Provincializing Europe: Postcolonial Thought and Historical Difference*. With a new preface by the author. Princeton, NJ: Princeton University Press, 2008.

Chopra, Preeti. *A Joint Enterprise: Indian Elites and the Making of British Bombay*. Minneapolis: University of Minnesota Press, 2011.

Curtis, William J. R. "Modernism and the Search for Indian Identity." *Architectural Review*, August 1987, 32–38.

Dadi, Iftikhar. *Modernism and the Art of Muslim South Asia*. Chapel Hill: University of North Carolina Press, 2010.

Datta, Nonica, *Violence, Martyrdom and Partition: A Daughter's Testimony*. New Delhi: Oxford University Press, 2009.

French, Patrick. *Liberty or Death: India's Journey to Independence and Division*. London: Flamingo, 1998.

Getachew, Adom. *Worldmaking after Empire: The Rise and Fall of Self-Determination*. Princeton, NJ: Princeton University Press, 2019.

Gupta, Atreyee. "Dwelling in Abstraction: Post-Partition Segues into Post-War Art." *Third Text* 31, nos. 2–3 (March–May 2017): 9–17.

Khilnani, Sunil. *The Idea of India*. New York: Farrar, Straus and Giroux, 1997.

Mathur, Saloni. *India by Design: Colonial History and Cultural Display*. Berkeley: University of California Press, 2007.

Mitter, Partha. *The Triumph of Modernism: India's Artists and the Avant-Garde, 1922–1947*. London: Reaktion, 2007.

Muzaffar, M. Ijlal. "The Periphery Within: Modern Architecture and the Making of the Third World." PhD dissertation, Massachusetts Institute of Technology, 2007.

Perera, Nihal. *Society and Space: Colonialism, Nationalism, and Postcolonial Identity in Sri Lanka*. Boulder, CO: Westview, 1998.

Said, Edward W. *Orientalism*. New York: Pantheon, 1978.

Sharma, Alpana. "Decolonizing the Modernist Mind." *South Asian Review* 33, no. 1 (July 2012): 13–29.

Talbot, Ian. *A History of Modern South Asia: Politics, States, Diasporas*. New Haven, CT: Yale University Press, 2016.

Zamindar, Vazira Fazila-Yacoobali. *The Long Partition and the Making of South Asia: Refugees, Boundaries, Histories*. New York: Columbia University Press, 2010.

ARCHITECTURE: GENERAL REFERENCES AND SURVEYS

Ashraf, Kazi K. *The Hermit's Hut: Architecture and Asceticism in India*. Honolulu: University of Hawai'i Press, 2013.

Bhatt, Vikram, and Peter Scriver. *After the Masters: Contemporary Indian Architecture*. Ahmedabad, India: Mapin, 1990.

Bozdogan, Sibel. "Orientalism and Architectural Culture." *Social Scientist* 14, no. 7 (July 1986): 46–58.

Brown, Rebecca M. "Reviving the Past: Post-Independence Architecture and Politics in India's Long 1950s." *Interventions* 11, no. 3 (2009): 293–315.

Chang, Jiat-Hwee. *A Genealogy of Tropical Architecture: Colonial Networks, Nature and Technoscience*. London: Routledge, 2016.

Chattopadhyay, Swati. "India." In *Encyclopedia of Twentieth Century Architecture*. Vol 2, *G–O*, 673–74. Edited by R. Stephen Sennott. New York: Fitzroy Dearborn, 2004.

Desai, Madhavi. *Women Architects and Modernism in India: Narratives and Contemporary Practices*. London: Routledge, 2017.

Dutta, Arindam. *The Bureaucracy of Beauty: Design in the Age of Its Global Reproducibility*. New York: Routledge, 2006.

Elser, Oliver, Philip Kurz, and Peter Cachola Schmal, eds. *SOS Brutalism: A Global Survey*. Zurich: Park Books, 2017.

Forty, Adrian. *Concrete and Culture: A Material History*. London: Reaktion, 2012.

Frampton, Kenneth, and Rahul Mehrotra, eds. *World Architecture 1900–2000: A Critical Mosaic*, vol. 8, *South Asia*. Vienna: Springer, 2000.

Ghose, Rajeshwari. "Design, Development, Culture, and Cultural Legacies in Asia." *Design Issues* 6, no. 1 (Fall 1989): 31–48.

Guha, Sudeshna. "Decolonizing South Asia through Heritage- and Nation-Building." *Future Anterior* 16, no. 2 (Winter 2019): 30–45.

Haque, Saif Ul. "Towards a Regional Identity: The Evolution of Contemporary Architecture in Bangladesh." *Architecture + Design* 4, no. 4 (May–June 1988): 24–45.

Holod, Renata, ed. *Architecture and Community: Building in the Islamic World Today—The Aga Khan Award for Architecture*. Millerton, NY: Aperture, 1983.

Holod, Renata, and Hasan-Uddin Khan. *The Contemporary Mosque: Architects, Clients and Designs since the 1950s*. New York: Rizzoli, 1997.

Hosagrahar, Jyoti. *Indigenous Modernities: Negotiating Architecture and Urbanism*. London: Routledge, 2005.

———. "South Asia: Looking Back, Moving Ahead; History and Modernization." *Journal of the Society of Architectural Historians* 61, no. 3 (September 2002): 355–69.

Jazeel, Tariq. "Tropical Modernism/Environmental Nationalism: Politics of Built Space in Postcolonial Sri Lanka." *Fabrications* 27, no. 2 (2017): 134–52.

Kagal, Carmen, ed. *Vistāra: The Architecture of India*. Bombay: Tata Press, 1986.

Karim, Farhan. *Of Greater Dignity than Riches: Austerity & Housing Design in India*, Pittsburgh, PA: University of Pittsburgh Press, 2019

Khan, Hasan-Uddin. "Developing Discourses on Architecture: The Aga Khan Award for Architecture, the Journal *Mimar: Architecture in Development*, and Other Adventures." *Journal of Architectural Education* 62, no. 2 (March 2010): 82–84.

Kumar, Ashok, Sanjeev Vidyarthi, and Poonam Prakash. *City Planning in India, 1947–2017*. London: Routledge, 2021.

Lang, Jon, Madhavi Desai, and Miki Desai. *Architecture & Independence: The Search for Identity—India 1880 to 1980*. New Delhi: Oxford University Press, 1997.

Lee, Rachel, and Kathleen James-Chakraborty. "*Marg* Magazine: A Tryst with Architectural Modernity,"*ABE Journal*, no. 1 (2012), https://doi.org/10.4000/abe.623.

Le Roux, Hannah, "The Networks of Tropical Architecture." In *Narrating Architecture: A Retrospective Anthology*, 379–97. Edited by James Madge and Andrew Peckham. London: Routledge, 2006.

Levin, Ayala. "Beyond Global vs. Local: Tipping the Scales of Architectural Historiography," *ABE Journal*, no. 8 (2015), https://doi.org/10.4000/abe.10869.

Lim, William Siew Wai, and Jiat-Hwee Chang, eds. *Non West Modernist Past: On Architecture & Modernities*. Singapore: World Scientific, 2011.

Lu, Duanfang, ed. *Third World Modernism: Architecture, Development and Identity*. London: Routledge, 2011.

Mehrotra, Rahul. *Architecture in India since 1990*. Mumbai: Pictor, 2011.

Mehrotra, Rahul, and Kaiwan Mehta. *State of Housing*, vol. 1, *Aspirations, Imaginaries and Realities in India*. Mumbai: Spenta, 2018.

Mumtaz, Kamil Khan. *Modernity and Tradition: Contemporary Architecture in Pakistan*. Karachi: Oxford University Press, 1999.

Pieris, Anoma. *Architecture and Nationalism in Sri Lanka: The Trouser under the Cloth*. London: Routledge, 2012.

———. "South and Southeast Asia: The Postcolonial Legacy." *Fabrications* 19, no. 2 (2010): 6–33.

Prakash, Vikramaditya, Maristella Casciato, and Daniel E. Coslett, eds., *Rethinking Global Modernism: Architectural Historiography and the Postcolonial*. New York: Routledge, 2022.

Rewal, Raj, Jean-Louis Véret, and Ram Sharma, eds. *Architecture in India*. Paris: Electa Moniteur, 1985.

Scriver, Peter, and Vikramaditya Prakash eds. *Colonial Modernities: Building, Dwelling and Architecture in British India and Ceylon*. London: Routledge, 2007.

Scriver, Peter, and Amit Srivastava. *India. Modern Architectures in History*. London: Reaktion, 2015.

Shikoh, Murtuza, and Zain Mankani. *Architecture after Independence: 55 Architects of Pakistan*. Karachi: Arch Press, 2016.

Srivastava, Amit. "The Struggle with Modernity, 1870s–1920s." In *A Work of Beauty: The Architecture & Landscape of Rashtrapati Bhavan*, 44–61. Edited by Narayani Gupta. New Delhi: Sahapedia, 2016.

Subramanian, Ajantha. *The Caste of Merit: Engineering Education in India*. Cambridge, MA: Harvard University Press, 2019.

Tuck, Eve, and K. Wayne Yang. "Decolonization is Not a Metaphor." *Decolonization: Indigeneity, Education & Society* 1, no. 1 (2012): 1–40.

Woods, Mary N. *Women Architects in India: Histories of Practice in Mumbai and Delhi*. London: Routledge, 2017.

ARCHITECTURE: CITIES/PROJECTS/ARCHITECTS

Ali, Zainab F., and Fuad H. Mallick. *Muzharul Islam, Architect*. Dhaka: Brac University Press, 2011.

Ashraf, Kazi Khaleed. "Muzharul Islam, Kahn and Architecture in Bangladesh." *Mimar*, no. 31 (March 1989): 55–63.

Ashraf, Kazi Khaleed, and James Belluardo, eds. *An Architecture of Independence: The Making of Modern South Asia; Charles Correa, Balkrishna Doshi, Muzharul Islam, Achyut Kanvinde*. New York: Princeton Architectural Press, 1998.

Avermaete, Tom, and Maristella Casciato. *Casablanca Chandigarh: A Report on Modernization*. Zurich: Park Books, 2014.

Baweja, Vandana. "Otto Koenigsberger and Modernist Historiography." *Fabrications* 26, no. 2 (2016): 202–26.

Bittner, Regina, and Kathrin Rhomberg. *The Bauhaus in Calcutta: An Encounter of Cosmopolitan Avant-Gardes*. Ostfildern, Germany: Hatje Cantz, 2013.

Chattopadhyay, Swati. *Representing Calcutta: Modernity, Nationalism, and the Colonial Uncanny*. London: Routledge, 2005.

Chusid, Jeffrey M. *An Innocent Abroad: Joseph Stein in India*. Occasional Publication 18. New Delhi: India International Centre, 2010.

———. "Joseph Allen Stein's Experiments in Concrete in the U.S. and India." *APT Bulletin: The Journal of Preservation Technology* 48, no.1 (2017): 23–31.

Daechsel, Markus. *Islamabad and the Politics of International Development in Pakistan*. Cambridge, UK: Cambridge University Press, 2015.

Damluji, Salma Samar, and Viola Bertini. *Hassan Fathy: Earth & Utopia*. London: Laurence King, 2018.

Das, Samit. *Architecture of Santiniketan: Tagore's Concept of Space*. New Delhi: Niyogi, 2003.

Deulgaonkar, Atul. *Laurie Baker: Truth in Architecture*. Pune, India: Jyotsna Prakashan, 2015.

Falvo, Rosa Maria, and Ramprasad Akkisetti, eds. *Christopher Benninger: Architecture for Modern India*. Milan: Skira, 2015.

Glover, William J. *Making Lahore Modern: Constructing and Imagining a Colonial City*. Minneapolis: University of Minnesota Press, 2008.

Guerrieri, Pilar Maria. *Negotiating Cultures: Delhi's Architecture and Planning from 1912 to 1962*. New Delhi: Oxford University Press, 2018.

Gupta, Pankaj Vir, Christine Mueller, and Cyrus Samii. *Golconde: The Introduction of Modernism in India*. 2010. 2nd ed. New York: Actar, 2021.

Ismail, Mohamed A., and Caitlin T. Mueller, "Engineering a New Nation: Mahendra Raj and His Collaborations Across Disciplines." In *Black Box: Articulating Architecture's Core in the Post-Digital Era*, 562–66. 107th ACSA Annual Meeting Proceedings. Edited by Jeremy Ficca, Amy Kulper, and Grace La. Washington, DC: Association of Collegiate Schools of Architecture, 2019.

Jadeja, Hiralba. "Architecture of Habib Rahman: A Critical Inquiry into the Reinterpretation of His Early Influences into the Context of India." Undergraduate thesis, CEPT University, Ahmedabad, 2013.

Jayewardene, Shanti. *Geoffrey Manning Bawa: Decolonizing Architecture*. Colombo: National Trust Sri Lanka, 2017.

Jazeel, Tariq. *Beyond Bawa: Modern Masterworks of Monsoon Asia*. London: Thames & Hudson, 2007.

Jones, Robin. "'Thinking' the Domestic Interior in Postcolonial South Asia: The Home of Geoffrey Bawa in Sri Lanka, 1960 to 1998." *Interiors* 3, no. 3 (2012): 203–26.

Kahn, Nathaniel, Raymond Meier, and William Whitaker, eds. *Louis Kahn Dhaka: Construction*. Zurich: Dino Simonett, 2004.

Kalia, Ravi. *Chandigarh: The Making of an Indian City*. New Delhi: Oxford University Press, 1988.

———. *Gandhinagar: Building National Identity in Postcolonial India*. Columbia: University of South Carolina Press, 2004.

Kanvinde, Vindra. "Tracing Architectural Authorship through the Archive of Indian Modernist Achyut Kanvinde." Master's thesis, Harvard University, 2021.

Karim, Farhan. "Between Self and Citizenship: Doxiadis Associates in Postcolonial Pakistan, 1958–1968." *International Journal of Islamic Architecture* 5, no. 1 (March 2016): 135–61.

Karim, Farhan Sirajul. "MoMA, the Ulm and the Development of Design Pedagogy in India." In *Western Artists and India: Creative Inspirations in Art and Design*, 122–39. Edited by Shanay Jhaveri and Devika Singh. London: Shoestring, 2013.

Khan, Hasan-Uddin, ed. *Charles Correa*. Singapore: Concept Media, 1987.

Kreutzmann, Hermann. "Islamabad: Living with the Plan." *Südasien-Chronik/South Asia Chronicle*, no. 3 (2013): 135–60.

Kries, Mateo, Khushnu Panthaki Hoof, and Jolanthe Kugler, eds. *Balkrishna Doshi: Architecture for the People*. Weil am Rhein, Germany: Vitra Design Museum, 2019.

Lee, Rachel. "Constructing a Shared Vision: Otto Koenigsberger and Tata & Sons." *ABE Journal*, no. 2 (2012), https://doi.org/10.4000/abe.356.

Mahsud, Ahmed Zaib Khan. "Rethinking Doxiadis' Ekistical Urbanism." *Positions*, no. 1 (Spring 2010): 6–39.

Mathur, Saloni. "Charles and Ray Eames in India." *Art Journal* 70, no. 1 (Spring 2011): 34–53.

Mankani, Zain. *Mehdi Ali Mirza: Pioneer of Architecture in Pakistan, 1910–1962*. Karachi: ARCH Press, 2012.

Mehta, Vandini, Rohit Raj Mehndiratta, and Ariel Huber, eds. *The Structure: Works of Mahendra Raj*. Zurich: Park Books, 2016.

Misra, Manjusha. "Laurie Baker's Contribution to the Continuation of Vernacular Architecture in India." *International Journal of Environmental Studies* 73, no. 4 (August 2016): 631–50.

Moffat, Chris. "Building, Dwelling, Dying: Architecture and History in Pakistan." *Modern Intellectual History* 18, no. 2 (June 2021): 520–46.

von Moos, Stanislaus, ed. *Chandigarh 1956: Le Corbusier, Pierre Jeanneret, Jane B. Drew, E. Maxwell Fry; Photographs by Ernst Scheidegger*. Zurich: Scheidegger & Spiess, 2010.

Morshed, Adnan. "Modernism as Postnationalist Politics: Muzharul Islam's Faculty of Fine Arts (1953–56)." *Journal of the Society of Architectural Historians* 76, no. 4 (December 2017): 543–49.

Naz, Neelum. "Development of Architectural Education in Pakistan: A Historical Perspective." *Global Built Environment Review* 7, no. 1 (2010): 31–42.

Pieris, Anoma. *Imagining Modernity: The Architecture of Valentine Gunasekara*. Colombo: Stamford Lake, 2007.

Pillai, Jayesh S., ed. *Masterpiece of a Master Architect: Centre for Development Studies*. Thrissur, India: COSTFORD, 2014.

Prakash, Vikramaditya. *Chandigarh's Le Corbusier: The Struggle for Modernity in Postcolonial India*. Seattle: University of Washington Press, 2002.

———, ed. *One Continuous Line: Art, Architecture and Urbanism of Aditya Prakash*. Ahmedabad, India: Mapin, 2020.

Rahman, Ram. "Habib Rahman: A Bauhaus Legacy in India." *Bauhaus Imaginista* website, November 4, 2019. http://www.bauhaus-imaginista.org/articles/6220/habib-rahman.

Rahman, Tariq L. "Enabling Development: A Housing Scheme in Rural Pakistan." Master's thesis, University of Oregon, 2016.

Rajagopalan, Mrinalini. *Building Histories: The Archival and Affective Lives of Five Monuments in Modern Delhi*. Chicago: University of Chicago Press, 2016.

Ramzi, Shanaz. "Retrospective: Yasmeen Lari" *Architectural Review*, September 2019, 16–25.

Rewal, Raj, Peter Davey, Kenneth Frampton, Suha Ozkan, and Suparna Rajguru. *Raj Rewal: Innovative Architecture and Tradition*. Noida, India: Om Books International, 2013.

Richards, James Maude, Ismail Serageldin, and Darl Rastorfer. *Hassan Fathy*. Singapore: Concept Media, 1985.

Robson, David. *Geoffrey Bawa: The Complete Works*. London: Thames & Hudson, 2002.

Robson, David, and Channa Daswatte. "Serendib Serendipity: The Architecture of Geoffrey Bawa." *AA Files*, no. 35 (Spring 1998): 32–33.

Said, Anwar, ed. *Anwar Said Architect: Complete Works*. Self-published, 2017.

Sane, Prajakta. "Modern Temples for Post-Independence India: Institutional Architecture of Achyut Kanvinde." PhD thesis, University of New South Wales, 2016, http://unsworks.unsw.edu.au/fapi/datastream/unsworks:40403/SOURCE02.

Shaw, Annapurna. "Town Planning in Postcolonial India, 1947–1965: Chandigarh Re-Examined." *Urban Geography* 3, no. 8 (November 2009): 857–78.

Siddiqi, Anooradha Iyer. "Crafting the Archive: Minnette de Silva, Architecture, and History." *Journal of Architecture* 22, no. 8 (2017): 1299–336.

Singh, Devika. "Approaching the Mughal Past in Indian Art Criticism: The Case of *MARG* (1946–1963)." *Modern Asian Studies* 47, no. 1 (January 2013): 167–203.

Steele, James. *The Complete Architecture of Balkrishna Doshi: Rethinking Modernism for the Developing World*. London: Thames & Hudson, 1998.

Taylor, Brian Brace. *Geoffrey Bawa*. Singapore: Concept Media, 1986.

Tironi, Giordano. *Humanisme et architecture: Raj Rewal, construire pour la ville indienne*. Lausanne, Switzerland: L'Âge d'Homme, 2013.

"Tribute: Habib Rahman, 1915–1995" Special issue, *Architecture + Design* 13, no. 2 (March–April 1996).

Ubbelohde, M. Susan. "The Dance of a Summer Day: Le Corbusier's Sarabhai House in Ahmedabad, India." *Traditional Dwellings and Settlements Review* 14, no. 2 (Spring 2003): 65–80.

Williamson, Daniel. "Modern Architecture and Capitalist Patronage in Ahmedabad, India, 1947–1969." PhD thesis, New York University, 2016.

ACKNOWLEDGMENTS

An endeavor with the range and complexity of *The Project of Independence: Architectures of Decolonization in South Asia, 1947–1985* would not be possible without the input and support of a great number of individuals both inside and outside the Museum. We owe our profound thanks to all of them.

During the many years of research that accompanied the formation of this project, we were aided by numerous individuals who helped us gain access to architects and sometimes difficult-to-find buildings. Of particular importance was the opportunity to explore South Asian modern architecture on the occasion of a series of trips to the region, starting in early 2016, organized through MoMA's Contemporary and Modern Art Perspectives (C-MAP) program. Our heartfelt thanks go to Jay A. Levenson, Director, International Program, and Carol Coffin, Executive Director, International Council, as well as to Rattanamol Singh Johal, former C-MAP Fellow for Asia, who was a knowledgeable travel companion and instrumental in making it possible to visit numerous sites.

For guiding us through multiple cities and locations on various visits to India, we are particularly indebted to Gautam Bhatia, Devika Daulet-Singh at PHOTOINK, Nigar Gajjar at the Sarabhai Foundation, Salima Hashmi, Khushnu Panthaki Hoof at the Vāstu Shilpā Foundation, Aparajita Jain, Shanay Jhaveri, Tanishka Kachru and Shreyasi Parikh at the National Institute of Design, Geeta Kapur, Saman Quraishi and Kartikeya Shodhan at CEPT University, Ram Rahman, Arun Rewal, Dipti and Dattaraj V. Salgaocar, Seher Shah, Tejal Shah, Dayanita Sinha, Gayatri Sinha, Vivan Sundaram, and Gayatri Uppal. Moreover, we thank Jeffrey M. Chusid and Prajakta Sane for providing valuable references, and Projjal Dutta for his introduction to Ethan and David Stein at the Joseph Allen Stein Collection.

In Pakistan, we were warmly welcomed and helped by various representatives of the Institute of Architects, Pakistan, including Faisal Arshad, Ramiz Baig, Arif Changezi, Mariam Nabi, Umar Saeed, and Wasim Shekhani. We are further indebted to Nayyar Ali Dada, Raza Ali Dada, Farida Ghaffar, Adil Kerai, Saad Mahmood Khan, Kamil Khan Mumtaz, Naeem Pasha, Shazia Qureshi, Qudsia Rahim, Mahwish Khawja Ghulam Rasool, Anwar Said, Syed Faisal Sajjad, and Murtuza Shikoh.

In Bangladesh, we are greatly indebted to Diana Campbell Betancourt for her introduction to Bangladeshi modern and contemporary architecture, and to Nurur Rahman Khan, Director, Muzharul Islam Archive at the University of Asia Pacific.

In Sri Lanka, we are especially grateful to the Board and Trustees of the Geoffrey Bawa and Lunuganga Trusts. We thank, in particular, Shayari de Silva, Curator of Art and Archival Collections, as well as Channa Daswatte, Shanth and Saskia Fernando, Ajit Gunewardene, Annoushka Hempel, Amila de Mel, Milinda Pathiraja, Suhanya Raffel, Rohan de Soysa, Chandragupta Thenuwara, and Jagath Weerasinghe for their commitment to the exhibition.

The following parties have been instrumental in providing images for the catalogue and the exhibition: Ashfaq Ahmad and Yasmeen Lari at the Heritage Foundation of Pakistan, Robert G. Boughey, Kate Dunham, Isabelle Griffiths at the Aga Khan Trust for Culture, Rafique Islam, Kiran Kakad and Manoj Das Gupta at the Sri Aurobindo Ashram, Rohit Raj Mehndiratta, Meg Partridge at the Rondal Partridge Archives, Helga Perera, Maya and Daniela Plesner, Sebastian Posingis, Raj Rewal, David Robson, and Dominic Sansoni.

The numerous interactions with the members of our curatorial advisory board (see p. 238) along the way were essential in shaping the overarching thesis and narrative of our project. Several members of this group met for an initial workshop in New York in November 2018, followed by another in January 2019 in Colombo, Sri Lanka. We are indebted to all those who participated in these study days for their invaluable insights, and to Jocelyn Wong, a former Curatorial Assistant in MoMA's Department of Architecture and Design, for smoothly organizing them. In addition, a number of individuals generously shared knowledge and opinions that allowed us to further refine the project's aspirations. We are particularly grateful to Homi K. Bhabha, Swati Chattopadhyay, Farrokh Derakhshani, Frank Escher, Ravi GuneWardena, Jyoti Hosagrahar, Kathleen James-Chakraborty, Ram Rahman, Anooradha Iyer Siddiqi, and Vazira F-Y Zamindar.

*The Project of Independenc*e provided an opportunity to produce a number of newly built models in collaboration with the Irwin S. Chanin School of Architecture at The Cooper Union. We are greatly indebted to Dean Nader Tehrani and former Associate Dean Elizabeth O'Donnell for their unwavering and enthusiastic support of this undertaking, as well as to James Lowder for directing the class. The models were built over the course ofcountless hours by the following students, and we are in awe of their dedication and persistence throughout the coronavirus pandemic and many months of remote learning: Risako Arcari, Taesha Aurora, Jesse Bassett, Javier Blancas, Bo Cai, Thomas Choi, Junmin Chung, Tilok Costa,

Claudia D'Auria, Samuel Dobens, Xinyi Guo, Jiwon Heo, Isaac Islas-Cox, Mudong Jung, Sanjana Lahiri, Maksymilian Mamak, Jyhun Park, Fredrick Rapp, Karim Sabry, Hyun Woo Song, Maren Speyer, Tracy Tan, Brandy Vazquez, and Wei Hong Xie.

We are grateful to Randhir Singh, from whom we commissioned a set of contemporary photographs illustrating a selection of modern South Asia's outstanding architectural achievements, which he took during a number of field trips throughout the region. His task was complicated not only because of the political realities in the region, but also on account of the severe impact of the pandemic, as a result of which many key buildings in Sri Lanka and Pakistan could not be included. We are immensely thankful for his persistence in surmounting many obstacles in order to present us with a compelling portfolio of images.

The vast majority of the materials presented in this book and the accompanying exhibition come from a substantial number of generous lenders on three continents, both institutional and private. We are deeply indebted to their tireless efforts to secure the most outstanding representations of modern architecture from the region, once again under often unideal and complicated pandemic circumstances. In addition, we thank Balsam Abdul-Rahman and Ola Seif at the American University in Cairo; Elaine Catherine Phillips at the Auroville Town Development Council; Raphaële Bianchi and Frédéric Migayrou at the Centre Pompidou; Surane Gunasekara; Dominique Jahn and Ann-Marie Wieckhorst at the Vitra Design Museum (who arranged the exhibits on loan from the Vāstu Shilpā Foundation); Charles Hind at the RIBA British Architectural Library; Sanjay Kanvinde at the Kanvinde Archives; Anupama Kundoo; Anuradha Mathur; Nondita Correa Mehrotra and Tahir Noronha at the Charles Correa Foundation; Kiran Nadar and Roobina Karode at the Kiran Nadar Museum of Art; Giota Pavlidou at the Constantinos A. Doxiadis Archives; Prarthana Tagore at the Swaraj Art Archive; Martien de Vletter at the Canadian Centre for Architecture; and William Whitaker at the Architectural Archives, University of Pennsylvania.

This project would not have come to fruition without the extraordinary dedication of many colleagues in various departments across The Museum of Modern Art. We are deeply grateful to Glenn D. Lowry, for his initial enthusiasm and consistent support and guidance of this project, as well as Ramona Bannayan, former Senior Deputy Director of Exhibitions and Collections, for her steady hand. The following colleagues and their teams made key contributions to the success of this project, and we owe them our sincere thanks: Aimee Keefer for her compelling exhibition design,

Margaret Aldredge-Diamond from Exhibition Planning & Administration for managing the project, Registrar Sacha Eaton for guaranteeing a smooth installation, Conservators Lee Ann Daffner, Roger Griffith, Erika Mosier, and Lynda Zycherman for their meticulous attention to the manifold objects on view, and Tom Krueger and his team of art handlers for putting everything in the galleries in perfect place with great care. Stephanie Katsias, Jack Spielsinger, and Meg Montgoris from Communications were instrumental in conveying our curatorial vision to the media and the outside world.

This book is owed not least to the tireless efforts and great care of our colleagues in the Department of Publications. We are greatly indebted to Don McMahon, Editorial Director; Marc Sapir, Production Director; Hannah Kim, Business and Marketing Director; Curtis Scott, Associate Publisher; Naomi Falk, Rights Coordinator; and Sophie Golub, Department Manager. We owe particular thanks not only to the authors but also to Alexander Scrimgeour, who edited the essays assembled in this volume with extraordinary attention to detail and provided numerous suggestions that greatly improved the coherence of the argument. We are also deeply grateful to the anonymous peer reviewer for their incisive comments on the originally submitted manuscripts, as well as to the members of Studio Lin for their congenial book design.

We owe our utmost gratitude to the members of the Department of Architecture and Design, who were the mainstay of the entire project throughout the long period of its gestation. Assistant Curator Evangelos Kotsioris not only oversaw the logistics of this complex undertaking with great professionalism and dedication, but also proved an invaluable interlocutor in many conceptual conversations. Former C-MAP Fellow for Asia Prajna Desai, Mellon-Marron Research Consortium Fellows Da Hyung Jeong and Y. L. Lucy Wang, and former Curatorial Assistant Arièle Dionne-Krosnick provided deep research and assisted in many tasks along the way, as did twelve-month interns Pooja Annamaneni and Aaron Smithson, along with seasonal interns Neha Garg, Larissa Guimarães, Mayuri Paranthahan, Jean Wong, and Virginia Zangs. Collection Specialist Paul Galloway provided assistance with works from MoMA's collection, as did Department Manager Emma Presler and Department Assistant Katya Hall in coordinating everyone's efforts.

Finally, the curators wish to thank their partners, friends, and families for their encouragement and support.

Martino Stierli
Anoma Pieris
Sean Anderson

IMAGE CREDITS

Images have been provided in many cases by owners or custodians of the work. Individual works of art appearing herein may be protected by copyright in the United States of America or elsewhere, and may not be reproduced in any form without the permission of the rights holders. In reproducing the images contained in this publication the Museum obtained the permission of the rights holders whenever possible. Should the Museum have been unable to locate a rights holder, notwithstanding good-faith efforts, it requests that any contact information concerning such rights holders be forwarded so that they may be contacted for future editions.

Aga Khan Award for Architecture
    © Aga Khan Trust for Culture/Jacques Bétant (photographer): 223, 224 [top], 225 [bottom], 232 [bottom], 233 [all];
    © Lari Associates: 154 [figs. 9, 10], 224 [bottom], 225 [top];
    © Anwar Said Architect: 232 [bottom], 233 [all].
The Architectural Archives, University of Pennsylvania
    Antonin Raymond and Noémi Pernessin Raymond Collection: 171;
    David L. Leavitt Collection: 172 [top];
    Anant D. Raje Collection: 50 [fig. 14];
    Henry Wilcots Collection: 30 [fig. 23].
Architectural Press Archive/RIBA Collections: 121 [fig. 8].
Courtesy Avery Architectural & Fine Arts Library, Columbia University: 122 [fig. 1], 139 [fig. 7].
Kazi Khaleed Ashraf: 22 [fig. 12].
Sri Aurobindo Ashram Trust: 172 [bottom], 173 [all].
Courtesy Bajaj Heritage, Mumbai: 142 [fig. 1].
Courtesy Robert G. Boughey: 203, 204 [all], 205.
Margaret Bourke-White/The LIFE Picture Collection/Shutterstock: 111 [fig. 2].
Courtesy the Brian Brake Estate and Museum of New Zealand Te Papa Tongarewa (E.004270/23): 179.
Canadian Centre for Architecture
    Luc Durand fonds, Gift of Luc Durand, © Harji Malik: 167 [fig. 10];
    Aditya Prakash fonds, Gift of Vikramaditya Prakash: 227, 228 [all], 229 [all].
CEPT Archives. © CEPT University: 131 [figs. 3, 4].
Charles Correa Foundation: 123 [figs. 4, 5], 124 [fig. 6], 127 [fig. 10], 152 [figs. 6, 7].
COSTFORD. Drawing by Jayesh Pillai and Rutu Panchal: 217 [top].
Dinodia Photos/Alamy Stock Photo: 157 [fig. 2].
Daniel C. Dunham, Courtesy Kate Dunham: 164 [fig. 7].
Imogen Cunningham Trust: 162 [fig. 2], 183, 184 [all], 185 [bottom];
William J. R. Curtis: 122 [fig. 2].
© Constantinos and Emma Doxiadis Foundation: 54 [fig. 18], 55 [figs. 19, 20], 112 [fig. 3], 113 [fig. 6], 139 [fig. 6], 187, 188 [all], 189 [all].
Nihal Fernando/Studio Times Ltd.: 211.
Films Division, Govt. of India: 140 [fig. 8].
© F.L.C./ADAGP, Paris/Artists Rights Society (ARS), New York 2021: 114 [fig. 7].
The Getty Research Institute: 13 [fig. 2].
Heritage Foundation of Pakistan, © Lari Associates: 22 [figs. 12, 13].
Valentine Gunasekara Archive: 44 [fig. 8], 212 [all], 213 [all];
© Ariel Huber: 191, 193.
Courtesy IIMA Archives, Indian Institute of Management Ahmedabad: 50 [fig. 15].
Muzharul Islam Archives, Courtesy architect Nurur Rahman Khan: 29 [fig. 21], 58 [fig. 22], 126 [fig. 9], 144 [fig. 5], 154 [fig. 8], 207, 208 [all], 209.
Courtesy Rafique Islam, from *First Faculty of Architecture in Dhaka*: 132 [fig. 5], 133 [fig. 6].
Kanvinde Archives: 24 [figs. 14, 15], 26 [figs. 16,17], 35 [fig. 1], 47

[figs. 9, 10], 48 [fig. 12], 118 [fig. 3], 120 [fig. 7], 144 [fig. 4], 146 [fig. 8].
The Laurie Baker Centre for Habitat Studies: 29 [fig. 22], 39 [fig. 3].
Living Architecture, Scandinavian Design: 196.
© The Lunuganga Trust: 26 [fig. 18], 42 [figs. 4, 5], 146 [fig. 7], 150 [fig. 3], 151 [figs. 4, 5], 162 [fig. 3], 163 [figs. 5, 6], 195.
Courtesy Madan Mahatta Archives and PHOTOINK: 14 [fig. 5], 18 [fig. 8], 119 [fig. 6], 125 [fig. 8], 185 [fig. 4], 219, 220 [top], 235.
Abhilash Mallick: 33 [fig. 25].
Courtesy Anuradha Mathur: 39 [fig. 2].
Courtesy The Marg Foundation, Mumbai: 135 [fig. 1], 136 [figs. 2, 3].
MIT Libraries
    Aga Khan Documentation Center: 147 [fig. 10].
    G. E. Kidder Smith Image Collection: 48 [fig. 13].
José Moscardi/FAU USP: 14 [fig. 4].
Musée National d'Art Moderne, Centre Georges Pompidou, Paris, France. © CNAC/MNAM, Dist. RMN - Grand Palais/Art Resource, NY: 221 [all], 237 [all].
© The National College of Arts, Lahore: 156 [fig. 1].
National Geographic Images: 116 [fig. 1].
National Institute of Design—Archive, Ahmedabad: 130 [fig. 2], 158 [figs. 4, 5], 159 [fig. 6].
PAP/Archive: 137 [fig. 4].
Drawings by Milinda Pathiraja: 44 [figs. 6, 7].
Ulrik Plesner Archives: 118 [fig. 4], 197 [all].
Sebastian Posingis: 28 [fig. 19], 163 [fig. 4].
Virendra Prabhakar/Hindustan Times: 165 [fig. 8].
Courtesy Vineet Radhakrishnan: 33 [fig. 24], 140 [fig. 9], 216 [top].
Courtesy Ram Rahman: 138 [fig. 5], 166 [fig. 9].
© Ram Rahman, Habib Rahman Archives: 123 [fig. 3], 161 [fig. 1], 175, 176 [all], 177 [all].
Courtesy Mahendra Raj Archives: 18 [fig. 6].
    Mahendra Raj: 22 [fig. 11], 192 [all], 236 [all].
© Rare Books and Special Collections Library, The American University in Cairo: 113 [figs. 4, 5].
RCS Photograph Collection, Fisher Collection, University of Cambridge: 129 [fig. 1].
Private archive of David Robson: 28 [fig. 20], 149 [fig. 2].
Anwar Said Architect: 231, 232 [top].
Barbara Sansoni Archives, Courtesy Dominic Sansoni: 145 [fig. 6], 159 [fig. 7].
Courtesy Sarabhai Foundation—Calico Museum of Textiles, Ahmedabad, India: 47 [fig. 11].
Minnette de Silva, *The Life & Work of an Asian Woman Architect* (Colombo: Smart Media Productions, 1998): 149 [fig. 1], 180 [all], 181.
© Randhir Singh: Portfolio [all], 215, 216 [bottom].
Stella Snead: 118 [fig. 5].
Courtesy Robin Spence. Photograph: Jack Skeel (ARPS): 217 [bottom].
© 2022 Stiftung Ernst Scheidegger-Archiv, Zurich: 9 [fig. 1].
Swaraj Art Archive, Noida: 13 [fig. 3], 117 [fig. 2].
Tigerman McCurry Archive, Ryerson and Burnham Art and Architecture Archives, The Art Institute of Chicago. Digital File #201703_210706-001.tif.: 55 [fig. 21].
Vāstu Shilpā Foundation Archives: 18 [fig. 7], 20 [fig. 10], 52 [figs. 16, 17], 122 [fig. 2], 147 [fig. 9], 199, 200 [all], 201 [all].

The exhibition is made possible by Allianz,
MoMA's partner for design and innovation.

Leadership support is provided by Xin Zhang
and Shiyi Pan.

Generous funding is provided by
The International Council of The Museum of
Modern Art.

Additional support is provided by the Graham
Foundation for Advanced Studies in the Fine Arts.

Published in conjunction with the exhibition *The Project of Independence: Architectures of Decolonization in South Asia, 1947–1985*, at The Museum of Modern Art, New York, February 20–July 2, 2022. Organized by Martino Stierli, The Philip Johnson Chief Curator of Architecture and Design, The Museum of Modern Art; Anoma Pieris, a professor at the Melbourne School of Design, The University of Melbourne; and Sean Anderson, Associate Professor, Department of Architecture, Cornell University; with Evangelos Kotsioris, Assistant Curator, Department of Architecture and Design, The Museum of Modern Art.

The exhibition is made possible by Allianz, MoMA's partner for design and innovation.

Leadership support is provided by Xin Zhang and Shiyi Pan.

Generous funding is provided by The International Council of The Museum of Modern Art.

Additional support is provided by the Graham Foundation for Advanced Studies in the Fine Arts.

Produced by the Department of Publications, The Museum of Modern Art, New York

Hannah Kim, Business and Marketing Director
Don McMahon, Editorial Director
Marc Sapir, Production Director
Curtis R. Scott, Associate Publisher

Edited by Alexander Scrimgeour
Designed by Studio Lin
Production by Marc Sapir
Proofread by Kyle Bentley
Printed and bound by Conti Tipocolor, Florence

This book is typeset in Monotype Times New Roman Small Text. The paper is 150 gsm Condat Matt Périgord and 120 gsm Fedrigoni Arena White Smooth.

Published by The Museum of Modern Art
11 West 53 Street
New York, NY 10019-5497
www.moma.org

© 2022 The Museum of Modern Art, New York. Certain illustrations are covered by claims to copyright noted in the Image Credits on p. 245.

All rights reserved.

Library of Congress Control Number: 2021948782
ISBN: 978-1-63345-124-7

Distributed in the United States and Canada by
ARTBOOK | D.A.P.
75 Broad Street
Suite 630
New York, NY 10004
www.artbook.com

Distributed outside the United States and Canada by
Thames & Hudson
181A High Holborn
London WC1V 7QX
www.thamesandhudson.com

Printed and bound in Italy

TRUSTEES OF THE MUSEUM OF MODERN ART

Marie-Josée Kravis
Chair

Ronnie F. Heyman
President

Sid R. Bass
Mimi Haas
Marlene Hess
Maja Oeri
Richard E. Salomon
Vice Chairmen

Glenn D. Lowry
Director

Richard E. Salomon
Treasurer

James Gara
Assistant Treasurer

James E. Grooms
Secretary

Ronald S. Lauder
Honorary Chairman

Robert B. Menschel
Chairman Emeritus

Jerry I. Speyer
Chairman Emeritus

Agnes Gund
President Emerita

Wallis Annenberg*
Lin Arison**
Sarah Arison
Sid R. Bass
Lawrence B. Benenson
Leon D. Black
David Booth
Clarissa Alcock Bronfman
Patricia Phelps de Cisneros
Steven Cohen
Edith Cooper
Paula Crown
David Dechman
Anne Dias Griffin
Elizabeth Diller**
Glenn Dubin
Lonti Ebers
Joel S. Ehrenkranz
John Elkann
Laurence D. Fink
H.R.H. Duke Franz of Bavaria**
Glenn Fuhrman
Kathleen Fuld
Maurice R. Greenberg**
Agnes Gund
Mimi Haas
Marlene Hess
Ronnie Heyman
AC Hudgins
Barbara Jakobson
Pamela Joyner
Jill Kraus

Marie-Josée Kravis
Ronald S. Lauder
Wynton Marsalis**
Robert B. Menschel
Khalil Gibran Muhammad
Philip S. Niarchos
James G. Niven
Peter Norton
Daniel S. Och
Maja Oeri
Eyal Ofer
Michael S. Ovitz
Emily Rauh Pulitzer
David Rockefeller, Jr.*
Sharon Percy Rockefeller
Lord Rogers of Riverside**
Richard Roth
Richard E. Salomon
Ted Sann**
Anna Marie Shapiro
Anna Deavere Smith
Jerry I. Speyer
Jon Stryker
Daniel Sundheim
Tony Tamer
Steve Tananbaum
Yoshio Taniguchi**
Jeanne C. Thayer*
Alice M. Tisch
Edgar Wachenheim III
Gary Winnick
Xin Zhang

EX OFFICIO

Glenn D. Lowry
Director

Bill de Blasio
Mayor of the City of New York

Corey Johnson
Speaker of the Council of the City of New York

Scott M. Stringer
Comptroller of the City of New York

Sarah Arison
Chair of the Board of MoMA PS1

Sharon Percy Rockefeller
President of The International Council

Randall Gianopulos and Tom Osborne
Co-Chairs of The Contemporary Arts Council

Alvin Hall and Nancy L. Lane
Co-Chairs of The Black Arts Council

*   Life Trustee
**   Honorary Trustee